Joel and Obadiah

Dr Irv Busenitz is currently the Vice President for Academic Administration and Professor of Old Testament at The Master's Seminary, Sun Valley, California. He became a founding member of The Master's Seminary Administration and Faculty in 1986. From 1974 to 1986 he was a member of the Bible and Old Testament Faculty at Talbot Theological Seminary. He has also done post-doctoral studies at The American Institute of Holy Land Studies in Jerusalem and has been published in books, journals, and periodicals. Dr Busenitz and his wife Karen have been actively involved in the various ministries at Grace Community Church, Sun Valley, since 1977. They have been married for over thirty years and are the parents of two sons.

Joel and Obadiah

A Mentor Commentary

Irvin A. Busenitz

ⅢENTOR

ISBN 1-85792-861-X
ISBN 978-1-85792-861-7

First published in 2003
Reprinted in 2010
in the
Mentor Imprint
by
Christian Focus Publications,
Geanies House, Fearn,
Ross-shire, IV20 1TW, Great Britain

www.christianfocus.com

Cover design by Daniel van Straaten

Printed and bound in the USA.

Contents

Joel

Contents

Obadiah

Charts and Map

In loving memory of my parents,
for their faithful instruction in the truths of
God's Word and their lives which
pounded them deep.

Joel

JOEL: ZEALOUS FOR THE WORSHIP OF YAHWEH

THE DAY OF YAHWEH

Contemporary Day of Yahweh
(1:1-20)

Source of the message
(1:1)

Command to comtemplate the devastation
(1:2-4)

Completeness of the Devastation
(1:5-12)

Call to repent in light of the devastation
(1:13-20)

Impending Day of Yahweh
(2:1-17)

Alarm sounds
(2:1)

Army Invades
(2:2-11)

Admonition to repent
(2:12-17)

Eschatological Day of Yahweh
(2:18-3:21)

Introduction
(2:18-20)

Material restoration
(2:21-27)

Spiritual restoration
(2:28-32)

National Restoration
(3:1-21)

Historical:
Day of Yahweh Experienced

Transitional:
Day of Yahew Illustrated

Eschatological:
Day of Yahweh Described

1.
Introduction to the Prophecy

The Man

Apart from his name and that of his father, the prophecy itself provides only scant information about the author. Attempts to ascertain his exact identity are further limited by the commonness of his name, for the Old Testament mentions at least a dozen different men by the same name (1 Sam. 8:2; 1 Chron. 4:35; 5:4, 8, 12; 6:33, 36; 7:3; 11:38; 15:7, 11, 17; 23:8; 26:22; 27:20; 2 Chron. 29:12; Ezra 10:43; Neh. 11:9). Acts 2:16 provides the only New Testament reference.

The name Joel is a compound form of two Hebrew designations for deity, Yahweh and Elohim, and means 'Yah[weh] is El[ohim].' The Hebrew name carries over into the Septuagint (LXX) and the New Testament with the same meaning.

Assuming the date of Joel is correct (see later discussion), the name of the contemporary prophet Elijah is similar, meaning 'my El[ohim] is Yah[weh].' The name itself is either a tribute to the faith of the parents, reflecting on their piety, or a confession of faith made by the prophet when he selected the name.

Joel distinguishes himself from others who had the same name by giving the name of his father. Pethuel means 'open-heartedness' or 'sincerity toward/of God' and, like the name of his son, reflects well upon his character. Facts concerning his father are equally obscure, this being the only occurrence of the name. The substitution of 'Bethuel' in the LXX is unfounded, being either a scribal error or an attempt to relate the prophet with the patriarchal period (Gen. 24:15).

Due to the prophet's profound interest in the various aspects of the temple worship and his zeal for the continuation of the prescribed sacrifices, it has been suggested that Joel was of priestly descent. Some have even connected Pethuel with Pethahiah (1 Chron. 24:16), giving additional support to this theory. It is doubtful, however, that Joel was a Levite. In 1:13-14 and 2:17 he addresses the priests objectively, distinguishing himself from them as a group to which he did not belong.[1] Furthermore, his frequent reference to the pastoral and agricultural life, as well as his familiar contacts with people, implies a background other than the normal seclusion of the priesthood.[2]

His considerable knowledge of the temple and the levitical procedures has led others to classify Joel as a 'temple-prophet' or as belonging to one of the schools of the prophets.[3] This conclusion is strengthened further by the contention that the prophecies possess the dramatic movement of ritual, borrowed from the cultic liturgy and designed to be spoken on the occasion of a great festival.[4] While the composition of the book will be discussed below, it should be noted that the utilization of certain liturgical

---

1. Cf. J. A. Bewer, *A Critical and Exegetical Commentary on Obadiah and Joel, in The International Critical Commentary* (Edinburgh: T & T Clark, 1974), 67.

2. Cf. J. Hardee Kennedy, *Joel*, in *The Broadman Bible Commentary*, ed. by Clifton J. Allen (Nashville: Broadman Press, 1972), 61.

3. Cf. A. S. Kapelrud, *Joel Studies* (Uppsala: Almquist and Wiksells, 1948) 176. Due to the visible zeal of Joel for the maintenance of religious rituals, some contend that many of the prophets were temple servants, receiving their support from the temple revenue (cf. A. A. MacRae, 'Prophets and Prophecy,' in *The Zondervan Pictorial Encyclopedia of the Bible*, ed., Merrill C. Tenney [Grand Rapids: Zondervan, 1975] IV: 889-890).

4. John D. W. Watts, *The Books of Joel, Obadiah, Jonah, Nahum, Habakkuk and Zephaniah*, in *The Cambridge Bible Commentary* (Cambridge: University Press, 1975), 12.

phrases and forms merely implies an active participation in the religious and does not necessarily suggest that he was a 'temple-prophet.'

Extra-biblical tradition records that Joel was from the tribe of Reuben. Pseudo-Epiphanius in *Vitae Prophetarum* as well as the end of G[22] suggest that he came from Bethom.[5] The legend is unsupported, however, having been derived apparently from 1 Chronicles 5:4 where a certain Joel is mentioned as the descendant of Reuben. The impression emanating from the whole prophecy is that Joel was a Judean who made his home either in Jerusalem or in the immediate vicinity. He speaks from the temple, bidding the priests to blow the trumpet in Zion (2:15) and gather the nation for a solemn assembly in the house of God (1:13-14; 2:15-17); he envisions the enemy besieging and entering Jerusalem (2:9); he addresses the people as the sons of Zion (2:23), Judah, and Jerusalem (3:6). In all of these he speaks as one who is intimately related and personally acquainted with them. The tone of a stranger is absent. The existence of the northern ten tribes of Israel goes unmentioned, except for their inclusion with Judah in three eschatological references to Israel (2:27; 3:2, 16) which describe God's restoration of the fortunes of His covenant people. 'The absence of any direct promise of the extension of those blessings to the ten tribes (such as occur in Hosea and Amos) implies that he had no office in regard to them.'[6]

The Date

Not only is the book undated in the superscription but there is a noticeable absence of significant temporal references within the text. Consequently, dating is dependent upon internal allusions, references that are at best sketchy and have multiple explanations. Although the position of Joel in the Hebrew canon implies an early date and this

---

5. Bewer, 67. This town, sometimes called Bethharan, was located north-east of the Dead Sea on the border of Reuben and Gad. It should not be confused with the city of Bethhoron (Beit Ur) located ten miles northwest of Jerusalem.

6. E. B. Pusey, *The Minor Prophets*, in *Notes on the Old Testament* (Grand Rapids: Baker Book House, 1973), I, 143.

is supported by Jewish tradition, the arrangement is only suggestive and not decisive. A pre-exilic date for the book of Joel was generally accepted until the early nineteenth century.[7] More recently, dating has fallen primarily into the two broad categories of pre- and post-exilic authorship, with opinions ranging from the ninth century down to the third century BC. Each of the numerous temporal allusions will be considered individually.

Chronological Markers

The occurrence of the locust plague possesses little value as a chronological indicator. There is no record elsewhere of this widespread calamity, a catastrophe that occurred all too frequently to be of much help. If there is to be any assistance whatsoever, it is to be found in the fact that the prophet's intense absorption with the catastrophe seems to reflect primarily an agricultural and pastoral community, such as Israel was prior to the eighth century.

1. The first matter centers on the cultic development in Israel. It is contended that the use of the phrase 'holy mountain' (2:1; 3:17) as a designation for Zion, together with the location of the temple in Jerusalem, implies a time subsequent to the reforms of Josiah in 621 BC (cf. 2 Chron. 34-35).[8] Many mountains, it is contended, were holy prior to his reforms, thus making the designation meaningful only after

---

7. This view was first questioned in 1831 by Karl A. Credner in *Der Prophet Joel ubersetzt und erklart* and in 1835 by Wilhelm Vatke in *Die Religion des AT nach den kanonischen Buchern*. Since then, a number of different dates have been advanced. Of a ninth century BC date, advocates include Hobart E. Freeman, *An Introduction to the Old Testament* (Chicago: Moody, 1968), 147-149; Gleason L. Archer, Jr., *A Survey of Old Testament Introduction* (Chicago: Moody, 1974), 304-305; and Walter C. Kaiser, Jr., *The Messiah in the Old Testament* (Grand Rapids: Zondervan, 1995), 139. Richard D. Patterson, *Joel* in *The Expositor's Bible Commentary*, ed. by Frank E. Gaebelein (Grand Rapids: Zondervan, 1985), 7:231-233, suggests an early eighth century BC date. A late pre-exilic date has been put forth by Arvid S. Kapelrud, *Joel Studies* (Uppsala: Almquist & Wiksells, 1948), 191. Post-exilic dates have been espoused by Leslie C. Allen, *Joel*, in *NICOT* (Grand Rapids: Eerdmans, 1976), 19-25; and R. K. Harrison, *Introduction to the Old Testament* (Grand Rapids: Eerdmans, 1969), 876-879.

8. So Marco Treves, 'The Date of Joel,' *Vetus Testamentum* 7 (1957), 149-156.

the reforms. Furthermore, Joel makes no mention of the local high places or of the idolatry that the pre-exilic prophets condemn. Bewer defends this rationale by observing that there is

> an emphasis on daily cult and the value of daily sacrifices and on the importance of the regularity of the temple services which stands in striking contrast to the attitude of the pre-exilic prophets. And all this centres in the temple of Jerusalem, no other sanctuaries are named and no hint is given that any of the ancient much combated sanctuaries outside Jerusalem are still in existence.[9]

These arguments lack credence, however, since they are predicated upon presuppositions that lack biblical support and historical accuracy. First of all, it is based upon the false concept that Israel had multiple places of worship with no central sanctuary until the time of Josiah's sweeping reforms in 621 BC. This belief, namely, the evolutionary concept of religion, basically asserts that Israel's religion slowly evolved, developing from the simple to the complex. Since having one central sanctuary depicts a higher, more developed form of religion, it could not have occurred until a period in the late monarchy. This contention wrongly suggests that Israel's religion was man-made and denies that God supernaturally revealed Himself to His chosen people and divinely instructed them regarding where and how they were to worship. While it is true that Israel did at times resort to idolatry and the erection of various high places throughout her nation, God expressly forbade such practices from the beginning (cf. Exod. 20) and established a central place for worship.[10]

Second, the absence of any mention in Joel of local high places or idolatrous practices referred to by other pre-exilic prophets is not as significant as it might first seem. Post-exilic prophets such as Haggai, Zechariah, Ezra, Nehemiah, and

---

9. Bewer, 57.

10. Acceptance of a late date on the basis of this argument demands the adumbration of a late date for the bulk of the Pentateuch in which God sets forth the religious prescriptions.

Malachi, all of whom lived subsequent to the reforms of
Josiah, are filled with numerous warnings and stern rebukes
regarding idolatrous practices.[11] Although there is no mention
of the high places or the idolatry which the pre-exilic prophets
condemn, the prophet does exhort the people to 'rend your
hearts and not your garments' (2:13). The admonition does
imply the leaving of sins. And while the early prophets frequently and strongly exhorted the people to a godliness of the
heart and not mere ritualism, the situation is not significantly
different in Joel. The book hardly represents a superseding
religion of liturgy and legalism; it merely expresses the desire
to carry out the prescriptions of God's law.

Furthermore, such desire could be evidence of an
earlier, pre-exilic date. If many of the pre-exilic prophets
continually spoke out against an overemphasis on the
liturgical, then for the prophet to describe the horror
of the people at the interruption of the liturgy they so
strongly pursued fits well with this pre-exilic overemphasis. Kirkpatrick concludes:

> There is an entire absence of indications that the prophet
> is living in a small, struggling, despised community. The
> temple worship is firmly established and regularly organized.
> There is no sign of the apathy and neglect which Haggai and
> Zechariah rebuke, or the contemptuous indifference which
> Malachi censures.[12]

Indeed, there were periods of reformation at other, earlier
times in Israel's history, when the law was being carefully
observed, which could certainly explain the absence of any
mention of idolatry in Joel. The omission does not force the
book to be dated after the reforms of Josiah. The whole point
is based upon silence and so carries little, if any, weight. Even

---

11. Ahlstrom correctly claims that the religious practices of the second temple
cannot have been free from the accusation of being syncretistic and idolatrous. Pointing to Malachi 2:10ff and Ezra 9-10, he contends that post-exilic
Judah could be reproached for taking part in cultic practices which were
contrary to the *pure* worship of Yahweh (Gosta Werner Ahlstrom, *Joel and
the Temple Cult of Jerusalem*, in vol. 21 of *Supplements to Vetus Testamentum*
[Leiden: E. J. Brill, 1971] 125-129).

12. A. F. Kirkpatrick, *The Doctrine of the Prophets* (New York: Macmillan, 1897), 71.

Bewer, who holds to a post-exilic date, admits: 'It is true that Joel does not rebuke them for moral and social sins either, so that this point may not count for much.'[13] Young adds:

> The absence of mention of the *bamoth,* or high places, proves nothing as to date, since there seems to be no particular reason why they should have been mentioned. And even Oesterly and Robinson do admit that such absence might apply to a time considerably before Amos. Hence, nothing can really be made of the lack of such mention.[14]

Finally, it should be observed that the circumstances that underlie the book are not in significant agreement with those of the post-exilic period. Thus, 'advocates of the post-exilic date generally avoid the difficulty by placing the book in the interval between Zechariah and Ezra or some considerable time after Malachi—two periods of which we know practically nothing.'[15]

2. A second consideration involves the fact that the temple is present. Religious worship and practices are being carried out on a regular basis, except for a shortage of offerings caused by the locust plague and famine (Joel 1:9, 13-14). This certainly eliminates the period from 586-516 BC. The offerings of the temple are primarily the grain offering and libation (1:9, 13; 2:14). These, it is contended, 'are best understood as referring to the post-exilic *tamid* or daily temple offering.'[16] Passages such as Nehemiah 10:33, Daniel 8:11, 11:31, 12:11 and Acts 26:7 are said to be indicative of the great importance with which the regularity of the daily meal and drink offerings was regarded in later Israelite history, especially

---

13. Bewer, 57.

14. E. J. Young, *An Introduction to the Old Testament* (Grand Rapids: Eerdmans, 1977) 256.

15. Kirkpatrick, 70.

16. Allen, 20. Robert Pfeiffer agrees: 'Moreover (as in Dan. 8:11; 11:31; 12:11), the daily offering and libation in the temple (i.e., the *tamid*) had become not only the main office in religion but an indispensable symbol for the maintenance of correct relations between Jehovah and His people (1:9, 13; 2:14)' (*Introduction to the Old Testament* [New York: Harper, 1941] 576).

17. G. A. Smith, *The Book of the Twelve Prophets* (NY: Harper, n.d.): II, 382.

when compared with the dissimilar way the earlier prophets speak.[17]

On the other side, however, the reference to these offerings cannot be used to indicate a late date, unless one is also willing to accept the critical theories which late date Exodus, Numbers, and the writings which introduce these offerings (cf. Exod. 29:38-42; Num. 28:3-8). Any acceptance of the critical theories that late date much of the Pentateuch deals a serious if not fatal blow to the integrity of the Old Testament. And furthermore, such evidence is really inadmissible, in that one has arbitrarily concluded that the passages that emphasize the daily sacrifices are late. Such emphasis could have been earlier, especially in light of their Pentateuchal origins.

In an argument of a similar nature, Smith quotes from Josephus' records of the siege and fall of Jerusalem to the Romans. In these accounts, Josephus details the horror generated by the interruption of the daily sacrifices, adding that such had not occurred in any previous siege of the city (Ant. XIV, iv, 3).[18] Thus, it is assumed that the siege of Jerusalem by Nebuchadnezzar did not cause such a horror because the daily sacrifices had not been instituted yet. This argument is untenable, however, for not only is it from silence concerning the events surrounding the siege of Nebuchadnezzar, but it again plays havoc with the integrity of the Pentateuch and its prescription of the daily offerings.

3. In 3:1-2, 2:27 and 3:16 Judah is called Israel. This fact, it is argued, coupled together with the absence of any allusion to the northern kingdom, suggests a date after the fall of the northern kingdom to Assyria in 722 BC and possibly even subsequent to the Babylonian Captivity after which there was significant amalgamation between Judah and Israel.

Although the locust plague and drought undoubtedly extended into the northern kingdom and was not merely confined to Judah, there appears to be no particular occasion or reason for the prophet to mention them. His immediate concern is for the state of affairs in Judah. His prophetic

---

18. Smith, II, 382.

discourses are directed toward and limited to Judah. The use of 'Israel' as synonymous with Judah need not reflect a date after 722 BC; Israel was a name which belonged to the southern kingdom as well as to the northern. In fact, Joel's interchange of names may not only reflect a conviction that Judah was the true heir of Jacob but may also have been an attempt to strengthen the call to repentance by using nomenclature with significant covenantal overtones (cf. Gen. 35:10).

4. The reference to the restoration of the fortunes of Judah and Jerusalem (3:1[4:1]) and the scattering among the nations (3:2[4:2]) does not necessarily describe the restoration from the Babylonian captivity. The expression 'I shall restore the fortunes' is ambiguous and may speak of the restoration of divine favor and prosperity, as it does in Job 42:10. In any case, it is certainly not an argument for a post-exilic date. The phrase envisages a future restoration, a future time when divine favor is restored to His people (cf. Hosea 6:11; Amos 9:14).

Joel 3:2 [4:2] is another passage that has been used to postulate an exilic or post-exilic date. It is claimed that '3:2f. is most naturally to be understood as a reference to the cataclysmic events of 587 B. C.'[19] If this is a reference to the destruction of Jerusalem by Nebuchadnezzar, then Joel would have been written sometime later. In support of this claim, Allen notes that Jeremiah 50:17 does use the verb 'scatter' in reference to the Babylonian captivity, while Lamentations 5:2 records the loss of lands and homes to foreigners during that time.[20]

It is doubtful, however, that Joel is describing the historical takeover of Israel by Babylon. Smith observes: 'The supporters of a pre-exilic date either passed this over or understood it of incursions by the heathen into Israel's territories in the ninth century. *It is, however, too universal to suit these.*'[21] Although Smith believes that the passage points to a post-ex-

---

19. Allen, 24.

20. Allen, 20-24.

21. Smith, II, 374 (emphasis mine).

ilic date, the observation he makes is a correct one. The reference is too universal to fit any historical account, including the Babylonian exile. The context does not support an historical, Babylonian fulfillment. First, Joel 3:2[4:2] speaks of gathering 'all the nations' (plural, not singular as expected if referring to Babylon). Why would all nations be summoned if Babylon alone was the culprit? Second, the scattering is described as being carried out by the nations, not just one nation as in 587 BC. Third, Babylon did not really scatter Israel among the nations; in fact, she allowed a considerable number of Israelites to remain in the land. This is especially noteworthy when compared with the procedures followed by the Assyrians, who displaced most of the inhabitants of the ten northern tribes and supplanted them with foreigners (cf. 2 Kings 17:6, 23-24). Although some Judeans did flee to Egypt prior to the coming of Nebuchadnezzar, such could hardly be seen as the fulfillment of multi-national scattering. Fourth, she did not divide up the land as Joel here describes. And finally, the statement is too universal to accurately reflect the wounds inflicted by Nebuchadnezzar.[22] In the case of 3:2b-3 [4:2b-3], the scattering of the people and the division of the land is spoken of in terms that would allow it to have occurred any time prior to the coming of the judgment depicted in 2:28-3:2a [3:1-4:2a]. R. K. Harrison correctly asserts that the reference 'cannot be used decisively as an argument for either an exilic or a post-exilic date.'[23]

5. The summons of all the inhabitants of the land to assemble in the house of the Lord (1:14) has been propounded as evidence that 'the ancient numerous Israelite nation, with its populous capital, many cities, and twelve tribes, had dwindled to the small Judea of the Persian and Ptolemaic periods, a provincial town clustered around its Temple and surrounded by a few villages.'[24] It is assumed

---

22. See C. F. Keil, *Commentary on the Old Testament, Joel*, by C. F. Keil and Franz Delitzsch (Grand Rapids: Eerdmans, rpt 1975), 219-222.

23. R. K. Harrison, *Introduction to the Old Testament* (Grand Rapids: Eerdmans, 1975), 877.

24. Treves, 151.

that since the entire population was summoned the entire population would and could have fit into the Temple area.

But the assumption is only that—an assumption. In view of similar phrases in Jeremiah 26:2, 7-19 and 36:6, 9, the summons of the whole community need not suggest a small population. The context emphasizes the fact that not only the priests and elders but the entire community needed to repent—not that all would fit into the confines of the Temple.

6. A considerable amount of weight has been given to the absence of any reference to a king or princes. The prominence of the priests and elders, apparently acting in the capacity of governmental officials, has led to a number of different interpretations. Specifically, some have concluded that since it was the priests and elders who summoned the people to an assembly (1:13-14; 2:1, 15-17), it is reasonable to conclude that there were no royal princes or ruling king in Jerusalem at the time.[25] The calling of an assembly was the privilege/responsibility of the king (cf. 1 Kings 8:1; 2 Kings 10:20; 2 Chron. 5:2; 29:20); consequently, many have promoted a post-exilic time when there was no monarchy in Israel.

There are a number of considerations, however, which cast doubt upon this conclusion. Essentially, the argument is from silence. The absence of any mention of royalty cannot be used to prove its nonexistence. As Kirkpatrick has rightly claimed, 'too much stress must not be laid on the absence of all mention of the king and his court. The book of Micah contains no reference to Hezekiah, except in the title, though, as we know from the book of Jeremiah (26:18), he came into close personal relations with him.'[26] Nor do the books of Nahum or Zephaniah mention the monarchy. While the passages in Kings and Chronicles describe the king as doing the summoning, they do not preclude the priests and the elders from doing so. Second Kings 10:20 also describes the king as the one who requested the assembly, but it was the priests and prophets who actually proclaimed it. In

---

25. Cf. Bewer, 57.

26. Kirkpatrick, 69.

Numbers 10:1ff, the calling of an assembly was the duty of the priests.

Nowhere in the Old Testament are the priests prohibited from proclaiming a solemn assembly. In fact, their response to this crisis is quite appropriate, for they are the ministers of the sanctuary.[27] They are the ones who are expected to express the greatest alarm at the inability to carry out their divinely ordered responsibilities. No special authority is given to them; they are merely bidding the people to face the difficulty and initiate the appropriate changes. Furthermore, the absence of the mention of any kings may be due to the nature of Joel's prophecy, centered around the inability to carry out the prescribed offerings.

Others have used the absence of any mention of royalty to date the book during the time when Joash (sometimes referred to as Jehoash) was still too young to be king and Jehoiada the priest was regent (2 Kings 11-12).[28] Although the condition of affairs that existed during the early years of Joash may accord with the nature of Joel's prophecy in general, there are certain specifics which do not. First of all, Joel nowhere mentions the Syrians, yet by the reign of Joash, the Syrians, under the long and successful reigns of Hazael (841-801 BC) and his predecessor Benhadad I (890-841 BC), were 'not only prominent to the thoughts of Israel but had already been felt to be an enemy as powerful as the Philistines or Edomites'[29] (cf. 1 Kings 20; 2 Kings 5-8). Consequently, the omission suggests a date earlier than the reign of Joash, a time when Syria had not yet come into conflict with Judah.

Second, the moral and spiritual level of the nation intimated by the prophet does not coincide with the early years of the reign of Joash. The 'Joash view' demands that Joel's prophecy be written either during the very earliest years of

---

27. Bewer's contention that Joel's designation of priests as 'ministers of Yahweh' (1:9) is an evidence of post-exilic literature (57), is another argument from silence and is 'not as assured as might be imagined' (Harrison, 878).

28. See Kirkpatrick 60-61; Gleason L. Archer, Jr., *A Survey of Old Testament Introduction* (Chicago: Moody, 1974), 304.

29. Smith, II, 379.

his reign or during the time when the queen mother Athaliah usurped the throne and Joash was still in hiding (2 Kings 11). Yet the moral and spiritual level of Judah was very low during the reign of Athaliah (841-835 BC) and during the preceding reigns of Ahaziah (841 BC; cf. 2 Chron. 22:3-5) and Jehoram (853-841 BC; cf. 2 Chron. 21:6, 11-13). Therefore, the excessive wickedness in which the nation wallowed from 853-835 BC is difficult to equate with the absence of reference to any specific sin in the book of Joel. Rather, these factors seem to indicate an earlier date, possibly during the godly reign of Jehoshaphat (873-848 BC; cf. 2 Chron. 20:32).

7. The mention of the city wall in 2:7, 9 has been set forth repeatedly as evidence of a post-exilic date. Treves writes that 'the mention of the wall of the city shows that Joel wrote after the wall had been rebuilt by Nehemiah.'[30] In spite of the frequency with which this argument is embraced, nothing of certainty can be deduced from the reference to the city wall.[31] First of all, the walls of Jerusalem were not totally destroyed in the takeover by Nebuchadnezzar. That some were left standing is strongly intimated by the prophet Jeremiah (41:5) and by Nehemiah (3:8). Thus the reference to the city wall need not demand a post-exilic period. A more important consideration is the literary nature of the passage. The language is picturesque and colorful, depicting the onslaught of the locusts in metaphorical terms.[32] The point of the text is not to report the actual scaling of the city wall but to communicate the massive and awesome locust devastation in a most descriptive fashion.

8. Considerable discussion regarding the date of Joel has centered around the mention of the Greeks (3:6) and their involvement in the slave trade. Specifically, Joel states that Jewish slaves had been sold to the Grecians. Advocates of

---

30. Treves, 151. Also cf. G. B. Gray, *Critical Introduction to the Old Testament* (New York: Scribner & Sons, 1913) 208.

31. Cf. William F. Albright, 'Book Review of R. H. Pfeiffer's Old Testament Introduction,' *Journal of Biblical Literature* 61 (1942) 120-121; Smith II 379; and Jacob M. Myers, 'Some Considerations bearing on the Date of Joel,' *ZAW* 74 (1962), 191.

32. See chapter two regarding the discussion of whether or not the locusts depict a literal advancing army.

a late date note that the Greeks are not mentioned by any other Hebrew writer before the exile. Smith, for example, admits that this argument cannot deny the possibility of a ninth century BC date; yet he does contend that such an early date is improbable, especially in light of the fact that Amos (pre-exilic) does not mention the Greeks when describing the Phoenicians as slave traders (cf. Amos 1:6-10).[33]

In response to this argument, it should be noted first of all that it is inaccurate if one adheres to a conservative dating of Isaiah. In Isaiah 66:19, the nation of Greece is mentioned under the ancestral name of 'Javan' (cf. Gen. 10:2, 4; 1 Chron.1:5, 7). Second, while the majority of references depicting a relationship between Palestine and Greece is exilic and post-exilic, it is very possible that the commercial trafficking of slaves between Palestine and Greece occurred much earlier (cf. Amos 1:6-10 where similar activity was present at an early point in Israel's history). Harrison observes that 'the Ionians [Greeks] appeared in Assyrian literary sources[34] as early as the eighth century BC, so that this allusion cannot be used as an assured basis for a later rather than earlier date for the prophecy.'[35] Archaeological discoveries have asserted that by the eighth century BC the Greeks were well known throughout the Near East, controlled the trading routes that lead through Asia Minor and were the primary commercial competitors of the Phoenicians. As a result, 'it would be hazardous to assume that the people of the pre-exilic Judah had no knowledge of the Ionians.'[36]

Furthermore, the silence of Greek authors regarding the purchase of Jewish slaves until after the conquests of Alexander[37] carries no weight in light of the fact that both Homer[38] (*ca* eighth

---

33. Smith, II, 379.

34. Cf. *Ancient Near Eastern Texts*, ed. by James B. Pritchard (Princeton: Princeton University, 1955), 284ff.

35. Harrison, 877.

36. Ahlstrom, 117.

37. Cf. Treves, 152. For an extensive discussion of the lateness of the Greeks and Sabeans in Joel, see Myers, 178-190.

38. Indeed, Homer himself mentions the existence of slave trade between Phoenicia and Greece (*Odyss*, XV, 415ff).

century BC) and the Tell el-Amarna tablets (*ca* fifteenth century BC) refer to intercourse between Greece and the Phoenicians.[39] While the post-Alexandrian period witnessed the extensive settlement of Greek kings, noblemen, and rich men all over the Near East,[40] Joel's account that the slaves were removed 'far from their territory' (3:16 [4:16]) suggests a time when such Grecian colonization had not yet occurred.

Ultimately, the mention of the Greeks is of little value for determining the date of the prophecy. The incident(s) to which the prophet is referring could be understood as telling historical events, events which caused Yahweh to pronounce a similar judgment upon the guilty parties (3:4-8 [4:4-8]).[41] These events could have occurred anytime while Tyre, Sidon and Philistia were strong and able to execute the actions that Joel describes. The Grecian reference may be even less significant if it is given by Joel as representative of the nations to which the Jewish slaves had been traded. Kirkpatrick intimates this, suggesting that slaves may have been transported to Asia Minor with Joel selecting the Greeks for mention as the remotest region to which his countrymen had been carried away.[42]

Likewise, the mention of the Sabeans lacks chronological significance. As with the references to the other nations, the prophet's notation of the Sabeans provides only a suggestion. Says Albright: 'The reference to purchase of slaves by the remote Sabeans points to a time not later than the sixth century, since the Minaeans controlled Arab trade in the following centuries.'[43]

In 3:6 the reference to 'Greeks' is plural. This form is said to argue for a date close to the time when the Chronicles were written since such constructions accord with the style of the Chronicler. But, as Ahlstrom rightly observes, the Chronicles lack consistency in this matter, employing both the singular

---

39. Cf. Kirkpatrick, 70.

40. Treves,152.

41. Ahlstrom, 119.

42. Kirkpatrick, 70.

43. Albright, 120. But even this supposed *terminus ad quem* must be viewed in light of the eschatological nature of the context.

and the plural in similar references.[44] Kapelrud also notes that while the word 'prophet' is not a proper noun, the plural 'sons of the prophets' occurs in earlier literature (1 Kings 20:35; 2 Kings 2:3, 5, 7, 15; *et al*),[45] casting additional doubt upon the lateness of this plural form. Thus it is both difficult and precarious to assume the lateness of a particular construction on the basis of a single occurrence, making the attribution of any significance to the plural reference here doubtful.

9. It is contended that the blatant exclusion of foreigners from Jerusalem reflects a later, more advanced form of Jewish nationalistic thinking. In 3:17 [4:17], Joel states how the presence of Messiah in Zion will be accompanied by strangers passing through her no more. In the first part of the chapter, the prophet describes a day of vengeance against the heathen and the restoration of the fortunes of Judah and Jerusalem. Says Pfeiffer: 'These oracles belong to a time when possession of the law of Moses (canonized in the Pentateuch around 400) made the Jews regard themselves as God's favorites and the heathen as rejected by God—a feeling that Joel expresses in no uncertain terms.'[46] Proponents go on to claim that this apocalyptic genre is a product of the religious/political despair that gripped the Jewish people in the post-exilic era.[47]

This argument, however, is founded on non-biblical assumptions. It depends on the antisupernatural presupposition that God either cannot or did not divinely reveal Himself to Israel and upon the evolutionary concept of religion which, simply put, asserts that the religion of Israel developed humanistically out of a need for a god and therefore was not of divine origin. On the contrary, the narrow nationalistic exclusiveness intimated by the prophet may be due to its early date rather than late. The later prophets frequently anticipate the existence at least of a remnant of the nations. Such anticipation does not accord with a mentality of nationalistic exclusivity.

---

44. Ahlstrom (118) provides significant examples of this inconsistency.

45. Kapelrud, 154.

46. Pfeiffer, 576.

47. Critics also point to the mention of angelic armies in 3:11 as an evidence of lateness since the doctrine of angels *allegedly* did not come into existence in Israel's religion until the Intertestamental period.

It is the earlier prophets who often convey an attitude similar to Joel's. The pre-exilic prophet Hosea is mute regarding the destiny of the nations. Amos likewise foresees their conquest, not their conversion (9:12).[48] Smith also observes that 'in Joel's attitude toward other nations, whom he condemns to judgment, Ewald saw 'the old unsubdued warlike spirit of the times of Deborah and David.''[49]

10. A number of nations are singled out by the prophet as being especially menacing to Israel. In addition to Greece and her role as slave-trader (discussed earlier), Tyre, Sidon and Philistia (3:4ff [4:4ff]) are described as ones who had plundered the treasures of Israel's temple (or palaces) and had sold the people into slavery.

Some have connected these verses with the Philistine invasion of Judah during the reign of Jehoram (853-841 BC; cf. 2 Chron. 21:16-17). There are similarities between the two descriptions; however, the impact of the correlation is diminished by the fact that the Philistines were a major enemy of Israel for many years prior to the monarchy and continued to plague them through the early years of the monarchy. Thus the actions described could have occurred most any time during their period of strength (cf. the frequent exploits against Israel in Judges and 1 Samuel). If, on the other hand, Joel is referring to the invasion during the reign of Jehoram, then the prophecy could not be earlier than 853–841 BC.

The mention of Tyre and Sidon cautions against making any correlation between the invasion by Philistia under Jehoram's reign and the reference to Philistia by Joel. The prophet includes the Phoenicians as being active partners with Philistia in the slave-trading and plundering of Israel; yet there is no mention in the Old Testament of the Phoenicians being at enmity with Israel. Thus it is possible that the incident described by Joel does not have a biblical parallel.

The reference to Egypt and Edom (3:19 [4:19]) is similarly devoid of significant chronological evidence. While Egypt and Edom were ancient and perpetual enemies of Israel, the reason which the prophet gives for their punishment cannot

---

48. Kirkpatrick, 70.

49. Smith, II, 377.

be accounted for in the Old Testament. To explain 3:19 [4:19] by referring to 2 Kings 8:20-22 demands the assumption that a massacre of innocent Israelites occurred at that time. Gray questions the legitimacy of that assumption: 'Granted the assumption, in itself far from improbable, does a massacre during a regular war of independence justify the terms in which Joel speaks?'[50] Attempts to correlate 3:19 [4:19] with Shishak's attack of Rehoboam (1 Kings 14:25ff) and Edom's revolt during the reign of Jehoram (2 Kings 8:20-22)[51] are feeble at best. The historical information given is far too scanty to make an identification with any degree of substantiation.

As far as the fulfillment of the desolation upon Egypt and Edom which the prophet predicts, it must be remembered that the context is eschatological, describing the day when Messiah is present upon the earth (cp. 3:17-21 [4:17-21] with Zech. 12-14). Thus the reference has no historical fulfillment before which the prophecy must have been written.

Ultimately, little stress can be laid upon the mention of these enemy nations, except that essentially they were the early enemies of Israel. While the Old Testament does mention some post-exilic hostility with the Philistines (cf. Neh. 4:1; Zech. 9:5-7) and the Edomites (cf. Mal. 1:2ff), their enmity with Israel at that time was nothing more than a mere shadow of earlier hostilities. Beyond that, the historical information given in the Old Testament is only inferential. It is impossible to draw any significant or substantial chrono-logical conclusions from them here.[52]

11. Occasionally, some have given the book a late date as a result of the denial of the supernatural, prophetic element. Treves, for example, does rightly contend that the war described in 3:9-11[4:9-11] appears to be between the Lord and

---

50. G. B. Gray, 'The Parallel Passages in "Joel" in Their Bearing on the Question of Date,' *Expositor*, 8 (Sept 1893), 209.

51. See Allen, 19-20.

52. Although Milman concludes that 'the silence about the Assyrian power is conclusive as to this early period assigned to the prophecies of Joel' (Henry H. Milman, *History of the Jews* [London: J. Murray, 1883] I , 370), it is better to maintain a more cautious attitude. In eschatological contexts the special mention of some does not always necessarily exclude the exist-ence and involvement of others.

the foreign nations. But he incorrectly assumes that the absence of any mention of a Jewish army and only the presence of the Lord and His angels (3:11[4:11]) must indicate a time between 586-166 BC when the Jews had no national army.[53] The fulfillment of this passage cannot be found in history; it is eschatological, as the context reveals. The battle that the Lord fights on behalf of His people occurs in that future Day of Yahweh.[54]

12. The location of Joel in the Hebrew canon has been utilized by some to infer an early date of writing, while others have cast off the canonical order as meaningless. Most who reject a pre-exilic date attribute the canonical position of the prophet to literary similarities between Joel and other prophets from whom Joel supposedly borrowed.[55] Further proof is claimed from the Septuagint, which places the book fourth: Hosea, Amos, Micah, and then Joel.

Regardless of who borrowed from whom, the Hebrew order does suggest that those who formed the canon considered the prophecy to be early. 'Some of the Jewish writers, as Jarchi, Kimchi, and Abendana relate, make Joel contemporary with Elisha.'[56] Jerome asserts that he was a contemporary of Hosea.[57] Ultimately, this chronological consideration cannot be totally dismissed. While it is recognized that the order of the Minor Prophets is not strictly chronological, it cannot be denied that the arrangement is intended to be essentially chronological. There certainly appears to be a chronological distinction between the pre-exilic and the post-exilic prophets, regardless of whether one follows the order given in the Hebrew canon or the Septuagint. It is difficult to imagine how those who arranged the canonical order could have forgotten the date of the prophecy if the prophet lived and wrote after the exile.[58]

---

53. Treves, 154.

54. Compare 3:13 with Isa. 63 and Rev. 14:14-20. See additional discussion in the commentary section.

55. Cf. Allen, 21 and Watts, 12.

56. John Gill, *Gill's Commentary* (Grand Rapids: Baker, rpt 1980) IV, 638.

57. W. J. Deane, *The Book of Joel* (Grand Rapids: Eerdmans, rpt 1975) vii.

58. Bic adds that the book reflects a close affinity to Hosea and that its traditional position in the canon must, therefore, be taken seriously (Milos Bic, *Das Buch Joel* [Berlin: Evangelische Verlagsanstalt, 1960]).

Those who suggest that Joel borrowed from other writers do so primarily on the basis of linguistic analysis.[59] By analyzing the vocabulary of Joel and comparing it with the words used by other writers whose date of writing is more certain, many commentators have concluded that the book is one of the later prophecies of the Old Testament.[60] Gray, for example, concludes: 'The whole argument from the parallels, itself cumulative, points somewhat strongly to the conclusion that Joel is a post-exilic writing.[61]

The linguistic parallels, however, are not conclusive. The majority of parallels in phraseology exist between Joel and Amos. For example, Joel 3:16a [4:16a] and Amos 1:2a contain identical phrases: 'The Lord roars from Zion and utters His voice from Jerusalem.' While it is possible that Joel borrowed from Amos, the context suggests that it was the reverse. Amos appears to be quoting from Joel in an effort to show his hearers that he is continuing the work of his predecessor. Robinson correctly claims that Joel 3:16 [4:16] 'is obviously prior to Amos 1:2 .... For, in Joel it is the climax of a revelation; whereas Amos starts out with it, taking it, as it were, for his text.'[62] Pusey agrees: 'The whole force of the words, as employed by Amos, depends upon their being recognized by his hearers, as a renewal of the prophecy of Joel.'[63] The same thing can be said regarding the parallel between Joel 3:18 [4:18] and Amos 9:13. The phrase is firmly

---

59. For an exhaustive list of linguistic parallels between Joel and other books, cf. Heinrich Holzinger, 'Sprachcharakter und Abfassungszeit des Buches Joel,' *Zeitschrift für die Alttestamentliche Wissenschaft* (Giessen: J. Rickersche Buchhandlung, 1889), 89-136.

60. Proponents include G. R. Driver, 'Notes and Studies, Joel,' *The Journal of Theological Studies*, 39 (1938) 400-402; G. B. Gray, *Expositor*, 8 (Sept, 1893) 208-225; Holzinger, 89-136; Watts, 11-13; Bewer, 56-62.

61. Gray, *Expositor*, 222. The linguistic argument is often based upon a weak view of biblical inspiration. Bewer readily admits this predetermined perspective in his opening statement on the date of Joel: 'Since the book is not a unity we must try to determine the date of Joel, of the eschatological editor and of the author of 4:4-8' (56).

62. G. L. Robinson, *The Twelve Minor Prophets* (Grand Rapids: Baker, rpt 1979) 38.

63. E. B. Pusey, *The Minor Prophets* (Grand Rapids: Baker, rpt 1973), 144.

entrenched in Joel and is closely connected to his circle of ideas. Kirkpatrick summarizes the argument cogently:

> The Book of Joel closes with a vision of judgment on the nations, and a promise of prosperity for Judah. Amos takes up the thought of judgment, develops it in detail, and warns Judah that they will not escape. He then closes his prophecy (9:13) with a repetition of Joel's promise of marvelous fertility for the land of Judah (Joel 3:18), as though he would declare that, although the promise has not yet been realized, God's word cannot fail. Thus in respect both of threatening and of promise he (Amos) confirms the message of his predecessor.'[64]

It would seem quite natural for Joel, who was from Jerusalem, to speak of the Lord roaring from Zion and uttering His voice from Jerusalem (3:16 [4:16]) and to promise unprecedented productivity in light of the drought and locust invasion (3:18 [4:18]). On the other hand, Amos was from Tekoa (1:1) and mentions Zion and Jerusalem only once each elsewhere (2:5; 6:1).

Other words and phrases which both Joel and Amos employ appear to originate in Joel. The word 'pasture' occurs three times in Joel (1:19, 20; 2:22) and is more contextually appropriate than in Amos where it occurs only once (1:2). Amos' use of the word 'caterpillar' in 3:9 seems borrowed from Joel, for it is utilized elsewhere in the Old Testament only by Joel, where it depicts a kind of locust ('gnawing locust,' 1:4; 2:25).[65]

The prophecy appears to contain additional reflections of the earlier years of the monarchy. Smith elaborates: 'The vagueness of his representations in general, and of his pictures of the Day of Jehovah in particular, is attributed to the simplicity of the earlier religion of Israel.'[66] Kirkpatrick adds:

> It appears that the concept of 'The Day of the Lord' was an idea familiar to the people of the time of Amos (cf. 5:18ff.), even though they had misinterpreted its significance and were

64. Kirkpatrick, 64.
65. Cf. Kirkpatrick, 63-65.
66. Smith, II, 377.

claiming its blessings for themselves and the threats to their enemies. But such a misconception might easily have arisen from a one-sided and partial interpretation of the prophecy of Joel.[67]

In all of this it is admitted that who borrowed from whom cannot be conclusively demonstrated. Nevertheless, the point is that it is equally probable (if not more so) that Joel is early rather than late. The oft-cited parallels between Joel and other prophets find equal or greater contextual homogeneity within the prophecy of Joel as they do elsewhere. The resemblances of Joel with Zechariah 12–14 point to the same conclusion. Zechariah 12–14 is not based upon present circumstances, but is apocalyptic and eschatological rather than prophetic and didactic. Joel's prophecy, on the other hand, issues out of the actual circum-stances of his time. 'His thoughts on the future are in terms suggested by and closely related to the circumstances of the present.'[68]

A large proportion of Joel's vocabulary is classic and very suitable to an early period of literature. Smith attempts to explain this phenomenon by attributing their presence to wholesale borrowing from earlier authors.[69] But even Ahlstrom, who holds to a post-exilic date, admits that 'many of the words and phrases used as arguments for a late date are not late at all.'[70] Von Orelli cogently adds: 'The notion that a later epigon compiled the book of Joel out of older prophetic literature, is wrecked on the consideration that in Joel everything is of a piece, and the language is just as fresh and inspiring as the connection is original and unforced, which ill comports with tedious mosaic work.'[71] Thus it is not necessarily late at all; the stylistic and linguistic arguments bring virtually no verifiable chronological evidence to the discussion of date. Ultimately, it must be concluded

---

67. Kirkpatrick, 65.
68. Kirkpatrick, 71-72.
69. Smith, II, 376, 383.
70. Ahlstrom, 21.
71. C. von Orelli, *The Twelve Minor Prophets*, tr. by J. S. Banks (Minneapolis: Klock & Klock, rpt 1977), 77.

that 'there is no single element of the thought of Joel that is incompatible with a pre-exilic date for the prophecy.'[72]

13. In Joel 3:2, 12 [4:2, 12] the reference to the valley of Jehoshaphat suggests that the prophet ministered sometime during or shortly after the reign of King Jehoshaphat (873-848 BC). The location of this valley is uncertain, but the fact that it is attached to Jehoshaphat's name suggests a time period during or shortly after his reign. Some consider the mention of this valley to be an allusion to the supernatural defeat of the combined forces of Ammon, Moab and Edom while Jehoshaphat was king (cf. 2 Chron. 20), which allowed him to be at peace and to have rest from his enemies (2 Chron. 20:30). While this connection cannot be confirmed, it does provide a fitting picture of the future gathering of confederate forces at Jerusalem (cf. Zech. 12:3; 14:2) when Yahweh will again bring supernatural triumph and peace for His people.

Conclusion

There is no easy solution to the complex problem of dating the prophecy of Joel. Despite the multiplicity of arguments that both sides have hurled at the controversy, much of the evidence adduced is clearly indecisive. There are some chronological factors, however, that point to an early rather than late date for the book.

First is the canonical location of the prophecy in the canon among the pre-exilic prophets. While this does not carry conclusive weight, it cannot be dismissed. Post-exilic scribes would certainly have known of its lateness and would have included it with the post-exilic prophets.

Second, the contents of the book reflect the earlier years of Israel. The concept of the 'Day of Yahweh' had not yet fallen into misconception and misinterpretation as it did in the days of Amos (5:18ff). Furthermore, the ravages of a locust plague would have a substantial impact upon a strongly agricultural community such as Israel was in her earlier years. The prophecy presupposes that the nation was following a correct form of divine worship, for Joel does not mention any specific

---

72. Harrison, 878.

sin. The dismay that the plague would interrupt the daily sacrifices also reflects an earlier period. The call to repentance was not made with regard to any specific sin but in regard to sin as a whole—nationally, a situation which parallels the time period of Elijah (858–852 BC) and his struggle with Baalism. Throughout Israel's early years the nation was susceptible to the allurement of Baal worship which, since Baal was the god of fertility, promised agricultural prosperity (cf. Judg. 2:11ff; 3:7; 6:25ff; 8:33; 10:6ff; 1 Sam. 7:4; 12:10). In response to the Baal worship of Ahab and his Phoenician wife Jezebel, God sent a drought on Israel and Phoenicia. Through Elijah God supernaturally supplied food for the Phoenician widow and raised her son from the dead (1 Kings 17:14, 17-24), thereby demonstrating the superiority of Yahweh over Baal, the god of fertility, and over Mot, the god of death, to whom Baal was thought to be subject during times of famine. After the culmination of the confrontation at Mount Carmel, God sends rain, once again demonstrating His superiority over Baal. 'Many of Yahweh's deeds...parallel Baal's alleged accomplishments and demonstrate that Yahweh, not Baal, controls the elements of the storm and possesses authority over the forces of chaos and death.'[73]

Third, the mention of Israel's earlier enemies, such as Philistia and Edom, and the absence of any reference to her later enemies, such as Syria and Assyria who both invaded during the reign of Joash, intimate an early date.

Finally, the parallels between Joel and Amos attest that Joel was the earlier of the two. Similar passages found in both prophecies, when compared, are repeatedly found to be contextually more appropriate to Joel than to Amos. When Joel is compared with other Old Testament prophets, they appear to be dependent on, expand upon or presuppose the work of Joel (cp. Ezek. 30:2 with Joel 1:15, 2:1ff; Jer. 25:30-31 with Joel 3:11, 16 [4:11, 16]; Isa. 66:18 with Joel 3:2 [4:2]; Ezek. 47:1ff with Joel 3:18 [4:18]; Ezek. 38:17, 39:8 with Joel 3

---

73. Robert B. Chisholm, Jr., 'The Polemic Against Baalism in Israel's Early History and Literature,' *Bibliotheca Sacra*, 151:603 (July-September, 1994), 268. Also see Milos Bic, *Das Buch Joel* (Berlin: Evangelische Verlaqsanstalt, 1960).

[4]; and Isa. 2:4 and Micah 4:3 with Joel 3:10 [4:10], where the actual understandably precedes the ideal). Robinson remarks: 'Indeed, the general impression from reading Joel's book is that of smoothness and sequence of thought rather than of slavish reproduction.'[74]

It is suggested, therefore, that Joel was written in the middle of the ninth century BC (around 860–850 BC), during the latter years of the reign of Jehoshaphat. This would coincide with the ministry of Elijah and would identify the locust plague and drought of Joel with the great drought which occurred during the reign of Ahab (874–853 BC; cf. 1 Kings 17-18).

Ultimately, however, it should be remembered that the importance of dating the book for the purpose of interpretation is minimal. Unlike the nature of other prophecies in which knowledge of the time and history is significantly related to its understanding, the message of Joel is timeless. It forms a doctrine that could be repeated and applied in any age.

The Historical Situation

Although the historical situation is somewhat contingent on the date of the prophecy, many aspects of Joel's situation can be deciphered apart from any direct consideration of the date. The nation had been the victim of military escapades from her enemies to the west. Tyre, Sidon, and Philistia had inflicted severe blows upon the people (3:3, 6ff [4:3, 6ff]), the land (3:2 [4:2]), the temple and palaces (3:5 [4:5]).

Furthermore, the nation had suffered loss not only as a result of foreign military invasions but also due to the massive infiltration of locusts and drought. This natural calamity had caused the land to become economically devastated, so much so that the animals had no food (1:18ff) and there was nothing with which to bring an offering to Yahweh (1:13). Even the locusts themselves were forced to be satisfied with plants not known for their greenness (1:7, 12).

Spiritually, the people appear somewhat calloused and indifferent. No specific sins are mentioned by the prophet. Unlike many other prophets, he does not attack the people for their idolatry. Nevertheless, Joel does call them to a *bona*

---

74. Robinson, 37.

fide repentance. He admonishes them to 'rend your heart and not your garments' (2:13).[75]

The political situation is ambiguous. The people certainly were not enjoying the stability that characterized the monarchy under David and Solomon. Rather, internal evidence suggests a certain vulnerability, possibly arising out of political weakness. Economic devastation such as is described by the prophet often leaves a nation open to attack. However, the information is too scanty to allow for firm conclusions. The atrocities which were committed against Judah (3:3-7 [4:3-7]) are not chronologically specific and could have occurred at any time prior to the events of 2:18-3:2 [2:18-4:2].

Ultimately, an understanding of the historical situation is helpful but not crucial. As stated earlier, the message of the prophecy is timeless; its meaning and one's capacity for understanding it are not in any way diminished by the chronological ambiguity.

The Purpose and Theme

Purpose

The writing of the prophecy arises out of an exceptionally severe plague of locusts that was inflicting massive economic losses (1:2ff). As a result of this devastating calamity, the prophet is compelled to warn the nation of certain and imminent divine judgment (1:15) and to call all levels of society to earnestly mourn and repent (1:13ff; 2:12ff) in order that they might escape the coming doom and again enjoy Yahweh's mercy and favor.

Using this temporal divine judgment and the prospect of material prosperity following repentance, Joel points toward a more distant time. The future Day of Yahweh is in view, when God would cause spiritual blessings to be poured out upon His true worshipers (2:28-32 [3:1-5]), while divine judgment would issue forth upon the heathen and unrepentant (3:12ff [4:12ff]).

---

75. It is even possible that this testing and suffering were brought about, not because of sin, but to glorify God (cf. the book of Job; Luke 13:1-5).

Theme

Introduction. The theme of Joel is the 'Day of Yahweh.' Introducing the phrase to Old Testament prophecy,[76] the prophet seizes upon the catchword to rouse his countrymen from their complacency and stir them to repentance. This theme permeates all parts of Joel's message, making it the most sustained treatment in the entire Old Testament.

Although the Day of Yahweh has been long acknowledged as a predominant theme in prophetic discussions, there is diversity of opinion regarding its exact nature and character. The phrase is employed nineteen times by eight different authors of the Old Testament.[77] Related terms and phrases with varying degrees of variation occur more extensively throughout the Old Testament and also in the New. These include 'that day,' 'those days,' 'that time,' 'day of trouble,' 'great and terrible day,' 'the day' and 'last days.'[78]

The multitude of related passages has contributed to the absence of consensus when deciphering the exact nature of this day. Considerable difference of opinion as to which passages are legitimately related and therefore truly applicable has not allowed this consensus to be attained. Consequently, discussions herein relative to the Day of Yahweh commence with those passages which have the same phraseology; all other passages must be relegated to a supporting role.

Various attempts have been made to define the Day of Yahweh by seeking to establish its roots in Israel's history.

---

76. Cf. earlier discussions regarding the date of Joel's prophecy and his chronological relationship to the other prophets.

77. Cf. Isa. 2:12; 13:6, 9; Ezek. 13:5; 30:3; Joel 1:15; 2:1, 11, 31 [3:4]; 3:14 [4:14]; Amos 5:18 (2x), 20; Obad. 15; Zeph. 1:7, 14 (2x); Zech. 14:1; Mal. 3:23. In three of these texts (Isa. 2:12; Ezek. 30:3; Zech. 14:1) the phrase occurs with minor variation: 'Day belonging to Yahweh.' These three texts are included in the investigation, since the preposition that is attached to Yahweh reflects the occasional Hebraic practice of using the preposition 'to/for' for the purpose of denoting the definite object. While the phrase 'Day of Yahweh' already depicts whose day it is, affixing the preposition adds emphasis.

78. The 'Day of Christ' should not be confused with the eschatological Day of Yahweh. The Day of Christ is used essentially with regard to the glorification of the church (1 Cor. 1:8; Phil. 1:6, 10; 2:16) while the Day of Yahweh makes reference to God's covenantal dealings with Israel.

Sigmund Mowinckel, for example, maintains that it has its origin as a religious feast day, a day that commemorated and reaffirmed for successive generations Yahweh's deliverance of Israel from the enemy and the realization of peace and prosperity.[79] Ahlstrom concurs and, pointing to Amos 5:18-27, assesses:

> The only conclusion that can be drawn from Amos 5:18ff. is that the Day of Yahweh was a well known cultic day, which now will not be the usual festival of light, but instead will turn out to be a day of disaster for Israel. The prophet has used a common religious idea about a special cult day but turned it into its opposite.[80]

Others have contended that the Day of Yahweh should be understood from the perspective of the holy war traditions. Gerhard von Rad, an early proponent of this view, asserts that the Day of Yahweh 'encompasses a pure event of war.'[81] Proof for this derivation is attributed to the militaristic contexts of Isaiah 13, 34, Ezekiel 7, 30, Zephaniah 1, and Zechariah 14, as well as the blowing of a trumpet (Joel 2:1, 15) and the sounding of an alarm (Joel 2:1) to describe activities which occur in connection with holy war.

While these two definitions contain helpful insights, they are weak in two aspects. First, the conclusions are too narrow, for they are based (especially the religious festival concept) on only a limited number of passages which speak of the Day of Yahweh, specifically those which are *presumably* earliest. Since the phrase occurs without the article, and thereby emphasizes the *qualitative* nature of the day, any reference to a specifically celebrated, religious feast day is doubtful.

---

79. Sigmund Mowinckel, *Psalmenstudien* (Amsterdam: P. Schippers, 1961), II, 229.

80. Ahlstrom, 64-65. Cf. Watts (4-5) for a discussion regarding the constituent parts of such a celebration.

81. Gerhard von Rad, 'Origin of the Concept of the Day of Yahweh,' *Journal of Semitic Studies* IV: 97-108 (April 1959), 103. Also cf. Gerhardus Vos, *Biblical Theology* (Grand Rapids: Eerdmans, 1948) 313 and Hans Walter Wolff, *Joel and Amos*, tr. by W. Janzen, S. D. McBride, Jr., and C. A. Muenchow (Philadelphia: Fortress, 1977), 34, 47.

Second, the conclusions reflect a denial of divine propositional revelation, attributing the rise and development of such a concept to natural, evolutionary, non-supernatural forces such as tradition and myth. When more than one prophet employs the phrase, it is assumed that the later seer(s) merely borrowed from the one with whom the concept originated, a process owing to an inordinate emphasis being placed upon source criticism and *sitz im leben*. The particular chronological time frame and situation in which a prophet spoke cannot be allowed to dictate or choke the meaning of the Day of Yahweh; rather, the reality of an eternal God who disclosed Himself propositionally demands that all passages which contain this phrase must be allowed to speak, regardless of the century in which it was prophesied.[82]

Grammatical considerations. There are two primary elements to be noted regarding the grammatical construction of this phrase. The first is the word 'day.' It is utilized frequently in the sense of an indefinite period of time, such as the day of God's wrath (Job 20:28), day of trouble (Ps. 20:1), day of the Lord of hosts (Isa. 2:12). The word 'day,' when used in this particular phrase, always occurs without the definite article.[83] As such, it does not have reference to a chronological time period of twenty-four hour duration, but to a general period of time uniquely belonging to the Lord. The expression does not designate a definite extent of time but a definite happening in time, the exact nature of which is determined by its association with the personal name.

The second important aspect to be noted is the identity of the one to whom the day belongs; it is a day which

---

82. Others, cognizant of the difficulty in defining the Day of Yahweh, are more general in their assessment, stating only that it refers to a supernatural intervention of God in human history (cf. W. K. Price, *The Prophet Joel and the Day of the Lord* [Chicago: Moody, 1976] 18-19; S. Barabas, 'Day,' *Zondervan Pictorial Encyclopedia of the Bible*, ed. by Merrill C. Tenney [Grand Rapids: Zondervan, 1978] II, 45-46; and Colin Brown, 'Day of the Lord [Yahweh],' *Zondervan Pictorial Encyclopedia of the Bible*, II, 46-47).

83. Although the expression occurs without the article, the phrase is not indefinite, only anarthrous. Thus, while the phrase is definite in that it belongs to the Lord (it is *His* day), it is anarthrous and so emphasizes the qualitative nature of the day and not the quantitative.

belongs to Yahweh. The use of Yahweh is significant in that it is the Israelitish name for God. While El and Elohim are the generic and more universal names for God, Yahweh is recognized as a personal name specifically given to Israel.[84] Consequently the name brings a distinctively covenantal motif to the expression 'Day of Yahweh.' While the name almost certainly originates from or shares a common lineage with *hayah*,[85] it not only depicts an eternally existent God but also connotes His *active* existence on behalf of His covenant. The name brings together the two motifs of transcendence and immanence; He is both the God who possessed transcendent power and might (Exod. 3:14; 20:2) and the God who is vitally operative in human events. Thus the Day of Yahweh must be viewed as having special significance and particular ramifications for the covenant people, Israel.[86]

Objects/Recipients. The Day of Yahweh is directed toward Israel, Judah and Jerusalem in the majority of cases.[87] When employed elsewhere, the phrase refers to the Gentile nations in general (Joel 3:14; Isa. 13:6, 9)[88] and to Edom specifically (Obad. 15).[89]

Some conclude that the earlier conception of the Day of Yahweh as taught by Joel and Obadiah consisted of thoughts of hope and blessing for Israel, and that it was not until the preaching of Amos that Israel realized the Day of Yahweh could result in judgment for them as well.[90] However, while

---

84. Cf. Exod. 3:13-15. The name Yahweh is not known to exist outside of Israel. A connection with *Yw*, a god in the Ugaritic pantheon, is doubtful. Cf. A. Murtonen, *The Appearance of the Name YHWH Outside Israel* (Helsinki, 1951), 4-6.

85. Cf. Francis Brown, S. R. Driver, and Charles A. Briggs, *A Hebrew and Chaldean Lexicon of the Old Testament* (Oxford: Clarendon, 1968), 217-219.

86. Cf. further discussion in the commentary on 1:1.

87. Cf. Ezek. 13:5; Joel 1:15; 2:1, 11; Amos 5:18, 20; Zeph. 1:7, 14; Mal. 4:5.

88. While Isaiah 13 is specifically addressed to Babylon, verses 6ff move beyond the nation of Babylon to embrace the whole Gentile world in general, as verse 11 indicates.

89. Other passages which contain similar expressions are directed toward other nations also, such as Gog (Ezek. 38:9) and Egypt (Ezek. 30:3).

90. Cf. Keil, *Amos*, 287; Wolff, 256; von Rad, *Theological Dictionary of the New Testament*, ed. by Gerhard Kittel; tr. by Geoffrey W. Bromiley (Grand Rapids: Eerdmans, 1968), II, 945.

Amos does confirm the fact that the Day of Yahweh consists of judgment in Israel for those who are disobedient, the idea is introduced earlier by Joel. Joel's entire thrust, his call to repentance, centers around the very real potential of a coming divine judgment. In fact, the temporal disasters afflicting Israel (famine and locusts) were declared by the prophet to be forerunners of that judgment.

Consequently, from its earliest occurrence in the Old Testament the Day of Yahweh concept embraces more than just the idea of blessing on Israel and judgment on the nations; rather, it adumbrates the fuller conception of judgment for sin and blessing/vindication for obedience and faith, regardless of national identity. This is elucidated by the fact that the judgment prophesied against the nations was announced in the context of specific sins and acts of wrongdoing, not merely because they were Gentile. The fact that Israel chose to ignore this truth and that Amos needed to reiterate it cannot be used to justify the conclusion that the expression was devoid of its fuller meaning until the time of Amos; rather it should be attributed to a false theology, a false conception of the righteousness that God demanded. It is not that they considered the Day of Yahweh to bring only blessing to them, but rather that they, with the aid of the false prophets (cf. Isa. 13), had succeeded in deceiving themselves that they were righteously and faithfully executing the requirements of the law and therefore would not receive the judgment associated with the Day of Yahweh.[91]

General characteristics

1. Chronological aspects. Most of the Old Testament prophets look forward to the Day of Yahweh. They frequently stress its imminence, repeatedly using the adjective 'near.' In each occurrence, the writers employ it emphatically: '*near* is the Day of Yahweh' (cf. Isa. 13:6; Joel 1:15; 2:1; 3:14 [4:14]; Obad. 15; Zeph. 1:7, 14; Ezek. 30:3). They also describe it as a day which is 'coming' (cf. Isa. 13:9; Joel 2:1).

---

91. Acceptance of the alternative borders on the embracement of the evolutionary concept of Israel's religion, a concept which is diametrically opposed to the fact of supernatural, propositional divine revelation.

Zephaniah 1:14 adds that it is coming with 'exceeding haste.' Joel 2:11, while void of any specific chronological indicators, leaves no doubt as to the imminency of the day, for the following verse establishes the need for immediate repentance. Also, Joel 2:16-17 advocates setting aside the normal periods of non-involvement in Israelite society.

As a result, many have concluded that the Day of Yahweh is always an eschatologically fulfilled event. Cerny, for example, quite specifically maintains that it is always 'applied to the final and universal judgment, and not to any less decisive intervention of God in the course of human history.'[92] But such is not always the case. Sometimes the expression has a near historical fulfillment. The most specific instance is Ezekiel 13:5 where the prophet employs the phrase to speak of the Babylonian conquest and destruction of Jerusalem.[93]

The prophet Joel describes the Day of Yahweh similarly. The Day found partial fulfillment in the devastating drought and plague of locusts (cf. 1:15; 2:1). Note especially 2:11 where the Day of Yahweh is described as virtually being present. At the same time, however, it was designed to be a foretaste of the decisive, interventionary acts of God in the eschatological future, a time when Yahweh would dwell in the midst of His covenant people (2:27), pour out His Spirit (2:28-29 [3:1-2]), and render judgment and deliverance (2:30-32 [3:3-5]; also cf. Isa. 13:1-13).

Thus from a chronological point of view, the Day of Yahweh was employed by the prophets first to depict events which were fulfilled shortly after they were predicted, events where God intervened in the affairs of mankind (Joel 1:15; Ezek. 13:5; 30:3), and secondly to depict the more distant, eschatological Day of Yahweh, including both the Tribulation and the Millennium (Joel 2:31 [3:4]; 3:14ff

---

92. L. Cerny, *The Day of Yahweh and Some Related Problems* (Prague: Nakladem Filosoficke Fakulty University Karlovy, 1948), vii. Only the related reference in Lam. 2:22 does Cerny view as referring to a past event.

93. Related passages in which near historical fulfillments are mentioned include Lam. 1:12; 2:1; Jer. 46:10; and possibly Isa. 22:5.

[4:14ff]; Isa. 2:12; 13:6, 9). The historical fulfillment became illustrative of the eschatological event.

> The OT came to use the idea of the 'day of Yahweh' as short-hand for the belief that history is heading toward a goal. From our perspective it resembles a mountaineer making for a great peak but compelled by the terrain to climb other summits en route. Yet the interim climbs are not without purpose: each is a further guarantee that presently the final peak will be reached. So OT history proceeds in a series of promises and fulfill-ments. But as OT history progressed in this way, hope was mingled with disappointment as covenant institutions failed and covenant persons fell short of the promised ideal. But it was a theocentric hope so that well before the time of Amos it had been crystallized into the expectation of a climactic 'day of Yahweh' in and by which all would be consummated.[94]

This use of the expression reflects the very normative role of prophecy in the Old Testament. Prophecy never occurred in a historical vacuum; rather it was always given in a specific historical context. It was always proclaimed to meet the need of a specific situation.[95] The nature of the near fulfilled Day of Yahweh events provides a secure point of departure from which to investigate and understand the eschatological Day of Yahweh. That prophecy was always anchored chronologi-cally in a historical context is further evidenced by the fact that Old Testament prophetic thought revolved around two essential time elements. The first is the Exodus and God's judgment of Egypt and deliverance of Israel; the second is the eschatological Day of Yahweh, a day that will also encompass judgment and deliverance. The former chrono-logical time designation is frequently used by the prophets as a foundation from which to launch a discussion of the latter (cf. Isa. 11:16; 48:20-21; 51:10-11).

---

94. J. A. Motyer, 'Old Testament History,' *Expositor's Bible Commentary*, ed. by Frank Gaebelein (Grand Rapids: Zondervan, 1985), I, 255. Kaiser adds: 'This day is depicted as a period when the Lord will conclude his work of salvation and judgment on a universal and cosmic scale.... [T]he topic of that day is introduced by means of a contemporary calamity: in Joel's case, a severe locust plague...' (*The Messiah in the Old Testament*, 138).

95. This is most notably depicted in the prophecy of the virgin birth of Christ given by Isaiah to King Ahaz in Isaiah 7.

2. Descriptive elements. The manner in which the prophets speak of the Day of Yahweh is graphic and colorful. When describing that day, there are certain descriptive elements that recur frequently among the various writers:

- The Day of Yahweh is often marked by seismic disturbances. Manifestations and cosmic transformations are described as phenomena that will accompany the coming of this day. The sun, moon and stars lose their light (Isa. 13:6ff; Joel 2:1-11; 2:31 [3:4]; 3:14 [4:14]; Amos 5:18-20; Zech. 14:1ff). The heavens tremble and the earth shakes (Isa. 13:6ff; Joel 2:1-11; 3:14 [4:14]; Zech. 14:1ff). These types of cosmic phenomena are seen elsewhere in both the Old and New Testaments as accompanying divine intervention into human history, both historically (Judg. 5:4-5; 1 Sam. 14:15; Ps. 68:8; 77:18) and eschatologically (Isa. 34:4; Matt. 24:7; Luke 21:25-28; Rev. 6:12-17; 8:12).

- Closely related to the cosmic activity is the violent weather. While Ezekiel 13:5ff is the only Old Testament passage to mention it in connection with this day, it reappears elsewhere in conjunction with divine intervention (Gen. 19:24; Luke 17:29; Rev. 8:7).

- Another manifestation said to accompany the Day of Yahweh is the 'clouds' and 'thick darkness' (Joel 2:1-11; Zeph. 1:7ff; Ezek. 30:3ff). The 'cloud' has special significance in scripture, especially in connection with theophanies (Exod. 16:10; 19:16; 24:16; 34:5; Deut. 4:11; Matt. 17:5; Luke 21:27; Acts 1:9). 'Thick darkness' is almost exclusively used elsewhere in the Old Testament to describe the appearance of Yahweh (2 Sam. 22:10; Job 22:13-14; Ps. 97:2; Ezek. 34:12).[96]

- Joel indicates that the inhabitants of the day will observe blood, fire and columns of smoke displayed in the sky and on the earth (Joel 2:30 [3:3]; 2:3). The

---

96. Ezekiel 38:9, 16 speak of the massive armies of Gog and Magog being like a cloud covering the land of Israel.

prophet adds in 2:31 [3:4] that the cosmic upheaval will result in the moon turning to blood. Although Zephaniah 1:7ff makes no reference to blood specifically, it does liken the day to a sacrifice prepared by Yahweh; thus the concept of blood is not far removed. Isaiah 34:1ff closely associates the thought of blood and sacrifice with the idea of divine intervention in human affairs:

The sword of the Lord is filled with blood,
It is sated with fat, with the blood of lambs and goats,
With the fat of kidneys of rams.
For the Lord has a sacrifice in Bozrah,
And a great slaughter in the land of Edom
(Isa. 34:6; cf. Jer. 46:10; Isa. 63:1-6).

- The day is further described as 'destruction from the Almighty' (Joel 1:15; Isa. 13:6).[97] While Isaiah elucidates this day of destruction as one which is 'cruel, with fury and burning anger' (13:9), it is Zephaniah who defines it most graphically as a day of wrath, trouble, distress, destruction and desolation (1:14ff). Other prophets denote the day as being great, awesome and terrible (Joel 2:31 [3:4]; Zeph. 1:18; Mal. 4:5), an all-consuming day which demands that the trumpet be sounded and the battle cry be heralded (Joel 2:1; Zeph. 1:17).

- While the day of Yahweh is most prominently described in terms of destruction and catastrophe, it is depicted in terms of promise and hope as well. Joel notes that the day will be characterized by a pouring of the Spirit on all flesh, accompanied by prophetic utterances, dreams and visions (2:28-29 [3:1-2]). In a similar attitude, Malachi announces that the day will be marked by the coming of Elijah, an appearance depicted as bringing restoration and hope (4:5-6)

Consequences. The prophets of the Old Testament describe the impact and results of the Day of Yahweh with dramatic

---

97. In both instances there is a play on words which contributes significantly to the strength of the announcement.

and exacting language. The effects of the day are awesome, both constructive and destructive, affecting the entire spectrum of life: plant, animal and human.

The consequences awaiting those who are the enemies of God are grave. The enemies are often designated as Gentiles; yet the category is usually broadened to include all who are in opposition to Yahweh and His ways (Isa. 13:11), regardless of nationality. Tasker has correctly noted that it 'would be a day which God would vindicate "His own righteousness," not only against the enemies of Israel, but also against Israel itself.'[98]

With poetic vividness, Isaiah describes the day as a time when Yahweh will be exalted and the proud and lofty will be abased (2:11-22). Although Isaiah intimates how this will come about in 2:19, 21, he describes it explicitly in 13:6ff, stating that it will result in great terror: 'Therefore all hands will fall limp, and every man's heart will melt' (13:7). Furthermore, he adds that sinners will be exterminated (13:9, 12, 14-15; also cf. Ezek. 13:5; 30:3; Obad. 15; Zeph. 1:7ff). Joel 3:19 [4:19] mentions the destruction of Edom and Egypt specifically. Other physical atrocities will accompany these results. Houses will be plundered (Isa. 13:16; Zeph. 1:7ff; Zech. 14:2), wives will be ravished (Isa. 13:16; Zech. 14:2), and little ones will be dashed into pieces (Isa. 13:16). Few survivors will be left (cf. Isa. 2:10ff; Amos 5:18ff; Zeph. 1:18).

While grave consequences await the enemies of Yahweh on His day, great blessings will also be effected on that day for the godly remnant. The Day of Yahweh is not occupied with the judgment of God to the exclusion of the blessing of God. Both are integral parts of that day. Many of the contexts in which the phrase is located reflect with clarity the inclusion of blessing with that day.[99] Spiritual bless-

---

98. R. Tasker, *The Biblical Doctrine of the Wrath of God* (London: Tyndale, 1951), 45.

99. Cf. Kenneth L. Barker, 'Zechariah,' in *Expositor's Bible Commentary*, ed. by Frank E. Gaebelein (Grand Rapids: Zondervan, 1985), 7:619-620; W. C. Kaiser, Jr, *Toward an Old Testament Theology* (Grand Rapids: Zondervan, 1978), 191; A. B. Davidson, *The Theology of the Old Testament* (New York: Scribner's, 1907), 374-75; J. D. Pentecost, *Things to Come* (Grand Rapids: Zondervan, 1958), 230. Allen (59) also observes that the Day of Yahweh

ings will accrue to all who call upon the name of Yahweh (Obad. 15; Zech. 14:1ff; Joel 2:32 [3:5]). There will be dreams and prophesying (Joel 2:31 [3:4]) and restored familial relationships (Mal. 4:5). The goal and assured result of the day is that all will come to a true knowledge of Yahweh, a reality when the Day of Yahweh refers to an event with near fulfillment (Ezek. 30:3ff) as well as when it depicts an event with a more distant fulfillment (Joel 3:14ff [4:14]).

With the coming of Messiah on the Day of Yahweh, physical blessings will also result. The land's desolation, destruction and absence of agricultural and pastoral bounty (Isa. 13:6; Ezek. 30:3ff; Joel 1:15; 2:1ff; Zeph. 1:7ff) will be changed into fruitfulness and productivity. Joel describes how the sources and blessings of life will be restored and guaranteed in vivid contrast to the drought and locust plague of his day (2:21ff; 3:18 [4:18]; cf. Ps. 104:15; Judg. 9:13).

Joel adds that the rivers will flow with water (3:18 [4:18]). The Psalmist accounts for this as an abundant indication of God's favor to the earth and mankind (65:9-13). In Genesis 2:10 the same feature is depicted as a part of the paradise of the Garden of Eden (also cf. Ps. 46:4; 36:8-9).[100] It is described by other Old Testament prophets as a salient feature of the eschatological Millennial temple (Zech. 14:8; Ezek. 47:1ff). Revelation 22 mentions it in connection with the New Jerusalem.

Finally, the prophet Joel announces that Jerusalem, where Yahweh takes up His millennial residence, will not be profaned again: 'strangers will pass through it no more' (3:17 [4:17]). The holy city will be an inviolable city. Elsewhere the prophets utilize this motif in connection with the coming Millennium as well (Isa. 52:1; Obad. 17; Zech. 9:8; 14:21).

'theme oscillates in the prophets between woe and weal for God's people.'

100. Similarities have been found to exist in ancient Near Eastern religions where deities were thought to reside on a mountain located at the source of primeval waters. 'The Akkadian mountain of the gods was located *ina pi narati*, 'in the mouth of the rivers' or, as it could also be expressed, *ina berit pi narati killan*, 'between the mouth of the two rivers.' In Ugarit, El's abode was 'at the spring of the rivers in the midst of the stream of the (two) deeps'' (Ahlstrom, 87).

Thus the Day of Yahweh will result in universal resto-ration accompanied by the abasement, distress and death of the unrighteous and the exaltation of the Righteous One. It will result in the knowledge of Yahweh. Even the land will enjoy unprecedented fruitfulness and productivity; the godly remnant will enjoy peace, prosperity and the dwelling presence of Yahweh (Isa. 61:2ff).

Conclusion. The Day of Yahweh in the Old Testament refers to a time when God supernaturally intervenes in the course of human history. It possesses three basic features. First, the day is characterized by an explicit exhibition of the righteousness of God, namely, judgment poured out on sinners and blessing on the penitent. It involves cosmic upheavals as well as unprecedented prosperity and resto-ration. Second, it exhibits a strong covenantal motif, for it is *Yahweh's* day, a day having special significance for the covenant people, Israel. It is a reaffirmation of His covenant with His people. While God will vindicate His people on this day, it is primarily and foremost a day of the vindication of God. It is His epiphany day, the day on which He comes to unveil His true character—mighty, powerful, terrifying His enemies, bringing light and establishing righteousness. Thus it is not strictly a day of judgment on the Gentiles and blessings on Israel; rather, it is a day of judgment on sinners and blessing upon those who believe, regardless of eth-nicity. A third feature is that of imminency. Whether or not it makes chronological reference to a near fulfilled event or a more distantly fulfilled event, it is a day described as being 'near, at hand,' depicting not a chronological nearness neces-sarily, but an imminent, impending intervention of God.

The Day of Yahweh does not always refer to an event in the eschaton. Rather, the prophets repeatedly tie the histor-ical with the eschatological, the past with the future, essen-tially viewing these two aspects as though they were one corporate concept. It is the perspective of the current event that provides the prophets and the people with an illustra-tion of the future, eschatological visitation of Yahweh. Thus the Day of Yahweh passages maintain a secure anchor within the historical context. As with all predictive prophecy, it is

DAY OF YAHWEH
In the Old Testament

PASSAGE	FORM				OBJECTS								DESCRIPTIONS													RESULTS — Negative						RESULTS — Positive						FULFILLMENT			
	יום ליהוה	יום יהוה	Proud, lofty	False prophets	Commercialism	Idolatry	Physical creation	Israel	Babylon	Egypt	Edom	Nations in general	Light loss/darkness	Seismic activity	Violent weather	Darkness and gloom	Clouds and thick darkness	Blood	Fire and smoke	Great/awesome/terrible	"Destruction to Almighty"	Anger/fury/wrath	Pour out Spirit	Trumpet/battle cry	Coming of Elijah	Abasement	Death/annihilation	Destruction/desolation	Distress/terror	Houses plundered	Wives ravished	Fam. relat. restored	Land restored	Living waters	Dreams/prophesying	Salv. for remnant	Know Lord	Imminency	Near Hist - Eschat	Near Historical	Eschatological
Isa. 2:12	×		×		×		×					×														×		×	×												×
13:6		×	×						×												×					×	×	×	×	×	×							×	×		
13:9		×	×						×																	×	×											×			×
Ezek. 13:5		×		×				×							×					×																			×		
30:3		×								×						×	×											×										×	×	×	
Joel 1:15		×																			×						×	×										×		×	
2:1-11													×	×		×	×		×	×				×			×	×								×	×	×			
2:31 [3:4]													×	×				×	×	×		×	×					×							×			×			
3:14 [4:14]													×																			×	×	×	×			×			×
Amos 5:18-20		×										×	×														×									×	×	×			×
Obad. 15		×									×	×																										×		×	
Zeph. 1:7-18		×	×		×	×	×					×				×	×	×	×	×		×		×		×	×	×	×		×							×			

not heralded in a historical vacuum; rather its proclamation addresses the need of the hour, thereby providing a secure point of departure from which to understand the eschatological event.

The Composition of the Book

Unity

The prophecy of Joel has been regarded traditionally as the product of one author. It was not until the latter part of the nineteenth century that the unity of the book was questioned. Maurice Vernes in 1872 contended that Joel 2:28-3:21 [3:1-4:21] was not authored by the same person as 1:1-2:27. This perspective was propounded in 1896 by J. W. Rothstein and enthusiastically championed by Bernhard Duhm in 1911. The challenge was based upon the thesis that the first half (1:1-2:27) speaks of a contemporary disciplinary punishment—the locust plague and drought—while the latter portion (2:28-3:21 [3:1-4:21]) depicts an eschatological judgment of the heathen and the deliverance of Israel.[101]

The differences between the two parts of the book have been increasingly repudiated, however. Kapelrud, for example, argues for its unity, stating that the view of Duhm 'is no longer tenable' and that his 'arguments may be wholly dismissed, inasmuch as they were wholly subjective'[102] Rather than distinguishing between the two days of Yahweh, one historical and one eschatological, the majority of scholars now maintain that the locusts in the first portion were forerunners of the coming Day of Yahweh addressed in the last half. Within the natural progression of Joel's argument, Allen argues that 'there is a basic unity of content suggesting unity of authorship. To follow up an interpretation of the locusts as precursors of the Day with a description of the destruction the Day would cause is a natural development.'[103]

---

101. Cf. Bewer, 49ff for an adumbration and elaboration of this theory.

102. Kapelrud, 2. Others who support the unity include Allen, 25ff; Wolff, 6ff; and Smith, II, 387-388.

103. Allen, 26.

The advance of thought from chapter one to chapter two is abundantly portrayed. In chapter one, the natural calamity together with its attendant economic catastrophes is addressed while chapter two presents a coming judgment for Judah in light of the crisis of chapter one. Furthermore, Joel makes no mention of the heathen nations in chapter one, being caught up with the ravages of the locust plague. In chapter two, however, the prophet cries out in anticipation of a far more devastating enemy (2:2), turning his attention from the economic disasters of chapter one to a concern regarding the relationship of the nations to the people of God (2:17, 26-27). Wolff rightly asserts that the recurrence of the 'Day of Yahweh' phrase throughout these chapters 'makes it all the clearer that 1:15 and 2:1b, 2a, 11b do not represent extraneous matter. On the contrary, the relationship of chap. 1 to chap. 2, as well as many particular formulations beginning with 1:6a, become intelligible principally on the basis of these passages.'[104] The contention of Bewer that 'the references to the day of Yahweh in chapters one and two are interpolations'[105] must be rejected. Says Allen: 'To delete the 'Day of Yahweh' verses from the first part is arbitrary.'[106]

Style

Just as there is no compelling reason for multiple authorship found in a comparison of the contents, neither is there any discrepancy between the styles that the prophet employs to treat the subject matter. The call to repentance in light of the coming, final judgment is presented with stirring exhortation and description, with deviation of rhythm announcing changes in his mood and thought.[107] The author employs hexameter (2:12-14; 1:2, 5, 13; 2:18-20, 25-26), pentameter (2:17) and tetrameter with staccato movement (1:4, 8-12, 13-14, 16, 19-20; 2:5, 7-9, 15-16; 3:9-14 [4:9-14]) to powerfully convey his message.

---

104. Wolff, 7
105. Bewer, 50.
106. Allen, 26.
107. Cf. Harrison, 878; Bewer, 68-71.

Other stylistic characteristics include changes in the persons of verbs and pronouns ('my God' and 'your God' [1:13]; 'your God' [1:14] with 'our God' [1:16]), repetition in build up (1:4), the use of simile, metaphor (1:6; 2:3ff) and contrast (1:4ff; 2:19ff; 3:13ff [4:14ff]). The style, syntax and diction so characteristic throughout the prophecy not only attest to the unity of the book but also mark out the prophecy as a literary masterpiece. Although not a liturgy,[108] the prophet uses liturgical style and motifs in calling upon the civil and religious leaders as well as all aspects of society to lament and wail, thereby calling upon the assistance and mercy of Yahweh.

Arrangement

Following the superscription (1:1), the contents of the book are arranged under three basic categories. In the first section (1:2-20) the prophet describes the contemporary Day of Yahweh. The land is suffering massive devastation caused by a locust plague and drought. The details of the calamity (1:2-12) are followed by a summons to communal penitence and reformation (1:13-20).

The second section (2:1-17) provides a transition from the historical plague of locusts described in chapter one to the eschatological Day of Yahweh in 2:18-3:21 [2:18-4:21]. Employing the contemporary infestation of locusts as a backdrop, the prophet, with an increased level of intensity, paints a vivid and forceful picture of the impending visitation of Yahweh (2:1-11) and, with powerful and explicit terminology, tenaciously renews the appeal for repentance (2:12-17).

In the third category (2:18-3:21 [2:18-4:21]), Yahweh speaks directly, assuring His people of His presence among them (2:27; 3:17, 21 [4:17, 21]). This portion of the book assumes that the repentance solicited (2:12-17) has occurred and describes Yahweh's zealous response (2:18-19a) to their prayer. While earlier portions of the prophecy propound the accusation that God is absent from the midst of Israel (2:17), the latter portion

---

108. Cf. Ahlstrom, 130-37. The priests are exhorted to perform liturgical actions of sorrow and fasting, but it is not a lamentation *per se*. Rather, it is 'an actual situation in which a lamentation should be heard and performed' (Ahlstrom,131).

of the prophecy builds upon the absence of that charge, describing the blessings that would accrue as the result of His presence (2:27; 3:17, 21 [4:17, 21]).

Joel 2:18-20 forms the transition in the message from lamentation and woe to divine assurances of His presence and the reversal of the calamities, with 2:19b-20 introducing the essence and nature of that reversal. Yahweh then gives three promises that will assure the people of His presence among them. The first is the divine healing of the land (2:21-27). The people are promised material restoration to the extent that the losses suffered during the years of drought and devastation will be reimbursed and restored to overflowing. The second is the divine outpouring of the Spirit (2:28-32 [3:1-5]), a promise of spiritual restoration. The third is the divine judgment on the unrighteous, encompassing simultaneously the restoration of the faithful remnant of Israel to her rightful place among the nations (3:1-21).[109]

---

109. For alternative structural analyses, see Thomas J. Finley, *Joel, Amos, and Obadiah*, in *The Wycliffe Exegetical Commentary*, ed. by Kenneth Barker (Chicago: Moody, 1990), 9-14; and Duane Garrett, 'The Structure of Joel,' *JETS* 28 (1985), 289-97.

2.
The Contemporary
Day of Yahweh
(1:1-20)

Joel describes an actual plague of locusts and calls the people to repent, primarily to banish the effects of the plague so that they might continue the worship of Yahweh in their normal, prescribed fashion. Before describing the plague of locusts and the devastating effects it had deposited on the land, the prophet Joel briefly introduces himself and the origin of the message.

The Source of the Message (1:1)

The word of Yahweh which came unto
Joel, the son of Pethuel (1:1)

The identity of the prophet, apart from his name and the name of his father, is shrouded in obscurity.[1] The title, **Joel, the son of Pethuel,** is a form commonly found in Old Testament prophecy; yet for an author to give only his name and that of his father is unusual, occurring elsewhere only

---

1. See discussion regarding the man and his time in the introductory chapter.

in Jonah 1:1. The obscurity of this formula, however, does not cast a shadow upon the seer's credentials. The brevity of the introduction suggests that he was a well-known prophet, one who was a contemporary of the plague and of the people to whom he was speaking and, therefore, one who needed only to mention the name of his father to differentiate himself from others by the same name.

Furthermore, the prophet had no need for additional credentials to substantiate the message, for the locust plague was accomplishing that for him. The reality of the plague would provide a most persuasive and vivid argument that the utterance was of divine origin. And, lest there be any lingering doubt, Joel explicitly establishes the divine authority of his message with the familiar formula **the word of Yahweh which came unto.** This common introductory phrase, employed by the prophets to indicate that their message was divinely commissioned,[2] asserts that the message originated with Yahweh;[3] it was His word.

The utilization of the name Yahweh by the prophet discloses two basic yet significant things. The first is its relationship to the covenant. Being the distinctively Israelitish designation for God, it speaks of intimacy and a relationship bonded metaphorically through the covenant of marriage.[4] Thus the name carries special significance to those who were of the covenant (cf. Exod. 3:14; John 8:58; 18:5-6). The Old Testament frequently employs it in a covenantal context

---

2. Cf. Hosea 1:1; Micah 1:1; Zeph. 1:1. Mal. 1:1 is similar though not identical. Slightly varied forms are found in Jer. 1:2; Ezek. 1:3; Jonah 1:1; Zech. 1:1; 1 Sam. 15:10; 2 Sam. 24:11.

3. This is the rendering followed throughout the commentary. Other renderings include Jahweh, Yahwe', Jahve, 'the tetragrammaton,' and Jehovah, the last being a spelling devised by combining the four consonants of Yahweh (Y/J, H, W/V, H) with the vowels of Adonai. Its earliest appearance (i.e. 'Jehovah') dates from about the fifteenth century A.D., having been designed to avoid the actual pronunciation of the name, lest in speaking it one might violate the third commandment (cf. Exod. 20:7)

4. Hosea, in vividly portraying the marital relationship between Israel and her God, employs Yahweh in virtual exclusivity. In fact, he describes the marital separation as 'I will no longer be 'I am' (the verbal form of the proper noun Yahweh [cf. Exod. 3:14]) to you' (Hosea 1:9).

(*e.g.* Exod. 20:7 where it is the name that is not to be taken in vain; Lev. 24:16; Deut. 26:17-18; Jer. 11:3-4; 31:31-34; *etc.*). Second, the more dominant characteristic depicted is that of Yahweh's active manifestation on behalf of His people. Although the name was known as early as the time of Enosh (Gen. 4:26) and frequently declared in the history narratives of the patriarchs, it is uniquely associated with the work of God in the redemption of His people from Egypt. Exodus 20:2 reveals an intimate association between Yahweh's covenant with the people and the promise of redemption, 'I am Yahweh your God, who brought you out of the land of Egypt,' leading one to the inevitable conclusion that 'the heart of the Mosaic revelation of Yahweh was that He was going to redeem His people.'[5] The words of Exodus 6:2-3 give explicit evidence of the connection, indicating that the character expressed by the name was neither fully expressed nor comprehended in previous generations but would be so in the redemptive action: 'And God continued to speak unto Moses and said unto him, 'I am Yahweh, and I appeared to Abraham, to Isaac, and to Jacob as God Almighty, but by my name Yahweh I did not make myself known to them.'' As Motyer rightly contends: 'It was the character expressed by the name that was withheld from the patriarchs and not the name itself,'[6] an act which the following verses (6-8) make clear,

---

5. J. A. Motyer, *The Revelation of the Divine Name* (Leicester: Theological Students Fellowship, 1959), 24. Although Yahweh almost certainly originates from or shares a common lineage with *hyh*, the name is not limited to the idea of 'existence' or 'being' (as the LXX translation of Exod. 3:14; John 8:58, 18:5 would suggest). The Old Testament usage connotes much more than mere existence. Together with the fact that it is the imperfect tense which is used in Exodus 3:14, it embodies the idea of active existence or continual being in relation to working with His people (cf. S. Mowinckel, 'The Name of the God of Moses,' *Hebrew Union College Annual* [1961] 32:126-127).

6. Motyer, 15. He gives Exod. 6:2-3 the descriptive translation: 'And God spoke to Moses, and said to him: I am Yahweh. And I showed myself to Abraham, to Isaac, and to Jacob in the character of El Shaddai, but in the character expressed by my name Yahweh I did not make myself known to them' (*Ibid*, p. 12-13; also cf. R. Abba, 'The Divine Name Yahweh,' *Journal of Biblical Literature* (1961) 80:323; Mowinckel, 126; and C. Gianotti, 'The Meaning of the Divine Name YHWH', *Bibliotheca Sacra* (Jan-Mar 1985) 142:45-48.

declaring three times that He is Yahweh, the One who will actively manifest Himself in their deliverance from Egypt.[7]

Not only does the name depict an active manifestation in deliverance, but the Old Testament also joins it with an active manifestation in punishment and retribution. Yahweh's character is revealed both in His redemptive acts as well as in His retributive acts:

> Yet in spite of this, when they are in the land of their enemies, I will not reject them, nor will I abhor them so as to destroy them, to break my covenant with them, for I am Yahweh their God. But I will remember for them the covenant with their ancestors, whom I brought out of the land of Egypt in the sight of the nations, that I might be their God; I am Yahweh (Lev. 26: 44-45; also cf. 22:3).

This relation is continued in the writings of the prophets. Jeremiah, for example, in a context of divine judgment, explicitly states that the objective of the judgment is that Israel will come to truly know the meaning of the name Yahweh: 'Therefore behold I am going to make them know, this time I will make them know My power and My might; and they shall know that My name is Yahweh' (16:21). Ezekiel repeatedly reminds Israel of this when he calls to their attention the fact that in punishment 'they will know that I am Yahweh.' Not only does this phrase often occur in Ezekiel, it is found frequently in Exodus (cf. 7:5, 17; 8:10, 22; 9:14, 29, 30; 10:2; 11:7; 14:4, 18). Ezekiel also declares that the effectual character of the name Yahweh is not limited in scope to the people of the covenant, for the knowledge of Yahweh is repeatedly mentioned as the culmination of the punishment on the nations (cf. Ezek. 25-32).

Consequently, when the prophet Joel commences his prophecy in the name of Yahweh, the very mention of the name significantly calls to mind the awesome, active character of God, the One who redeems and the One who

---

7. Delitzsch observes that the emphatic expression 'I am Yahweh' at the close of verse 8 is given 'to show that the work of Israel's redemption resided in the power of the name Jehovah' (C. F. Keil and Franz Delitzsch, *Exodus* [Grand Rapids: Eerdmans, 1975 rpt], 468).

punishes. It would inevitably call to mind the past mighty acts of Yahweh on behalf of His people as well as the acts of punishment and retribution meted out against those who were disobedient. The very hearing of the name was a reminder that God would not fail to act in full accordance with the character of that name, not only in redemption and blessing but also in correction and judgment.

The Command to Contemplate the Devastation (1:2-4)

Hear this, O elders, and listen,
all inhabitants of the land!
Has anything like this happened in your days,
or in the days of your fathers? (1:2)

The message of Yahweh through the prophet Joel commences with a rousing appeal to contemplate the devastation that has fallen upon them; the gravity of the conditions demands the undivided focus of their senses. In an effort to arouse the attention of the hearers, the writer employs vivid and descriptive language, summoning them to *hear* and to *listen*, to pay close attention to what is about to be revealed. The terminology is frequently utilized by other writers in similar situations and for similar purposes (Deut. 32:1; Ps. 49:1; Isa. 1:2; cf. similar ideas in Deut. 32:7; Jer. 2:12; 6:19; Hosea 4:1; Amos 3:1; Micah 1:2). As early as Lamech, these words are used to demand attention (Gen. 4:23). In lament psalms the appeal is addressed to Yahweh (cf. Ps. 17:1; 55:2-3; 61:2; 102:1-3; 143:1). Kapelrud observes that 'the entire section, vv. 2-12, is characterized by the lamentation and its style: first, the demand to hear and to remember, thereafter a description of the calamity in detail, the lamentation itself.'[8]

The terminology is also commonly used in 'lawsuit' passages, such as Isaiah 1:2 and Hosea 4:1. While the context of Joel does not explicitly speak of a lawsuit brought by Yahweh against His people, the linguistic similarities between Joel 1:2 and the lawsuit passages intimates that the

---

8. A. S. Kapelrud, *Joel Studies* (Uppsala: Almquist and Wiksells, 1948) 12.

judgment presently being experienced may be the 'sentence' portion of a lawsuit in which Israel was found guilty.[9]

The impassioned appeal is presented by the use of two imperatives: **hear** and **listen**. The former verb, employed more than 1,000 times by the Old Testament writers, constitutes a very prominent part in Old Testament worship and study. The *Sh^ema* (Deut. 6:4-9) emphasizes the *hearing* of the Law as the foundation for obedience.[10] The term embodies more than the mere hearing of a sound; rather, it involves listening, obeying, perceiving a message. It denotes an effective hearing or listening—an understanding. Thus in Genesis 3:17, God describes the fact that Adam understood and followed the lead of Eve by stating: 'Because you listened to the voice of your wife . . .' Similarly, after the confusion of tongues, those at the tower of Babel could no longer 'hear'—i.e. not understand (Gen. 11:7). The word also embraces the idea of obedience (cf. Deut. 11:13; Ps. 81:11[12]; Prov. 12:15), an idea which was carried over into the New Testament (cf. Matt. 17:5; Mark 9:7; Luke 9:35).

The latter verb **listen** continues and strengthens the thought of the former. Literally it would be rendered 'and cause to give ear,' emphasizing the need to make a conscious, purposeful decision in the matter. As with the former, it is closely associated with perception and understanding. 'The ears are regarded as the instrument by which speech and orders are noted, not the brain, as with us. Hence the ear is the seat of "insight".'[11] Thus its usage frequently appeals for a response from the hearer (cf. Prov. 22:17; Hosea 5:1; Jer. 13:15; Job 12:11).

The significance of the ear (and hearing) in Israel's religion is further evidenced by its symbolism incorporated into her religious rituals. The bond-slave had a hole bored into his ear (cf. Exod. 21:6; Deut. 15:17; Ps. 40:6[7]), the priest was set apart by placing blood on the lobe of his ear (cf. Lev. 8:23-24; Exod. 29:20), blood and oil were applied to the ear lobe of the

---

9. Cf. J. C. Laney, 'The Role of the Prophets in God's Case against Israel,' *Bibliotheca Sacra* (Oct-Dec 1981), 138:318-323.

10. This emphasis is also exhibited in the New Testament (cf. Mark 4:24; Luke 2:20; Matt. 11:4; Heb. 2:3-4; 2 Cor. 12:4).

11. J. Horst, *Theological Dictionary of the New Testament*, ed. G. Friedrich (Grand Rapids: Eerdmans, 1975), I:546.

cleansed leper (cf. Lev. 14:14, 17), earrings were given to the bride by the groom at marriage (cf. Ezek. 16:12). The prophetic appeal is not to their hearing *per se* but to their knowledge and understanding in an effort to generate a response.

The entreaty is directed to the elders specifically and to all the people of the land in general. The Hebrew term relies upon the context to determine if old men or a ruling segment of society is intended.[12] While a comparison of *zaqen* with the latter portion verse 2 (where those most advanced in years are exhorted to scour their memories in search of a devastation parallel in magnitude) might suggest a translation of 'old men,' the designation of 'elders' is preferable.[13] First of all, **the elders** requires a parallelism not with the 'long memory' idea in the latter part of verse 2 but with the nearer, broader reference 'all the inhabitants of the land.' This parallelism would depict the elders who, as leaders and representatives in the land, are specifically called upon to respond to the seer's appeal together with the remainder of the general populace. Additional support is garnered from the comparison of 'elders' with 'all the inhabitants of the land' in 1:14, where the concept of 'long memory' is absent from the context.[14] As ruling representa-

---

12. The term is probably a derivative of *zqn* which means 'beard, chin' (F. Brown, S. R. Driver and C. A. Briggs, *A Hebrew and Chaldean Lexicon of the Old Testament* [Oxford: Clarendon Press, 1980], 278. While the Old Testament is ambiguous as to when one was considered a part of this group, Lev. 27:1-8 possibly suggests that the age of 60 separated the mature from the old. Elsewhere it is stated to be a time to be respected (Lev. 19:32; Prov. 23:22; Lam. 5:12; Job 32:4), intimating a significant number of years in which to earn such respect.

13. So Kapelrud, 12 and L. C. Allen, *Joel,* in *The New International Commentary on the Old Testament* (Grand Rapids: Eerdmans, 1976), 48. For the alternative view cf. E. Henderson, *The Twelve Minor Prophets* (Grand Rapids: Baker, 1980 rpt), 93.

14. The LXX also translates *zqn* with *presbuteros* instead of *gerontes*. Elders held considerable authority in Israel throughout her history, religiously (cf. Exod. 24:1, 9; Lev. 4:15; Num. 11:16B25; Deut. 22:15; Josh. 8:33; 23:2; 24:1), judicially (cf. Exod. 24:14; Deut. 19:12; 21:1ff; Josh. 20:4; Ruth 4:9, 11; Prov. 31:23), and politically (cf. 1 Sam. 8:14; 2 Sam. 5:3; 19:11[12]; 1 Kings 20:7; 21:8; 2 Kings 23:1). The importance and influence of the elders in the post-exilic years is evident from Ezra 10:8.

tives, the elders would provide the appropriate example for the 'inhabitants of the land,' leading the way in response to the message from Yahweh. The Hebrew *eres* is primarily used to denote either 'earth' in the cosmological sense (Gen. 1:9-13) or 'land' with specific reference to a particular land or territory, often Palestine. The reference here is undoubtedly to the land of Palestine, as the usage throughout the prophecy reveals.[15]

Having secured the attention of both the leaders and the general populace, the prophet now poses a dramatic and penetrating question. Appealing to their memory and driving them to reflect upon the magnitude of the devastation, he queries rhetorically:[16] 'Can you recall anything like this[17] ever happening, either in your days or in the days of your fathers?'[18] The question expects a negative answer.[19] The disaster, when history has been searched for a comparison, has no parallel.[20] It is unique, a 'one of a kind' event, thereby demanding that it be interpreted in the light of the providential purposes of Yahweh.

---

15. Of the 10 occurrences, it is used once to designate an unknown desert land (2:20). In the other 9 uses, 6 must refer to the land of Palestine (1:6, 14; 2:18, 21; 3:2, 19[4:2,19]). While the context of the remaining 3 (1:2; 2:1, 3) is not specific, the designation 'land' is preferred. In light of the fact that the previous 7 do not have a 'cosmological' meaning, it is unlikely that the remaining 3 do either.

16. Similar stylistic structure, in which a summons to listen is immediately followed by a rhetorical question, is employed both by the prophets (*e.g.* Isa. 1:10-11; 28:23-25), and by extrabiblical writers (e.g. Ras Shamra text, I AB, col. VI) (Kapelrud, 12-13).

17. 'This' has reference to the devastation caused by the locusts described in 1:4 (cf 1 Sam. 4:7 and Jer. 2:10 for similar usage).

18. 'Fathers' can refer beyond the immediate father or grandfather to a more remote ancestor, expressing the idea of 'forefather' (cf. Deut. 26:5; John 8:39; et. al.). The action called for is similar to that advocated by Moses regarding Yahweh's blessings (Deut. 32:7).

19. When the interrogative particle *h* is carried on by *im*, the answer 'no' is usually expected, especially in a rhetorical style. Although *im* is generally used as a hypothetical particle, it often carries the function of an interrogative particle, *e.g.* Gen. 17:17; 38:17; 1 Kings 1:27; Judg. 5:8 (Brown, Driver, & Briggs, 50).

20. Cf. similar language in Matt. 24:21.

Rehearse it to your sons,
And your sons to their sons,
And their sons to the next generation (1:3).

Because of the unprecedented nature of this cataclysmic event, it becomes an enduring memorial of Yahweh's mighty acts, and thus all who dwell in the land are to recite it to subsequent generations. Whether it be in the pouring down of judgment or the showering of blessings, the recitation of Yahweh's mighty acts brings glory to God.[21] The importance of carrying out this act is heavily underscored by the three-fold injunction to pass it on from generation to generation.[22] Scripture includes numerous exhortations calling the people to relate things to their children; here, however, the extent to which Joel emphasizes the point is 'cumulative beyond example.'[23]

The matter they are to relate to subsequent generations is introduced by *al*, the emphatic position indicating its pedagogical importance. While it is usually used as a preposition meaning 'on, upon, over,' here it has the meaning of 'concerning.'[24] On occasion it is also employed as a military term, being translated 'against' (*e.g.* Judg. 6:3; 1 Kings 14:25). The militaristic genre of chapter 2 corroborates this underlying idea. In Solomon's dedicatory prayer, he refers to a locust plague as 'an enemy [which would] besiege them in the land of their cities' (1 Kings 8:38). Together with the demonstrative 'this' in verse 2, the feminine suffix appended to *al* applies to what is reported in verse 4, denoting the cause or reason of the discourse.[25]

Furthermore, it is not merely the events themselves which are to be recounted to one's offspring, for the presence of *al*

---

21. The Old Testament, especially the Psalms, contains many examples of this command (cf. Exod. 10:1-6 [note the presence of the locust plague]; Deut. 4:9; 6:6-7; 11:19; 32:7; Ps. 78:5-7; 145:4-7; Prov. 4:1ff).

22. 'Textual tradition offers no basis for changing the tricolon into a bicolon (as proposed by Sellin, Robinson, and Weiser); the presence of a tricolon in verse 4, immediately following, argues against the proposal' (H. Wolff, 17; so also Bewer, 76).

23. Henderson, 93.

24. Brown, Driver, and Briggs, 754.

25. Brown, Driver, and Briggs, 754.

suggests that they are to relate the interpretation also. Bewer
observes that the use of *al* 'instead of the simple acc. indicates
that particulars and reflections are to be given about it.'[26] The
urgency with which the elders and the people were to relate
what they had witnessed and heard, together with its interpretation, is also indicated by the intensive term **rehearse,**
meaning to 'declare, tell, show forth.'[27] The Old Testament
designation 'scribe' is a derivative of this verb. As custodians
of the sacred text, the scribes were its teachers and interpreters (cf. Neh. 8:1-8). Therefore, in a sense, the elders and
people were to be 'scribes' to their progeny; they were to
relate the catastrophic event and to declare its meaning and
significance.

The significance was to be recounted **to your sons, and
your sons to their sons, and their sons to generations following. Generations,** derived from a word meaning 'circle,
ball,'[28] came to designate the cycle of one's life from birth
to death, apparently the meaning of Genesis 15:16 where
four generations cover the span of 400 years, conforming to
the length of life of the Hebrew patriarchs, reckoned at a
hundred years. Subsequently, the word came to mean 'the
circle of a man's life from his conception and birth until the
conception and birth of his offspring.[29] Such appears to be
the usage here.

> *What the cutting locust has left,*
> *the swarming locust has eaten;*
> *And what the swarming locust has left,*
> *the gnawing locust has eaten;*
> *And what the gnawing locust has left,*
> *the consuming locust has eaten* (1:4).

Following the summons to the elders and the entire population
of the land to contemplate the uniqueness of the catastrophe

---

26. Bewer, 76.

27. Brown, Driver, and Briggs, 707-708.

28. Brown, Driver, and Briggs, 189-190.

29. H. G. Stigers, *TWOT*, I:186. Similarly, the Roman *seculum* originally signi-
fied an age or generation of men and then later was employed to denote
a century.

and then to relate it to subsequent generations, the prophet rehearses in vivid fashion the devastation that has come upon them. Lest any should question the uniqueness of this plague, Joel abruptly and tersely reminds them of the ravages and complete destruction caused by the locusts. These insects occur characteristically in vast numbers (cf. Exod. 10:15; Jer. 46:23; Judg. 6:5; 7:12; Joel 2:10; Nahum 3:15), even to the point of restricting the sun with their innumerable quantity, and create considerable noise when in flight (cf. Joel 2:5; Rev. 9:9).

> No one who has ever seen the locust at work accuses the Bible account of hyperbole. In 1926 and 1927, small swarms of the African migratory locusts were spotted in an area 50 by 120 miles on the plains of the river Niger near Timbuktu. The next year swarms invaded Senegal and Sierra Leone. By 1930, ... swarms reached Khartoum, more than 2000 miles to the east of Timbuktu, then turned south, spreading across Ethiopia, Kenya, the Belgian Congo, and in 1932, striking into the lush farm land of Angola and Rhodesia. Before the plague finally sputtered out fourteen years after it began, it affected five-million square miles of Africa, an area nearly double the size of the United States.[30]

The locust is the most frequently mentioned insect in the Old Testament. The writers employ no less than nine Hebrew words to describe it,[31] indicating that, together with the

---

30. Daniel DaCruz, 'Plague Across the Land,' *Aramco World* (Nov-Dec 1967) 21. Locusts are from the order of Orthoptera ('straight-winged') and the family of Acridiidae ('short-horned grasshoppers'). With grasshoppers they belong to a subfamily of Saltatoria ('leapers') and were edible according to Jewish law (cf Lev. 11:21-22). Locusts from another subfamily, Cursoria, were considered unclean because they had legs formed only for creeping, not leaping. According to the Talmud, locusts that could be eaten had to have four feet, two hopping legs, and four wings which were large enough to cover their body (Hul. 59a). That locusts were a part of the Hebrew diet appears evident from Matt. 3:4 where it states that the food of John the Baptist consisted of 'locusts and wild honey.' Later, however, medieval rabbis forbade the eating of all locusts because of the difficulty of distinguishing the clean from the unclean.

31. While these terms generally designate some kind of locust or grasshopper, exact identification is difficult. The Talmud has twenty words for locust (cf. discussion by G. S. Cansdale, 'Locust,' *The Zondervan Pictorial Encyclopedia of the Bible* [Grand Rapids: Zondervan, 1978], 948-950).

biblical accounts of numerous infestations, the insect played an all-too-prevalent role in the lives of the Israelites.

The three-fold repetition of **has eaten** denotes grammatically and forcefully the voracious appetite of the locust, a creature which can eat its own weight daily.[32] The three-fold repetition of **has left** reinforces vividly the stark reality that nothing remains; all has been devoured![33]

There are two issues which arise out of the four-fold reference to the locusts. The first is whether the insects mentioned are symbols of human invaders or literal, actual locusts. Those who conclude that the locusts are symbols of human invaders argue that Joel 1:6; 2:7-9, 17, 20 refer to an actual invading army of human beings, not insects.[34]

That the reference here is to actual, literal locusts appears quite evident, however. First of all, the literal import of the activities ascribed to the locusts in 1:6, 2:9 is easily comprehended and even mandated when such descriptions are compared with Exodus 10:5-7. To deny literal locusts here is to intimate a non-literal plague in Exodus 10. Second, the numerous agricultural references in 1:5-20 strongly suggest a real locust plague and not a military invasion. An invading army can have an eroding effect on the crops, but the absence of any mention of ruination to things other than agriculture is inexplicable apart from an actual locust plague. Third, while extra-biblical literature does compare locusts with armies and armies with locusts, locusts are

---

32. *Ibid.* Cf. Exod. 10:12, 15; Joel 1:7, 12; Deut. 28:38; Ps. 78:46; 105:34; Isa. 33:4.

33. This fact is also heightened by the parallel phraseology used by the seer in which each division has four words with the words occurring in the same order in each subsequent division.

34. Cf. E. B. Pusey, *The Minor Prophets* (Grand Rapids: Baker, rpt 1973),148-157, who follows E. W. Hengstenberg, *Christology of the Old Testament* (Grand Rapids: Kregel, rpt 1973), 520-522. John Gill concurs, contending that the four locusts 'point at the several invasions and incursions of the Chaldean Army into Judea, under Nebuchadnezzar and his generals' (*Gill's Commentary* [Grand Rapids: Baker, rp 1980] IV:639). A. C. Gaebelein has suggested that the four are a type of the four great world powers of Daniel 2 and 7—Babylonia, Medo-Persia, Greece, and Rome (*The Prophet Joel*, [New York: Our Hope Publications, 1909], 39-40).

never symbols of people or their rulers.[35] Fourth, it is highly
unlikely that the seer would have described an invading
army with phrases as '*like* **soldiers**,' or '*like* **horsemen**.'
Because the locusts are compared to lions (1:6), horses (2:4),
warriors (2:5, 7), and thieves (2:9), to interpret this otherwise would be very strange, awkward, and confusing, for
one would have similes within a simile.[36]

Furthermore, it is doubtful that there is any connection
with the four world empires and Daniel 2 and 7. While
Medo-Persia did pass through the land (during Cambyses'
campaign against Egypt [530–522 BC]), she cannot be
accused of wasting or denuding the land in the manner
here described. Nor can invasions by the other three world
empires (Babylonia, Greece, Rome) be made to fit the
details. For example, immediately after the third invasion
of Nebuchadnezzar, the land is still said to have contained
summer fruit, oil, and wine in great abundance (cf. Jer. 39:10;
40:10-12).

It is even more doubtful that the book is an apocalyptic work which was never delivered orally but drafted
solely for the benefit of the people living during the Day
of Yahweh, in which case the locusts would be viewed as
supernatural portents preceding that day.[37] Support for
this view has been encouraged primarily by the poetic and
hyperbolic language with which Joel describes the locusts.
However to extract the contemporaneous, literal element
out of the prophecy is to reduce the urgent summons
which Joel makes (1:2, 13, 14; 2:13, 14) to insignificance. The
command to pass on the memory of the visitation to future
generations loses it force if the visitation is yet future.
Second, the abrupt manner in which Joel has introduced
the topic argues strongly that an actual, historical plague
had occurred, an event that amply provided the necessary

---

35. Cf. J. A. Thompson, 'Joel's Locusts in the Light of Near Eastern Parallels,'
    Journal of Near Eastern Studies 14 (1955) 52; H. W. Wolff, 28.

36. Marco Treves, 'The Date of Joel' *Vetus Testamentum* 7 (1957) 149.

37. In this view, the northern army is identified with Gog and Magog of Ezek.
    38 (for a fuller discussion, cf. Kirkpatrick, 52-57). Some proponents have
    also looked to Rev. 9:3-11 for support (so R. Pfeiffer, 574).

foundation from which to launch the impassioned appeal. The people did not need an extensive introduction to the word he had received from Yahweh; such had been well provided by the presence of an unprecedented plague.

The second question concerns the four different designations employed here for locusts. If literal insects are intended by the author, then to what do the four names refer? A prominent view is that they refer to four different stages or phases of the development of the locust.[38] This perspective, championed by Sellers,[39] contends that on the basis of etymology and historical accounts[40] the terms designate the various stages of locust development. For this to be done, however, the order of the names in 1:4 must be altered to fit the order given in 2:25. Armed with a realigned text, Sellers suggests that the **swarming locust** is the general term for locust, possibly the migrating swarm,[41] the **creeping locust** is the young, wingless locust which jumps but cannot fly,[42] the **stripping locust** describes the pre-flight, pupa or nymph stage, and the **gnawing locust** refers to the locust that has just arrived at the adult stage and is ready to fly.

Against the view that the four names denote four stages in the development of the locust, it is argued that, first of all, the identification of the Hebrew names with developmental stages cannot be verified and represents nothing more than hypothesis.[43] The Old Testament occurrences of these terms are too varied and accompanied by too little information to assign developmental stages to them. Second, when they

---

38. While some have maintained that different kinds of insects are meant (so L. Koehler, *Lexicon in Veteris Testamenti* [Leiden: Brill, 1953] 178, 319, and the *King James Version*), most are agreed that locusts are intended.

39. O. R. Sellers, 'Stages of Locust in Joel,' *The American Journal of Semitic Languages* 52 (1935/36), 82-84.

40. Primary reference is made to the locust invasion of Palestine in 1915, as described by John D. Whiting in *National Geographic Magazine* (December 1915), 511-550.

41. The Targum rendering may mean 'excavator,' thus alluding to the depositing of eggs in holes in the ground by female locusts.

42. This idea is derived from the possible relation to the Assyrian *ilqitu*, denoting the leaping gait of a camel.

43. Wolff, 27.

are mentioned elsewhere (2:25), the names do not appear in same order. This alone contradicts the idea that they represent four different stages, unless the text is altered to fit the interpretation, something which is neither warranted nor defensible. Third, the different names need not refer to different insects because originally different designations for the same locust were employed in different regions.[44]

It appears best to view the four designations as poetical equivalents.[45] By employing these poetical equivalents, Joel rhetorically rehearses for the people the dramatic and climatic impact of the devastation. It has been total and complete! 'The four names are used to exhaust the category and to describe the completeness of the destruction.'[46] The number four is frequently utilized in the Old Testament to denote this very concept, the preponderance of uses occurring in the context of judgment (cf. Jer. 15:2-3; 49:36; Ezek. 14:21; Amos 1-2; Zech. 6:1, 5; Prov. 30:15-31).

The Completeness of the Devastation (1:5-12)

In verses 2-4 the prophet focuses on the devastation from the vantage of the massive numbers of locusts, employing four different names as poetical equivalents to emphasize the totality of the event. Now, beginning in verse 5, the seer rehearses the same point from the perspective of the recipients of the plague. No one has been able to escape its tenacious grasp. Since all levels of society benefit from the vine, the fig tree, and the crops, therefore all have been affected.

The three societal groups most directly impacted, however, are the wine drinkers who delight in its abundance, the priests who utilize the fruit in the offerings, and the farmers who plant, cultivate and reap the harvest. Thus they are elevated to prominence and singled out as examples in preparation for the call to communal lamentation in 1:13-20. The prophet commences his address to each group with (1) an imperative, a call for decisive action, followed (usually)

---

44. Wolff, 27.

45. Keil notes that these 'poetical epithets never occur in simple plain prose, but are confined to the loftier (rhetorical and poetical) style' (*Joel*, 181).

46. Bewer, 75. Cf. the similar accumulation of terms in Job 4:10-11.

by (2) the vocative to designate those addressed, and by (3) a statement describing the cause for the lamentation.[47]

The Wine Drinkers (1:5-7)

Awake, drunkards, and weep;
And wail, all you wine drinkers,
On account of the sweet wine
That is cut off from your mouth (1:5).

The first group addressed is that of the drunkards. The vocative term **drunkards** usually has a negative, unfavorable connotation, though not always (cf. Gen. 43:34; Num. 28:7; Deut. 14:26; Prov. 31:6; Song 5:1). The usage here is not necessarily good or bad, though the implication is that those addressed were accustomed to making themselves drunk through excessive consumption. When compared with the subsequent, parallel phrase **all you drinkers of wine,** it appears that the seer has reference to the broader class of all who were imbibing intoxicating drinks. Pusey's contention that the passage is not speaking of literal drunkards is doubtful. The conclusion that the recipients of the message were to 'shake off the sleep of your insensibility, and oppose by watchful lamentations that many plagues of sin, which succeed one to the other in the devastation of your hearts'[48] is contrary to the context and would, if one were to embrace it consistently, require a non-literal interpretation of the 'ministers' and 'priests' in verse 8 and the 'farmers' in verse 11.

That at least some of the wine drinkers may have been intoxicated is also implied by the command for them to **awake.** While the word is used for awaking from a variety of conditions, here (as in Prov. 23:35) the reference is to one who would awake from a drunken stupor.[49] Henderson's obser-

---

47. Wolff, 21. Calls to communal lamentation were not infrequent in Israel (cf. 2 Sam. 3:31; 1 Kings 21:9, 12; 2 Chron. 20:3; Ezra 8:21; Isa. 14:31; 22:12; 23:1-14; 32:11-14; Jer. 4:8; 6:26; 7:29; 22:20; 25:34; 36:9; 49:3; Amos 5:16; Jonah 3:7-8; Zeph. 1:11; Zech. 11:2).

48. Pusey, I, 161.

49. A cognate is used similarly in Gen. 9:24. Awaking from other conditions include: (1) from sleep: 1 Sam. 26:12; Ps. 3:6; 73:20; 139:18; Prov. 6:22; Isa. 29:8; (2) from prophetical ecstasy: Jer. 31:26; (3) from death: 2 Kings 4:31; Jer. 51:39, 57; (4) and the resurrection: Job 14:12; Ps. 17:15; Isa. 26:19; Dan. 12:2.

vation that since 'the persons addressed had been deprived
of the means of intoxication, the prophet is rather borrowing
the term from the state in which they had too often been
found'[50] has some merit. Indeed the fruit of the vine had
been devoured by the locusts! But it is not apparent that the
stockpile of wine, harvested from previous years, had been
consumed. The admonition to **awake!** implies they needed
to awake to the realization that their wine would be no more.

Having come to their senses, the wine drinkers were to
mourn and lament their obvious loss. The prophet implores
them to **weep** and **wail** over their condition. Those who
drink to excess are accustomed to drowsiness and gaiety,
not to being awake and consumed with mourning and lamentation. The former imperative means 'to weep bitterly,
intensely, grievously,'[51] and is employed in 2:17 with regard
to the priests and ministers of the temple. It occasionally
speaks of joyful weeping (cf. Gen. 29:11; 33:4; 46:29), but
usually describes a spirit of intense sorrow (cf. 1 Sam. 1:10;
Isa. 30:19; 33:7; Jer. 22:10; Lam. 1:2; Micah 1:10). In Ezekiel 8:14
it is used in reference to the fertility cult in which one would
weep for the dead vegetation god during the fall of each
year (also cf. 1 Kings 18:26-29; Hosea 4:11-13; Amos 2:6-8;
6:4-7).[52] In this instance, however, the prophet is summoning
them not merely to weep over the loss of the wine harvest,
though that is surely involved, but to exercise a weeping of
repentance, sorrow arising out of having offended God (cf.
2:12-13; Hosea 7:14). Whereas **weeping** is associated with
crying and the eyes, the latter command **wail!** is associated
primarily with the voice. The verb means 'to howl, make
a howling.'[53] In other words, having awakened, they are to

---

50. Henderson, 95.

51. Brown, Driver & Briggs, 113.

52. Cf. Kapelrud, 17-23.

53. Brown, Driver & Briggs, 410. Except for Deut. 32:10 and Ps. 139:3, the
    term occurs only in the prophets. It is used both of the sorrow for sin
    (i.e. repentance) and sorrow for the judgment awaiting the sinner (cf.
    Babylon, Isa. 13:6; Moab, Isa. 15:2).

weep aloud. The severity of the devastation calls for public, communal mourning, not private.

They were to weep and wail, not on account of the absence of any wine to drink, but on account of the loss of the sweet wine, the next promising vintage that would bring future enjoyment. They apparently had sufficient supplies for the moment. Rather, it was the future that was being endangered, for the prophet goes on to give the reason for the aforementioned public lamentation. The occasion of the weeping and wailing is **on account of** [54] **the sweet wine that is cut off from your mouth.** The religious overtones of this phrase and its contribution to the message of Joel should not be overlooked. First of all, the word 'cut off' is frequently employed in the Old Testament in the technical phrase 'to cut a covenant' (cf. Gen. 15:18; 21:27, 32; 26:28; Exod. 24:8; *etc.*). Its choice introduces for the first time in Joel the significant correlation between the devastation of the crops and the proper execution of the divinely ordained sacrifices. While the prophet explicitly establishes the connection in 1:16, the relationship is not obscure in the earlier calls for lamentation (cf. 1:9, 13, 14).

The prophet's use of **sweet wine** also brings with it a fullness of meaning. Whereas the common word for wine (*yayin*) unquestionably represents fermented wine in the Old Testament, the sweet wine (*asis*) is more difficult to define precisely. The sweet wine mentioned here is usually said to refer to freshly squeezed wine, grape juice that has been recently pressed. But its use in Isaiah 49:26 indicates that it did possess intoxicating qualities. Harris remarks: 'The usual definition "sweet wine" may mislead. "Sweet" wine today is wine that has had the fermentation stopped and has some unfermented sugar. "Sweet" wine of antiquity seems to refer to stronger wine. It may mean wine that was stronger because made from sweeter juice.'[55]

The Old Testament frequently utilizes wine to graphically depict a state of joy and rejoicing (Deut. 14:23, 26;

---

54. Cf. the treatment of this preposition in 1:3.
55. R. L. Harris, *TWOT*, II:686. The Targum renders it 'pure wine.'

Num. 28:7), and thus it is not difficult to understand how the 'sweet wine' idea came to be used by some of the prophets to represent unbounded agricultural fertility and a state of bliss in general. In 3:18 [4:18], Joel describes the eschatological Day of Yahweh as one in which 'the mountains will drip sweet wine' (cf. Amos 9:13). The love poem in Song of Solomon 8:1-2 confirms and advances the same thought by including the 'juice (lit. 'sweet wine') of my pomegranates' as an indispensable accompaniment to love's blissful moments. Thus, in the eyes of the seer, the cutting off of the sweet wine represented more than just the absence of the fruit of the vine; it metaphorically represented the loss of intimacy between lovers (Hosea 1-3 and Ezekiel 16 are significantly analogous) and the departure of spiritual bliss and divine blessing.

> For a nation has invaded my land,
> Mighty and without number;
> Its teeth are the teeth of a lion,
> And it has the fangs of a lioness (1:6).

The destruction of the vine and the subsequent loss of its product (1:5) express the immediate reasons for the sorrow and lamentation. Now, in verses 6-7, the prophet descriptively portrays the instruments which God has ordained to carry out the mission of devastation and annihilation. Using the preposition **for** to provide the connection between verse 5 and verses 6-7, he announces the cause for the action so urgently called for in verse 5.

The reason is simple and obvious; a nation of locusts has invaded the land! The imagery is unmistakable. The locusts are represented as a warring nation that has come against the land, a metaphor which is further developed by the writer in chapter 2. The representation should not cause one to infer that the plague is only figurative and not literal.[56] Scripture frequently employs the animal creation to picture people (cf. Prov. 30:25-27; Num. 13:33; Isa. 40:22; Jer. 51:14). The object of the invasion is *my* **land**. Keil has suggested that

---

56. Charles L. Feinberg, *The Minor Prophets* (Chicago: Moody, 1977), 73; Keil, 183.

the possessive 'does not refer to Jehovah, but to the prophet, who speaks in the name of the people, so that it is the land of the people of God.'[57] However the prophet here speaks not in the name of the people, but in the mode of a prophet—as a spokesman for God. He is speaking in the name of God. God is the owner of the land; it is His land. The law of Moses made that explicitly clear: 'The land, moreover, shall not be sold permanently, for the land is Mine' (Lev. 25:23; also cf. Num. 36:2; Ezek. 38:16).

The locusts are represented under the figure of an invading nation because they are characterized as being **mighty and without number.** In this context their might does not infer brute, physical strength or power; rather, the meaning is expressed through the two following factors: massive numbers and sharp teeth. It is their massive numbers, together with their sharp teeth, that makes them strong. The Old Testament frequently uses locusts to illustrate the count-less multitudes (cf. Judg. 6:5; 7:12; Jer. 46:23; 51:14). The term 'mighty' is often associated with innumerable masses (cf. Exod. 1:7, 20; Ps. 40:5, 12; 139:17), as it is here.

The strength of the locusts is defined not only by their numbers, but also by their voracious appetite and ability to devour anything in their path. And thus the seer describes these hostile, countless intruders as possessing some formid-able weapons: **the teeth of a lion and the fangs of a lioness.** The lion[58] is often used to picture enemies who attack the people of God (cf. Jer. 4:7; 5:6; 49:19; 50:44; Nahum 2:11-13). In typical Hebrew poetical style, the locust's ability to tear and shred is described by a parallel phrase: **And it has the fangs of a lioness.** The lioness is occasionally employed as a symbol of violence (Gen. 49:9; Num. 23:24) and of the violent awesome nature of God's judgment (Isa. 30:6; Hosea 13:8).[59]

---

57. Keil, 183.

58. The word is thought to come from a root which means to 'pluck, gather' (Brown, Driver & Briggs, 71). It is interesting to note that Ps. 80:12 uses it with reference to the plucking of grapes from the vine, a connection that is not foreign to this context.

59. Contrary to the suggestion of some (*e.g.* Gaebelein, 46-47), it is unlikely that the representation extends beyond the locusts to include a reference to the Babylonians. The silence of the context regarding this world empire

The power to destroy and devastate is so graphically illustrated by a comparison of their teeth with the teeth of a lion. Teeth in Scripture speak of power and the capability for destruction (Ps. 3:7; 58:6). That locusts were endowed with this destructive power was well known in the ancient world, so much so that the locust became a commonly used illustration of it (cf. Job 29:17; Jer. 4:7; Rev. 9:8). Feinberg notes that the correlation was a most appropriate one: 'The teeth of the locust are likened to those of a lion and a lioness, because the two jaws of the locust have saw-like teeth like the eye teeth of the lion and the lioness.'[60] The **fangs** of the lioness are found only in parallel with **teeth**[61] (Job 29:17; Ps. 58:6; Prov. 30:14), reiterating and reminding the people of the destructive ravages of the locusts.

> *It has made my vine a waste,*
> *And my fig tree splinters.*
> *It has stripped them bare and cast them away;*
> *Their branches have become white* (1:7).

The trail of destruction left by the teeth of the lion and the fangs of the lioness is now exposed in verse 7, where the last two parallel phrases of verse 6 are further developed. After announcing the alarm (v. 5a) and the reason for the alarm (v. 5b-6), the prophet furnishes explicit proof for the drastic actions demanded in verse 5. Describing the extent of the damage and graphically detailing the destructive tactics of the invading locusts, he reminds them that it is not just one year's fruit that has been cut off from their mouth! On the contrary, the drunkards and the wine drinkers are to awake and lament the loss of multiple harvests. The damage inflicted will demand years of labor to restore.

The possessive suffixes used here continue the thought begun in verse 6. The prophet is not mourning the loss of

---

does not permit the analogy to advance beyond the historical plague (cf. corollary discussion on 1:4).

60. Feinberg, 73.

61. Wolff, 29. For a discussion of the obscure meaning and etymology of 'fangs,' cf. Mitchell Dahood, *Psalms II* in *The Anchor Bible* (Garden City, New York: Doubleday, 1974), 61.

his own vineyard; he is speaking on behalf of God. It is *His*
land, *His* vine, *His* fig tree (cf. Hosea 2:9)! The concept of
ownership is enhanced by the fact that the vine is frequently
employed in Scripture metaphorically for the people of
Yahweh (Ps. 80:8, 14; Isa. 5:1-7; 27:2; Hosea 10:1). The fig tree
has similar symbolical significance (Hosea 9:10; Matt. 21:19;
Luke 13:6-7). But here they are very literal; the vine and the
fig tree have been ruined, and all who partake of its produce
are to mourn its destruction. Contrary to their normal Old
Testament use as symbols of prosperity, happiness and
peace (1 Kings 5:5; Micah 4:4; Zech. 3:10), the vine and the
fig tree had become visual reminders of divine judgment.[62]

Instead of the vine and the fig tree bearing fruit for the
people's sustenance and enjoyment, as divine gifts of blessing
(cf. Hosea 2:14-15), the vine has been set for desolation and
the fig tree for splintering. The antecedent of the verb **it
has made** is the **nation** (v. 6) that has invaded the land. The
locusts, with their countless numbers and sharp teeth, have
caused disastrous conditions to prevail. Utilizing a play on
words, the prophet claims that the locust has ordained or
purposed[63] to waste or desolate the vine. They had invaded
with a specific goal in mind, as if executing a well-devised
military plan. The latter term generally incorporates the
concept of devastation and desolation resulting from divine
judgment, either by foreign invaders (Hosea 5:9) or by some
great disaster. The 'splintering' of the fig tree is parallel in
thought to the wasting of the vine. It too has been devastated
through the planned, designed attack of the army of locusts.

The action of the locusts is further described as one of
stripping and discarding. The infinitive absolute followed by
the finite verb 'stripping' denotes an ongoing, excessive act
of destruction that continues for what undoubtedly seems
an interminable period of time. The voracious appetite of
the locusts refused to be filled; they continually stripped the
vine and fig tree bare, casting away the undesirable parts.
With the bark peeled off, the branches become white, pre-

---

62. Kapelrud, 30.
63. Brown, Driver & Briggs, 962-64. Exodus 8:12 [8:8] has a similar grammatical construction and translation.

destining many of the exposed trees and vines to almost certain death.

The Priests and Ministers (1:8-10)

Having completed in the first stanza (1:5-7) a description of the complete and total devastation caused by the locust plague, the prophet now commences the second stanza (1:8-10). Like the first, it contains the basic, usual elements of a call to communal lamentation: the command to lament and mourn, the identification of the parties who are to respond, and the reason for the call (cf. 1:5).[64] But unlike the first stanza, the second turns from an emphasis on the more luxurious, peripheral 'necessities' to focus on a more essential element of life: maintaining a right relationship with Yahweh. He says,

> *Wail like a virgin girded with sackcloth*
> *For the bridegroom of her youth* (1:8).

Having called the drunkards and the drinkers of wine to weep, lament and wail, he now prevails upon the religious leaders to do the same. The situation before the people was grave and thus the prophet employs yet another term, a synonym, in his attempt to roust them to a proper attitude before God. The priests are **to wail, gird themselves with sackcloth,** and **mourn** like a young maiden upon the death of her youthful husband. Although the imperative **wail,** used only here in the Old Testament, is feminine, the reference is probably neither to the land nor to the Judean community (both of which are feminine), as some have suggested.[65] Rather, the summons appears to be directed toward the priests and religious leaders. As the context indicates, they are the ones who are directly addressed (l:9, 10b). They are the ones whom the prophet calls upon to wrap themselves with sackcloth (1:13) to declare and exhibit their lamenta-

---

64. Although the vocative is missing from this second stanza (unlike stanzas 1 and 3), the addressees are quite evident. The context, especially verse 9, makes it clear that those who administer the religious activities were to heed the seer's call.

65. So Kapelrud, 31; Keil, 184; Wolff, 29; Allen, 52.

tion.[66] And the departure of the very things for which they were to mourn in 1:13 is the absence of those same items mentioned in 1:9-10.

The priests and ministers were to weep and lament in a manner that would demonstrate both the gravity of the situation and the true nature of their hearts. The overwhelming grief that was to characterize their lament is vividly illustrated by the analogy with the virgin who has just been bereaved of her husband. The term employed to describe the young woman here (*betula*) is generally translated 'virgin.' Von Orelli summarily claims that the word 'means virgin in the strictest sense, the lord of her youth cannot be her still youthful husband, but her betrothed.'[67] Wolff agrees, contending that the alleged contradiction between 'virgin' and 'husband' indicates a time of death between betrothal and the act of taking into the home.[68]

Although the word is frequently translated 'virgin,' Wenham has demonstrated that the meaning is broader and cannot be limited to it.[69] While his denial of the meaning of 'virgin' in every occurrence in the Old Testament appears overstated, the word does lack the notion of virginity in the majority of cases. Esther 2:17 and Ezekiel 23:3 are obvious instances where it cannot be made to designate virgins. Such is most likely the reference here. The combination of the word together with 'husband' points to a young maiden widowed shortly after marriage. Bruce Waltke explains: 'In Joel 1:8, where the *betula* is called upon to lament the death of her *ba'al* 'husband,' it probably does not mean 'virgin' for elsewhere *ba'al* is the regular word

---

66. Bewer admits that 'the fem. form of the imv. would show that either the land or the community was addressed. But the address is omitted, which is so awkward that some insert *my land*, or *daughter of my people*, or *Israel*. It is, however, not the people who mourn so, but the priests, as v. 13 shows' (80).

67. Von Orelli, 81. Henderson agrees, contending that the reference is to one who is 'affianced to a husband, and, in this sense, viewed as married to him' (p 97).

68. Wolff, 30-31; so also Bewer, 80-81.

69. G. J. Wenham, '*Betulah* "A Girl of Marriageable Age," ' *Vetus Testamentum* 22 (1972): 326-48.

for 'husband' and its usual translation by 'bridegroom' in the versions is otherwise unattested.'[70] The fact that she is young is not helpful in arriving at a conclusion, since the term **youth** (*na'ar*) is broad and affords a wide range of meanings. It is used both of an infant (2 Sam. 12:16) as well as of Absalom as an adult (2 Sam. 14:21; 18:5).

But regardless of whether the situation here depicts a betrothed woman or a recently married woman, the simile is acutely powerful. The young woman has exchanged the silky fabric of a wedding dress for the scratchy, coarse clothing of goat's hair! She has traded the music and gaiety of the wedding feast for the reverberating cry of the funeral dirge! In the ancient world, the donning of sackcloth was a customary rite used to visibly express one's state of mourning. Sackcloth was generally made of goat's hair or camel's hair (cf. Matt. 3:4) and was usually black or dark in color (cf. the analogy in Rev. 6:12). Wolff notes that 'after the rending of the garment (2 Sam. 3:31) the *saq* [sackcloth] was put on the bare body around the hips (Gen. 37:34; 1 Kings 21:27), often covering only the loins; at least it left the chest free for the 'beating' which was part of the mourning practice (Isa. 32:11-12).'[71]

The young maiden is to mourn over the premature death of her husband (*ba'al*). The covenantal significance of the metaphor presented here by the prophet should not be overlooked. In Isaiah 54:5-8, God is referred to as the husband (*ba'al*) of Israel, His wife (also cf. Jer. 3:14; 31:32). The picture is clear. The covenantal offerings and libations cannot be carried out; Israel, as the wife of Yahweh, must repent, lest her relationship with Yahweh become like that of the young maiden.

The significance of this covenantal motif is continued in verse 9.

> *The grain offering and the libation are cut off*
> *From the house of the LORD.*
> *The priests mourn,*
> *The ministers of the LORD* (1:9).

---

70. Bruce K. Waltke, *TWOT*, I:138.

71. Wolff, 29.

The cause of the great mourning for the priests and the ministers is herein introduced: the grain offering and the drink offering have been cut off. Although the conjunction 'for' or 'because' is omitted at the beginning of the verse, the causative nature of the phrase is clear from a comparison with 1:13 where the communal lamentation of the priests and ministers is tied directly to the cessation of the grain and drink offerings.

In the Hebrew text the prophet begins prominently with the verb 'cut off are.' Because the term is used so frequently with 'covenant,' the covenantal overtones of the word here, especially when coupled with the grain and drink offerings, cannot be dismissed. To cut off the offerings was to cut off the covenant. Such actions represented the ultimate of religious gravity for Israel, for it meant the cutting off of the one who failed to maintain his part of the covenant (cf. Gen. 15:12-18; also cf. the covenantal nature of the term in 1:5, 16).

Further anguish is generated by the prophet's use of the causative passive tense of the verb 'cut off.' In other words, the cutting off has been caused by someone else. Yahweh, who is the giver of the grain, the wine, and the oil (Hosea 2:8) is the One who has cut it off! He is the source of the 'withholding' (1:13) of the grain and drink offerings. Such a realization, of course, makes the situation that much more unbearable. Yahweh has cut off the grain, wine, and oil so that the priests can no longer administer the mandatory outward rituals of the covenant.

The inability of the priests to carry on the temple service is a grave matter indeed. First of all, it threatened their very own livelihood. They received a portion of their daily sustenance from the offerings (cf. Lev. 2:3, 10; 6:16; 10:12-13). This factor placed them, in a sense, on the same level as the wine drinkers in 1:5-7 and especially the farmers in 1:11-12. Lacking the daily necessities was serious enough, but secondly, the inability to minister before Yahweh demonstrated the ultimate of gravity. As Feinberg has elaborated: 'Even the worship of God's house was affected by the desolation. What ravages sin can introduce into every realm of life! No greater catastrophe in the spiritual and religious sphere could have overtaken them. This meant practically the setting aside of the covenant relationship between God and His people.'[72] Allen adds: 'Members of other cultures in which ritual traditions do not play a compulsive part can hardly understand the overtones of emotional horror with which the simple statement is invested.'[73]

Although all sacrifices were undoubtedly affected by the drought and locust invasion, the primary reference here is to the daily sacrifices, offered each morning and evening. Grain (flour), wine, and oil were ingredients which accompanied the daily sacrifices (Exod. 29:38-42; Num. 28:3-8), depicting the presence and communion of Yahweh with His people (Exod. 29:42-46). The **grain offering** is used to signify a gift or tribute given to acknowledge submission or subservience (cf. 1 Sam. 10:27; 1 Kings 4:21; 2 Kings 10:25; 17:4; 20:12; Isa. 39:1). As a result, the term came to designate either a meat offering (Gen. 4:4-5) or a grain offering (Lev. 2:1-16; 6:14-23). Since the grain offering designated the submission of the offerer's whole life to God (cf. Lev. 23:16), the inability to offer the grain offering would be viewed as a lack of submission on the part of the people to Yahweh.

Generally accompanying the grain and meat offering was the **drink offering** (Num. 15:1-10). Meaning 'that which is poured out,' the drink offering was an integral element of the religious life of Israel. A drink offering was poured out together with the morning and evening offerings, and was a part of many of the national feasts (Num. 28-29), as well as the ceremony marking the end of the Nazirite vow. Wine was the normal liquid used (Num. 15:1-10), although water (2 Sam. 23:16; 1 Chron. 11:18) and oil (Micah 6:7) were apparently employed on occasion.

It is not until the latter part of verse 9 that the writer reveals who should lament and wail like the virgin who has been bereaved of her husband. He is speaking to the **priests** and the **ministers** of Yahweh. The two designations are essentially synonyms. The former refers to those who actually stood before the altar and represented the people to God. The latter is

72. Feinberg, 73.
73. Allen, 53.

a broader term. It not only includes the priests (cf. Exod. 28:35, 43; Joel 1:13; 2:17) and those who assisted in the care and administration of the temple and its services (cf. 1 Sam. 2:11, 18; 3:1), but it also describes those who stood before men of high rank. In contrast to 'servant' which denotes the common slave, the name 'minister' was more dignified, often attributed to those who waited upon kings (2 Chron. 22:8; Esther 2:2), leaders (Gen. 39:4ff; Exod. 24:13; 33:11; Josh. 1:1), and prophets (1 Kings 19:21; 2 Kings 4:43; 6:15).[74]

The lamentation of the priests and the ministers is here described by yet another Hebrew synonym. The term **mourn** depicts an intense, emotional response of grief for one who has died (cf. Gen. 37:34; Micah 1:8; Ps. 35:14; Jer. 22:18; 48:36). The word coincides significantly with the conditions of drought and desolation which had swept over the land. Kapelrud explains: 'In order fully to understand the verb in Hebrew it is necessary to compare it with the Assyrian *abalu* which denotes to be, or to become dry, to dry out. As a matter of fact, traces of a similar usage are to no little extent to be found in the O.T., cf. Isa. 24:4, 7, 33:9, Jer. 4:28, 12:4, 11, 14:2, 23:10, Hos. 4:3.'[75]

Having given the resultant cause of the mourning in verse 9(a), namely that it is no longer possible to offer the grain offering and libation, the prophet Joel now turns the attention of the religious leaders to the originating cause of this inability. He elaborates:

> *The field is ruined,*
> *The land mourns,*
> *For the grain is ruined,*
> *The new wine dries up,*
> *Fresh oil fails* (1:10).

The reason underlying their inability to offer sacrifices[76] and thereby to fulfill the divinely ordained offerings is set forth

---

74. Cf. Isaiah 56:6 where these two terms are compared. The term 'minister' is usually employed in a religious context, though not always (cf. Est. 2:2; 2 Chron. 22:8; Gen. 39:4ff).

75. Kapelrud, 37.

76. The causal nature of the verse is evident contextually, for the very elements which were offered in the grain offering and the libation (v. 9)

in terse, staccato-like phrases, punctuated and heightened by repeated word-plays. 'Joel loads his clauses with the most leaden letters he can find, and drops them in quick succession, repeating the same heavy word again and again, as if he would stun the careless people into some sense of the bare, brutal weight of the calamity which has befallen them.'[77]

In each of the phrases, the prophet emphatically accentuates the action by positing the verb in front of the subject. In the first case, there is a play on words between **field** (*sadeh*) and **ruined** (*suddad*). The crops of the fields have been devastated and despoiled. The drought has halted the production of food (cf. vv. 17-20); the locusts have devoured and carried away every plant like an army taking the spoils of battle. Consequently the land mourns. He describes the ground as suffering the same condition as that of the religious leaders. The land, like that of the priests and ministers, is thwarted in its divinely appointed role of providing food and the elements necessary for the worship of Yahweh. His judgment affects all of His creation (cf. Rom. 8:19-22). And whatever affects creation also affects man and his worship of God. 'The fertility hailed in OT times as a pledge of the harmony between Israel and its God has disappeared. With his terminology of feebleness and humiliation the prophet almost personifies what are normally tokens of Yahweh's blessing. It is as if by their very absence they were engaging in some mute mourning rites of their own.'[78]

The prophet mentions the three crops which most specifically affect the religious routine: **the grain, the wine, and the oil**. The **grain** that was to be offered before Yahweh (Num. 18:12; Deut. 18:4) was ruined, having been stripped away by the invaders. Both physically and religiously, the situation was grave. A bountiful harvest was considered as Yahweh's blessing (Deut. 7:13; 11:14), while its decrease was viewed as His discipline (Deut. 28:51; Hag. 1:11).

---

are those mentioned in verse 10. The Septuagint corroborates this conclusion, inserting the preposition *hoti* [because] at the beginning of the verse.

77. G. A. Smith, 405.

78. Allen, 54. Cf. Ps. 65:13 where the productive valleys are said to 'shout for joy, yes, they sing.'

The **new wine**, referring to the juice of the grape in the unfermented state,[79] is dried up. While the context describes the entire situation as originating from God, the verb here is used in the causative stem and thus denotes the active work of God. God has caused the new wine to dry up.[80] Like grain, grapes need water in order to mature normally and provide juice for making wine.

The **fresh oil** too, a third and very familiar member of this agricultural triumvirate, has failed. The grain, wine and fresh oil frequently occur together in the Old Testament (cf. Num. 18:12; Deut. 7:13; 2 Kings 18:32; Joel 2:19; Hag. 1:11; Neh. 5:1-13). Throughout Israel's history, they were recognized as the staples of her agricultural community, providing economic stability and security (cf. 2 Chron. 32:28 where Hezekiah built storehouses for the purpose of stockpiling them).

The prophet graphically personifies the oil as 'wasting away' due to a condition of extreme exhaustion. The picture is one of utmost conservation; conditions demanded that every drop of oil be guarded carefully and dispensed only when absolutely necessary. But now the fresh oil has been exhausted; there is no more in the urn. The locusts and the drought have devoured the fruit of the olive tree, precluding a renewed supply. Later prophets appropriately employ this term to describe Israel's condition as a result of God's discipline (cf. Isa. 33:9; Jer. 14:2; Lam. 2:8). God's physical creation as well as His human creation are described here as the recipients of His discipline (cf. 2:19, 24 where the reversal is joyously announced).

---

79. Cf. discussion in 1:5. Also cf. Harris, *TWOT*, II, 969. The word is never used in reference to drunkenness, with the possible exception of Hosea 4:11 where it is associated with the fermented wine (*yayin*). Micah 6:15 indicates that fermented wine (*yayin*) was produced from new wine.

80. Because of the parallelism of the phrase with the following phrase 'Fresh oil fails,' it is better to retain the meaning 'dried up' rather than opt for the meaning of 'to be ashamed' (from *bosh*). The Old Testament frequently employs the term to describe the power and sovereignty of God in judgment (cf. Gen. 8:7, 14; Josh.. 2:10; 4:23; Job 12:15; Ps. 74:15; Isa. 40: 24; 42:15).

The Peasants (1:11-12)

> *Be ashamed, O farmers,*
> *Wail, O vinedressers,*
> *For the wheat and the barley:*
> *Because the harvest of the field is destroyed* (v. 11).

> *The vine dries up,*
> *And the fig tree fails;*
> *The pomegranate, the palm also, and the apple tree,*
> *All the trees of the field dry up.*
> *Indeed, rejoicing dries up*
> *From the sons of men* (v. 12).

Having directed the attention of the hearers toward the source of the grain offering and the libation in verse 10, the prophet now turns to address directly those who cultivate the soil and tend the vines, namely, the farmers and the vinedressers. The seer is moving toward a climax; his word pictures have been perfectly orchestrated and choreographed so as to lead his audience to a timely crescendo. With each strophe of the three part movement, the drama has increased.

In the first strophe (1:5-7), the luxuries of life have been withdrawn. In the second strophe (1:8-10), the elements with which to worship have been interrupted. In the third strophe (1:11-12), the essentials of life have been snatched away, leaving the most rudimentary element of life—food—in jeopardy! To lose the enjoyment of wine is one thing; to lose the ability to outwardly worship God is of greater significance; but to have nothing to eat is tantamount to a sentence of death! There is concern about the loss of wine and even greater distress that the priest has no offering. But the greatest pathos is aroused by the vision of a poor farm laborer who has nothing with which to feed his starving family. With such fervency the prophet compels the people to respond with lamentation, mourning and repentance.

Beginning the third stanza with the same ardor as the previous two (cf. 1:5, 8), he implores the farmer and the vinedresser. It appears that the reference here is to hired personnel and not landowners. Both 2 Chronicles 26:10 and Isaiah 61:5 suggest that they were agricultural and viticultural workers hired to plant, tend, and harvest the crop.

The designation of vinedresser here is not to be restricted to those who tend vines, but is intended to include all fruit growers in general, as verse 12a indicates.

Continuing to reinforce the urgency of the matter at hand through the use of imperatives, the prophet exhorts the farmer to **be ashamed!** (*hobisu*), thereby forming a play on words with the **dries up** (*hobis*) in the previous verse. The ruining of the grain and the drying up of the vines has brought cause for shame and audible distress. The causative form of the imperatives and the inherent nature of the verbs suggest that the response is not something one does willingly or by himself; it is a state to which he has come under coercion. While the primary emphasis of the English verb **be ashamed** focuses on the inner attitude or state of mind, by contrast the force of the Hebrew term connotes a public disgrace, a physical state to which the guilty party has been forcibly brought (cf. Jer. 14:4; Amos 5:16-17).[81]

The remainder of verse 11 and the first half of verse 12 give the reason for the open shame and distress of the farmer and the vinedresser, with verse 12b providing the summation of the causes. The prophet begins by rehearsing for the farmers the obvious cause for the shame: the wheat and the barley have been destroyed; there is nothing to harvest! Wheat is prominently mentioned in Deuteronomy 8:8 as one of the material blessings with which the land of Palestine abounded and to which the people of Israel could look forward. It was a highly valued grain and was raised in sufficient abundance that King Solomon could use it in trade with Hiram, king of Tyre (cf. 1 Kings 5:11; 2 Chron. 2:10, 15). Elsewhere it is used to symbolize God's abundant provision and care (cf. Deut. 32:14; Ps. 81:16; 147:14).

Barley,[82] of less value than wheat, could be grown on poorer soil and was cheaper to purchase, and thus it was generally considered to be the grain of the poor. Now, however, neither of them could be purchased—at any

---

81. John N. Oswalt, *TWOT*, 97-98 presents an excellent discussion on the fullness of the term.

82. The Hebrew designation is derived from the word 'hair,' supposedly due to the beard on the grain.

price. The harvest had perished! The descriptive manner used by the seer to express the total crop failure is most emphatic. Employing the term which both the Old and New Testaments transliterate '*abaddon*,' the word refers to something which constitutes great loss—often physical life, and sometimes even eternal punishment. The crop has expired; the life-sustaining principle has been withdrawn. The connection between the crops 'expiring' and the very real threat of physical 'expiring' brought on by starvation must have certainly served as a vivid and compelling motivation to heed the admonition of lamentation and repentance.

The vinedresser has equal cause for sorrow, for verse 12a indicates that, just as the farmer, he too has nothing to harvest. While verse 11b gives the reason for the farmer's shame, verse 12a provides the reason for the vinedresser's lament. The matter of the vine is interwoven throughout the prophet's complaint. Beginning in verse 7 the vine has been splintered by the voracious activity of the locust and, as a result, the libation has been cut off. In verse 10, with the added emphasis of word play, the wine has dried up (*hobis*), a situation that has obviously resulted from the vine drying up (*hobisah*) in verse 12.

In addition to the withering up of the vine, the fig tree also fails. Note the continued parallelism and word play with verse 10. Just as the wine dries up (v. 10) and the vine dries up (v. 12), so also the fresh oil fails and the fig tree fails. The picture is indeed bleak, for even the deep roots of the trees cannot withstand the torturous treatment administered by the locusts, especially when accompanied by an extended period of drought. Like the wheat and the vine, the fig tree was a significant part of the economy of Canaan. In Deuteronomy 8:8 the land which God had given to Israel was a land full of vines and fig trees, with samples having been brought back by the spies to demonstrate their abundance (Num. 13:23). Old Testament writers frequently employ the fig tree to illustrate the prosperity of the land and the abundant provision of God (cf. 1 Kings 4:25; 2 Kings 18:31; Micah 4:4). Likewise, the destruction of the fig is used to symbolize Yahweh's judgment (cf. Isa. 34:4;

Jer. 5:17; 8:13; Hosea 2:12), a thought that carried over into
the New Testament (cf. Matt. 21:19; Mark 11:13).

The non-selective, all-inclusive nature of the devastation is demonstrated by the breadth of the destruction. The
pomegranate, whose fruit was brought back by the spies
(Num. 13:23), did not escape. The delicious, brown colored
fruit of the pomegranate was a prominent architectural
piece in Solomon's temple (Jer. 52:22) as well as a part of the
hem of the priest's garment (Exod. 28:34). The date palm,
not known for green, succulent leaves, is not exempt from
the ravaging of the locust either. This tall, stately tree, with
its slender form naturally lending itself to depict columns
of smoke (Joel 2:30 [3:3]), dotted the Canaanite landscape.
It was used for food (Exod. 15:27), landmarks (Deut. 34:3;
Judg. 1:16; 3:13), and for the construction of 'booths' during
the feast of Tabernacles (Neh. 8:15-16). Realizing that
the dry bark and crisp leaves of the palm tree would be
an unlikely target of the locusts, the prophet prefaces its
mention with the preposition **even.** Even the palm tree
has been destroyed! Although it is known to subsist well
in a dry climate, it too suffers from the drought. The path
of destruction also includes the apple tree. The name is
possibly a generic designation for some kind of fruit tree
or, as many have suggested, a reference to the apricot tree
(cf. Prov. 25:11; Song 2:3; 8:5).[83]

And, lest the breadth of this gravity is overlooked, the
summary statement **all the trees of the field** is added. The
clause represents the traumatic realization that *all* the trees
have been destroyed. The language here, as noted earlier,
makes clear the fact that the unprecedented locust intrusion
of the land was simultaneously conjoined with a long and
devastating drought.

The prophet's final assessment of such a travesty is only to
state the obvious: **Indeed, rejoicing dries up from the sons
of men** (1:12b). Introduced by **indeed** (*ki*), the departure of
rejoicing is a final reason for the shame and lamentation so

---

83. Cf. Henderson, 99; Allen, 54; *et. al.* The word apparently is a derivative of
    napah ('to breathe, blow'), from which the aromatic scent of blossoms is
    derived, thus apple tree (BDB, 655-656).

compellingly demanded in verse 11a.[84] In summary fashion, the reference here includes all the groups mentioned in the three stanzas: the drunkards (1:5-7), the religious leaders (1:8-10), and the hired laborers (1:11-12). Human joy and delight has departed from all segments of society; none have escaped its tenacious grasp. The joy that normally accompanies the time of harvest has been replaced with despair.

The point must not be missed: there is *total* devastation, a situation emphatically enunciated by the almost redundant repetition of the word **dries up.'** Just as the vine and the trees of the field have dried up, so joy and rejoicing have unwillingly and reluctantly followed. Harvest was followed by a celebration, by the offering of the first sheaf of grain (Exod. 23:16; 34:22; Lev. 23:10). This year there would be no celebration, no offering, for the enemy had devoured the harvest (cf. Ps. 4:7; Isa. 16:9-10). The very things with which the land abounded (cf. Deut. 8:7-9) are now cut off. Allen summarizes the circumstances graphically:

> The prophet has gradually been building up a picture of ghastly desolation. Between his appeals have been interspersed grim cameos of the contemporary scene depicted with heavy brush-strokes. He has spoken of what his audience already knew and probably were loath to be reminded, but he has so analyzed the disaster as to present a series of arguments to bring them to their knees.[85]

The Call to Repent in Light of the Devastation (1:13-20)

Having descriptively and vividly recalled the state of affairs, he now implores them to respond appropriately, to repent!

---

84. Cf. Keil, 185; Wolff, 32. The suggestion (cf. Therese Frankfort, *Vetus Testamentum*, 10 [1960], 445-48) that the trees of the field have dried up because the workers ('the sons of men') were so distressed that they forgot to irrigate them, is doubtful. First of all, the generic phrase 'sons of men' is too broad a designation to be limited to the peasant laborers. Secondly, in times of imminent economic devastation, efforts to save at least some of the harvest are generally carried out to excess.

85. Allen, 55.

The Recipients of the Call (1:13-14)

The priests and ministers (1:13)

> *Gird yourselves with sackcloth,*
> *And lament, O priests;*
> *Wail, O ministers of the altar!*
> *Come, spend the night in sackcloth,*
> *O ministers of my God,*
> *For the grain offering and the libation*
> *Are withheld from the house of your God* (1:13).

The discourse returns to the theme so briefly enunciated earlier. The inability to present sacrifices, grain offerings and libations (cf. v. 9) once again occupies his thoughts. The temple services, especially those of a sacrificial nature, necessarily reflect the conditions of the people, upon whom the offerings and sacrifices depend. Even the livelihood of the temple workers is at stake (cp. 1 Cor. 9:13). The fervency of the appeal and the reason for it strikes a familiar chord (cf. 1:5ff). But the recipients of the appeal and the level of intensity expressed are new. The prescription here takes on a new level of magnitude and a more formal nature. The situation will not be placated merely by expressions of anguish and grief (vv. 5, 9); the occasion calls for penitence and prayer, by all constituents of society.[86]

The Law had clearly established the direct corollary between disobedience toward God and the presence of a locust plague (Deut. 28:15, 38). And the means of removing such punishment was also clearly set forth: prayer and repentance (1 Kings 8:37-40; 2 Chron. 6:28-31). Consequently, the prophet proceeds to call the priests and ministers to take action, by example first (1:13) and then by proclamation (1:14), to rally the elders and the people together for prayer and supplication (1:14). The priests are official administrators of the religious community, and as such it was their

---

86. Joel's treatise in 1:13-20 reflects structural similarities to that of communal lament psalms (*e.g.* Ps. 60). It incorporates a call to assemble [1:13-14], lamentations [1:15-18], and supplications [1:19-20](Watts, 21). Allen notes that 'the three parts are marked by a strongly religious emphasis: mention of Yahweh and his concerns are intensified to a final point of direct supplication' (Allen, *NICOT*, 57).

duty to proclaim penitence and fasting. The prophet turns to them, asking them to prepare what is necessary for these functions to ensue. 'Since the judgment and calamity have been public, the humiliation and repentance must also be.'[87]

The reference to both **priests** and **ministers** here does not connote two distinct groups of temple workers. Rather, they are synonyms and stand parallel to each other. Ezekiel 45:4, 46:24, for example, describe the duties of ministers as those of the priests, executing the official functions associated with the temple services.

Knowing that Yahweh is gracious, slow to anger, giving repeated opportunity to repent (cf. Amos 4:9ff), the prophet addresses the priest and ministers to **gird yourselves.** The same term is employed in verse 8, but here the imperative is used. In 1:8, the people are importuned to wail the lamentation of a virgin who has donned the clothes of mourning; in verse 13 the priests are instructed to likewise gird themselves with sackcloth for the same reason—to depict a heart of lamentation and mourning.[88] So grave were the circumstances that even those who stand before the Lord were bidden to replace their ornately embroidered robes (cf. Exod. 39), which they were divinely instructed to wear when serving before the Lord (Exod. 28:3, 4, 43), with the plain, scratchy sackcloth woven of goats' hair.

Although not stated specifically, there is no doubt that the priests and ministers themselves are to enrobe with sackcloth. As in Isa. 32:11, the verb is used elliptically, adding to the terseness of the command and the urgency of the action. The verb signifies 'to surround, to wrap around' and should not be restricted to mere girding.[89]

While sackcloth had varied uses,[90] it was commonly utilized in the ancient world, both in Israel and in other

---

87. Feinberg, 74.

88. The definite article attached to 'sackcloth' later in 1:13 also suggests a reference back to 1:8. Modeled after the virgin bereaved of her bridegroom, the priests are to put on the sackcloth.

89. Henderson, 99.

90. Uses include grain bags (Gen. 42:25), saddle bags for beasts of burden (Josh. 9:4), and even bedding (2 Sam. 21:10).

cultures (cf. Isa. 15:3; Jer. 49:3; Ezek. 27:31; Jonah 3:5), in contexts of lamentation (Gen. 37:34; 2 Sam. 3:31; 1 Kings 21:27) and penitence (Isa. 37:1; Neh. 9:1; Matt. 11:21).[91] Because the prophets' message was usually one of calling the people to repentance, it came to be a principal garment worn by the prophets (Matt. 3:4; Rev. 11:3). False prophets, too, would wear it to deceive their audience, hoping to generate credibility through an outward expression of self-abasement and humility (Zech. 13:4).

In 1:9, the priests and ministers are noted as already mourning the loss of grain offering and libation. But such expression is not enough. They are to intensify their present lamentation in a more public fashion. First, the prophet urges them to **lament.** Although the term is of uncertain origin, it is generally thought to incorporate the physical beating of the breast.[92] The LXX renders the verb *kopto*, which means 'to strike, to beat the breast.' Wolff explains: 'Since the chest is bared in the process of putting on the *saq* [sackcloth], there follows, in keeping with the ritual, the command "lament!" This command calls for striking one's chest, so as to add one pain to another.'[93]

Furthermore, they are commanded to **wail.** Joined with 'lament,' it indicates that mourning for death and destruction is in view. 'The emphasis is not on singing a dirge, although that is sometimes in view (cf. Amos 8:3), but rather on violent lamentation.'[94]

The location of this activity is suggested by the imperative **come!** Following closely on the heels of the references to 'altar' and the absence of any grain and wine to offer

---

91. Equally, putting off sackcloth was a sign of gladness (Ps. 30:11).

92. Cf. BDB, 704; R. D. Patterson, *TWOT*, II:630.

93. Wolff, 32. Also cf. Isa. 32:12. The term occurs frequently in reference to mourning for the dead as an expression of the most bitter of lamentations. 'This grief could be demonstrated in many ways: going barefoot, stripping off one's clothes, cutting one's beard or body, fasting (or banqueting), scattering ashes, or beating some part of the body' (Patterson, *TWOT*, II:630).

94. Paul R. Gilchrist, *TWOT*, I:380-381. For the content of mourning and lamentation, see Jer. 9:18-20, Lamentations. Also see Stählin (*TDNT*, III, 150-151) for ancient mourning customs.

the Lord, it is best to render the command, 'enter!' The priests were to enter the court of the temple (cf. Exod. 28:29; Luke 1:9), into the more immediate presence of Yahweh, to bewail the situation, to lament the circumstances, even to **spend the night in sackcloth.** The phrase 'spend the night' is an imperative meaning 'to lodge, to pass the night.' There is no conjunction between the two imperatives, making them more emphatic and forceful. Rest was not to suspend the intercession; on the contrary, it was to continue uninterrupted. 'From the connexion, it is obvious not one night only, but many nights are meant. The priests were not only to wear the habit of mourning during the day, they were to remain in it all night.'[95]

Joel asserts his authority by reminding them that they are ministers of **my God.** As a prophet of God, he has the right to direct them to respond in this way. He, as a mouthpiece for God (cf. Exod. 4:16; 7:1), is God's representative to the people. But while the prophet is God's spokesman to the people, they as priests have been given the divine responsibility to represent the people to God. Consequently, Joel reminds them of the impact of this calamity upon the **house of your God.** Unless this travesty can be alleviated, they can no longer minister their divinely ordained duties toward Yahweh, **for the grain offering and libation are withheld from the house of your God. For** completes the parallelism with verse 9 and introduces the reason the priests must respond in such a drastic fashion. In verse 9, the grain offering and libation have been 'cut off.' In verse 13, the verb changes to **withheld,** meaning 'to withhold, keep back, deny, restrain.' While in verse 9 the offerings were cut off, as though the cause was the natural calamity, in verse 13 the prophet makes it clear by his choice of verbs that God is involved; He is withholding it and therefore prayer is required of those who would represent the people to God.

The divinely instituted obligations of the vassals toward their God-King, as a part of the theocracy, were in danger of going unfulfilled.

---

95. Henderson, 99. Ps. 134:1 notes that at least a minimal amount of temple services continued during the night.

'The priests had responsibility for the maintenance of the ritual system whereby due praise was ascribed to God and his name was honored. Now the system of worship had broken down and they were obliged to cancel the traditional rites for which the missing ingredients of grain, oil, and wine were necessary. In this new emergency a new obligation was imposed on them by virtue of their sacred rank, namely, to intercede with their God in prayers of mourning day and night.'[96]

The Elders and the People (1:14)

In terse, staccato fashion, the seer stipulates the actions required for the moment. The imperatives are still toward the priests and ministers of verse 13. But now the focus shifts from a focus on themselves and their own penitence to that of the people and their obligation to spur them toward lamentation and repentance.

> Consecrate a fast,
> Proclaim a solemn assembly;
> Gather the elders
> And all the inhabitants of the land
> To the house of the LORD your God,
> And cry out to the LORD (1:14).

The first command is to **consecrate a fast.** Old Testament writers generally speak of 'proclaiming' or 'appointing' a fast. However, to emphasize the urgency of the situation and to generate special awareness as to its religious essence, Joel employs the verb 'sanctify' (cp. 2:15, 16; 3:9 [4:9]).[97] In the normal Hebrew calendar, the special feast days and convocations were 'holy' (sanctified) days—days set apart for the singular purpose of worshiping Yahweh. So here too, the act of abstinence is to be hallowed, a 'holy' day set apart for the singular purpose of averting God's judgment.

Fasting was practised in order that God may be petitioned to graciously forgive and withhold further calamity and destruction (cf. 2 Sam. 12:22; Job 2:12-14; Jonah 3:7-9).

---

96. Allen, NICOT, 58.

97. Not only was a fast considered the proper way to propitiate God during times of calamity, but it was also a most vivid object lesson, reflecting the problem of hunger and the absence of any harvest.

A cursory survey of the Old Testament demonstrates that the general purpose of fasting, whether by individuals or a nation as a whole, was to elicit compassion from God and avert or terminate calamity.

At all times, the fast was to be motivated by and representative of a humbled and/or repentant heart. This most likely arose out of the requirements for celebrating the Day of Atonement, where fasting was stipulated (Lev. 16:29-31; 23:27-29).[98] The absence of a humble and contrite heart during fasting led to non-acceptance before God (Isa. 58:3; Zech. 7:5-6).

The second imperative, **proclaim a solemn assembly,** is a parallel expression of thought to 'consecrate a fast.'[99] Directives for calling an assembly are given in Numbers 10:3, where they were to blow two trumpets to gather the people. Different than a ram's horn, these are made of hammered silver. Whether both were to be blown at the same time, or in unison, or in different pitches is not known. Nevertheless, when they would sound, the people were to meet at the door of the tent of meeting, the same place where Joel calls for the leaders and the people to meet. Although a solemn assembly was generally called for festive purposes (Deut. 14:8; Lev. 23:36; Num. 29:35; 2 Chron. 7:9; Neh. 8:18), it occasionally refers to times called for the purpose of mourning and lamenting.

During solemn assemblies, work in Israel was specifically proscribed (Lev. 23:36; Num. 29:35; Deut. 16:8). In fact, the prophet's choice of the word for **solemn assembly** is a very specific term that carries the idea of restraint. Every solemn assembly was a day in which they were to do no work. But

---

98. The phrase **humble your souls** is used prominently in the Torah to denote fasting on the Day of Atonement. Because of the prominence of fasting on that most holy day, it came to be known later as 'the Fast' (Acts 27:9).

99. John Hartley suggests that the word 'proclaim' may owe its use here to the practice of positioning official observers to look for the first sign of the new moon. On sighting the new moon, the observers would send out a call throughout the land, proclaiming the beginning of the high day (*Leviticus, Word Biblical Commentary*, ed. by David Hubbard & Glenn Barker [Dallas: Word, 1992], IV:375).

apparently the situation at hand required a more forceful restraint than a mere invitation. The prophet designates it as a day of restraint, a day in which they were being held back, prevented from labor.[100]

The third imperative calls for the priests to **gather the elders.** While 'elders' can denote those of old age (as the context suggests in 2:16), the term most likely refers to the office of elder, designating one who functioned as the natural representative of the people.[101] It was their practice to call on the elders of the people when a serious public matter demanded attention. The priests and ministers were to summon them **and all the inhabitants of the land to the house of the Lord your God.** In 1:2, Joel calls upon all the inhabitants of the land to reflect upon the dire circumstances, followed by specific appeals to the various sectors of the society. Now he has come full circle. All the inhabitants were called to assemble at the house of the Lord. The law prescribed that three times a year all males were to appear before the Lord (Exod. 23:17). But there is no such limitation here; the devastating situation required that all should participate.[102]

And cry out to the Lord specifies the activity in which the priests, ministers, elders, and people are to engage. This

---

100. Ronald B. Allen, *TWOT*, II:691. The term has a wide range of usages, such as that of preventing conception (Gen. 16:2), holding back a plague (Num. 16:48 [17:13]), or reigning under divine compulsion (1 Sam. 9:17). 'With Yahweh as subject, this verb contributes greatly to the doctrine of the sovereignty of God' (Allen, 691).

101. 'Elder' is frequently used in this manner (*e.g.* Isa. 3:14; Ezek. 8:1). The term literally means 'beard.' Age sixty seems to have separated the mature from the old (Lev. 27:1-8), although Levites apparently retired at the age of fifty (Num. 4:3, 23, 30). The Old Testament does not specify the age required to qualify one to be in the ruling body of elders or how one might be appointed to it.

102. 'Elders' has been taken as a vocative, rendering the phrase 'Gather, O Elders, all the inhabitants of the land.' However, since the priests were given the responsibility to proclaim the assembly, it is best to see 'elders' as an accusative, as it is rendered in most translations. Nor is it necessary to see the phrase 'all the inhabitants...' as apositional to 'elders' = 'all the elders who live in the land.' While the phrase has no 'and' separating 'elders' from 'all the inhabitants...,' none is required. Asyndeton is not uncommon in Hebrew (cf. Keil, 186).

is the reason they are to fast, to assemble, and to gather to the house of the Lord. It is the culmination of the imperatives of 1:13, 14. The 'cry' is not merely a prayer, but a crying out to Yahweh, the covenant-keeping God (cf. 1:1). It signifies a loud, importunate prayer, one borne out of fear and danger and impelled by the gravity of the moment.

The prophet begins by summoning the priests to take off their religious garments and put on sackcloth (1:13), to call the elders and people to a consecrated fast (1:14) and then to cry out to Yahweh in prayer. In Old Testament history, these three elements usually accompany each other—sackcloth, fasting and prayer (Ps. 35:13)—for the purpose, if possible, of propitiating God's favor and averting His judgment.

The Reason for the Call (1:15-18)

The contents of 1:15-18, and especially of verse 15, justify the urgency of the unilateral appeal made by Joel in 1:13-14. Slowly the thoughts of the prophet expand from the momentary affliction imposed by the locust plague. There is a crescendo building as the chapter unfolds, culminating in the announcement of verse 15. The present devastation, historically unprecedented (1:2), is perceived by him as a precursor of a far greater calamity to come, the great Day of the Lord!

> *Alas for the day!*
> *For the day of the* LORD *is near,*
> *And it will come as destruction from the Almighty* (1:15).

In the previous verses, the prophet enunciates to the different groups within the community reasons for the urgent call to mourn. Now he provides the ultimate, compelling cause for the nation to humble itself before God. As the people were urged to cry out to the Lord (1:14d), so now Joel cries out the warning, **Alas for the day! For the day of the** LORD **is near. Alas** is a cry of alarm, an exclamation laden with ominous overtones, employed especially by the prophets to urgently exhort the people toward repentance.

With the introduction of the phrase 'Day of the LORD,' Joel has reached the theme of the book.[103] As Wolff observes,

---

103. See full discussion of this phrase in the introductory section.

it 'permeates all further parts of the book as its *cantus firmus* (2:1-2, 11; 3:4; 4:14). Nowhere else in the Old Testament is the Day of Yahweh treated in as sustained a way as in the book of Joel.'[104] Later in the book (2:18ff; 3:1[4:1]; 3:18-21[4:18-21]) and elsewhere among the prophets, the Day of the Lord often designates blessing, prosperity, and exoneration for God's people and judgment and destruction toward Gentiles.[105] But here Joel directs the warning toward his own people. Unless they repent, Yahweh's visitation could have dire consequences instead of the blessings they had come to expect.

Reference to the Day of the Lord frequently includes the indication that it is 'near' (cf. Isa. 13:6; Ezek. 30:3; Obad. 15; Zeph. 1:7; Joel 2:1). The Hebrew word order is literally, 'Because near is the day of the Lord,' placing the emphasis on its nearness. The term does not denote the actual presence of something, but its speedy approach, in this case the fast approaching Day of Yahweh. The designation indicates that 'the writer does not mean that the plague of locusts is the day of Yahweh, but that the plague is pointing to a more awful period still future.'[106]

To describe the Day of the Lord, the prophet Joel employs a simile, stating: **And it will come as destruction from the Almighty.** Like the previous phrase, the Hebrew word order is reversed from the English: 'And as destruction from the Almighty it will come,' emphatically punctuating the terrifying activity that is near. The Hebrew term for 'destruction' (*shod*) means 'destruction, violence, havoc, ruin.'[107] This forms a powerful play on words in the Hebrew with *Saddai*, usually translated 'Almighty' or transliterated 'Shaddai.'[108]

While the meaning of the former is unquestioned, suggestions concerning the exact definition of the latter have been

---

104. Wolff, 33.

105. For example, Isa. 13:6 and Ezek. 30:3 direct the phrase against foreign nations.

106. Henderson, 100.

107. BDB, 994. The term has already been introduced in 1:10, where the prophet states that 'the field is ruined, ... the grain is ruined.'

108. Though the name can refer to false gods, such as Deut. 32:17, it usually has reference to the true God of Israel.

varied due to an uncertain etymology. Some have made a connection with the Hebrew term for 'breast' (*shad*). As such it would signify fruitfulness and prosperity.[109] Historically, it has been connected with *saddad*, which means 'to deal violently with, to devastate, despoil, ruin,'[110] a meaning still held by many. This would connect most closely with the LXX translation *pantokrator*, meaning 'almighty, omnipotent.'

More recently, some have suggested a relationship with the Akkadian word *sadu*, which means 'mountain.' Thus, El Shaddai would mean 'God of the mountain.' 'The name apparently refers to this El's localization in a mountainous region or to his theophany in a mountain storm.... In the time of Abraham, the deity was identified with the heavenly storm-god, Hadad, who was often as Baal among the Canaanites.'[111]

While etymological uncertainty is inevitable, the context makes the meaning quite clear. Without question and 'invariably, the scriptural use conveys the notion of invincible strength.'[112] Devastation and ruin, at the hand of an omnipotent God, is coming.

> The Hebrew ear was sensitively attuned to associations of sound, and this emotional effect was not infrequently exploited by the prophets. Joel has subtly created a strong sense of shock by suddenly transposing the natural plague to a higher plane of supreme judgment, and heightening the effect by producing a wordplay....[113]

---

109. So Robert P. Lightner, *The God of the Bible* (Grand Rapids: Baker, 1978), 111-112. He contends that the recurring characteristics garnered from the contextual uses of Shaddai focus on fruitfulness, both through comfort (Gen. 28:3; Ps. 91:1-2) and through chastening. Naomi (Ruth 1) is chastened by Shaddai and yet later made fruitful. So also with Job, where this name for God is used 31 times.

110. BDB, 994.

111. George A. Buttrick (ed.), *Interpreter's Dictionary of the Bible* (Nashville: Abingdon, 1962), II:412. Attempts to down-play the polytheistic origins of this conclusion are feeble at best. Victor Hamilton rightly counters that 'it is not to the hills (natural phenomenon) that these men of faith looked for confidence but to the lord of these hills, the Lord of the mountains (Ps. 121:1-2)' (*TWOT*, II:907).

112 Carl F. H. Henry, *God, Revelation & Authority* (Dallas: Word, 1976), II:193-194.

113. Allen, 60.

And so, the prophet carries his readers beyond a focus on the locust plague and drought conditions of the immediate. He is eager to use the contemporary situation as a platform from which to direct their attention toward a more awesome, terrifying day—the eschatological day of Yahweh. The present merely foreshadows a day yet to come.

Joel urges the religious leaders, the elders and the people in 1:13-15 using the second person. In 1:16-20, however, he changes to the more intimate first person, wishing to stand alongside the people as a fellow sufferer. His attention is directed toward the calamity and its consequences, not on the matter of guilt. He asks:

> *Has not food been cut off before our eyes,*
> *Gladness and joy from the house of our God?* (1:16).

As if the connection between the dire circumstances and the coming of the day of Yahweh is not vivid enough, Joel queries the people, asking them to ponder once again the calamitous straits of their situation. There is a cause and effect relationship that undergirds the whole matter (Jer. 5:24-25); the impact of the living illustration of the moment must not be lost.

The context of chapter one is clear that all food has been cut off. However, here the prophet is referring to the food defined more specifically in verse 10—the grain, the new wine, and the oil. It is the food that is destined for the temple services and the great feasts referred to in the latter phrase of the verse. But now there are no harvest festivals or daily sacrifices. It has been cut off **before our eyes.** The phrase stands first in the verse, emphasizing the helplessness of the people and reiterating the swift and thorough nature of the devastation—'Before our eyes, food has been cut off.' The phrase is commonly employed to refer to man standing back and watching in amazement the power of God working of his behalf (Deut. 3:21; 6:22; 1 Sam. 12:16).

Like the first part, the latter portion of verse 16, **Gladness and joy from the house of our God** is also inverted in the Hebrew text, placing emphasis on the phrase, 'From the house of our God.' Annual feasts were always occasions of great rejoicing (cf. Lev. 23:40; Deut. 12:12, 18; 16:10-11; 26:10-11). 'Gladness' is often associated with the heart and speaks of being glad or joyful with one's whole being (cf. Gen. 31:27; Ps. 104:15; 105:3; Prov. 15:30). And, being an agrarian society, the festivals were essentially agricultural in nature. Thus the Feast of Firstfruits/Unleavened Bread (marking the opening of harvest), the Feast of Weeks/ Pentecost (marking the end of harvest), and the Feast of Tabernacles (marking the end of vintage harvest) would be occasions of sorrow rather than gladness and joy. There would be no joyful meals eaten at the sanctuary during these three festive occasions each year.

The prophet Joel continues his description of the absence of food, moving from a focus on the locust plague to that of the drought. That drought conditions existed was intimated earlier (cf. 1:10, 12), but this is the first explicit indication of its presence (also cf. v. 20).

> *The seeds shrivel under their clods;*
> *The storehouses are desolate,*
> *The barns are torn down,*
> *For the grain is dried up* (1:17).

The facts of 1:16 are substantiated by the examples set forth in 1:17-18. Conditions are severe; attempts to plant (or replant)[114] are rewarded with futility: **The seeds shrivel under their clods.** The phrase is difficult to translate, since three of the Hebrew words occur only here in the Old Testament. The Hebrew word for 'seeds' is probably from a root meaning 'to separate or divide' and thus the noun could be 'separated ones' or 'seeds.' Similar terms in both Syriac and Aramaic suggest kernel, seed, berry or pebble.[115] Some have suggested that 'shrivel' is to be compared to a Chaldean term meaning, 'to rot.' However, 'it is with more propriety referred to the Arab. *siccus fuit.*'[116] Although the

---

114. 'This situation presupposes that the seed had been ploughed under before the beginning of the rainy season, or that it was sown as summer seed into parched land' (Wolff, 35).

115. BDB, 825. Also cf. Allen, 61.

116. Henderson, 100.

origin and exact meaning is uncertain, the translation of 'rot' does not fit as well with the presence of drought conditions as does 'shrivel.' Furthermore, Joel uses 'dried up' in the last part of 1:17. The symmetry of the verse suggests that, just as the two middle phrases are parallel in thought, so too the translation of the first and fourth phrases should be of a parallel nature.[117] The absence of rain and the presence of heat (drought) cause the seeds to lose their ability to germinate.

The final word, rendered **clods**, presents the greatest difficulty. It almost certainly is derived from a root which means 'to sweep away' and related nouns 'shovel, hoe.'[118] But because this meaning makes little sense in the phrase, many have rendered it 'clods.' While this makes good contextual sense, it lacks textual basis or etymological support. It is most likely that some textual corruption has occurred and, until further textual evidence is produced, the exact meaning of the phrase will remain obscure. In an effort to maintain loyalty both to the text as it has been given and to the context in which it is found, Allen suggests the following compromise: 'Allusion is evidently made to drought conditions. When ground in which seed had been sown showed no sign of green life, investigating *shovels* had uncovered the ungerminated grain.'[119]

The remainder of the verse needs little clarification. **The storehouses are desolate, the barns are torn down** continues to reflect the consequences of the severe conditions. 'Storehouse' is most commonly denoted as a treasury, whether belonging to the temple (*e.g.* 1 Kings 7:51), to the king (*e.g.* 1 Kings 14:26), or to an individual. The storehouse, or granary, was the storage location of the reaper's 'treasury.' The

---

117. The first phrase 'is in all probability nothing more than a corrupt variant of the following sentence' (Bewer, 89; cf. Henderson, 100). The significance of translating this verb should not be underestimated. The rendering of this verb has a direct bearing on the translation of the remaining two terms.

118. BDB, 175.

119. Allen, 62. Bewer's contention that an old scribe or editor added a corrected text immediately following the corrupted phrase (in the form of the next two phrases) is without manuscript basis (91).

harvest, whether it included grain, wine, or oil (Neh. 13:12), represented a portion of his wealth. **Barns** is a synonym for 'storehouse.'[120]

While the NASB gives both verbs ('are desolate/are torn down') an active translation, both are simple passives. As such, the translation **have been desolated/have been torn down** would reflect more accurately the situation described by Joel. The lack of harvest, caused by the locust plague and drought, has aided and even accelerated the deterioration of the granaries. In the absence of a crop, owners would have little motivation, and little money, to maintain the storehouses and barns.

The use of the verb **'have been desolated'** reiterates the divine involvement in the current situation. Inherent in the root is the idea of devastation caused by some great disaster, usually at the hand of the divine Judge. The verb **have been torn down** suggests that the demise of the barns has come as a result of the plague. They have fallen into disrepair through prolonged disuse and lack of upkeep.[121]

The prophet, in poetic parallelism, resumes the thoughts with which he began the verse (cf. 1:10, 12). The granaries have fallen into disrepair **For the grain is dried up. For** once again (see above) acknowledges the cause for the dilapidated state of the storehouses.

Having already noted the shriveled seeds in verse 17a, Joel now reiterates the grim evidence that there will be no crop or harvest next year either. Not only have the locust swarms devoured this year's produce, the drought has prevented the seeds from germinating. **Is dried up** means 'to be dried up, withered' and is employed as a synonym with 'shrivel.'

> *How the beasts groan!*
> *The herds of cattle wander aimlessly*
> *Because there is no pasture for them;*
> *Even the flocks of sheep suffer* (1:18).

---

120. Cf. Deut. 28:8; Prov. 3:9-10; Hag. 2:19.

121. Although the verb generally connotes a more active idea of tearing down, it is occasionally used with the more passive thought of becoming dilapidated through lack of proper maintenance (cf. Prov. 24:31).

There is no harvest, and consequently no grain offerings and drink offerings (libations) can be brought before the Lord (1:9, 13, 16). Using poetic anthropomorphisms, the prophet remarks how the land mourns (1:10) and how the people should lament and mourn and cry out to the Lord (1:13, 14). Now he describes, in heartfelt, compassionate terms, the effects on the animals—they too suffer the consequences of the locust plague and drought. All of creation appears to be groaning! (Rom. 8:18-22). Unless the Lord of the harvest and the Lord of all creation would stay the hand of the locusts and unlock the rain clouds, the circumstances could deteriorate to the level of those described a few centuries later by another prophet. Gazing at the imminent collapse of Jerusalem into the hands of Nebuchadnezzar, Jeremiah mourns:

'For the mountains I will take up a weeping and wailing,
And for the pastures of the wilderness a dirge,
Because they are laid waste, so that no one passes through,
And the lowing of the cattle is not heard;
Both the birds of the sky and the beasts have fled; they are gone'
    (9:10).

Joel begins by noting **How the beasts groan!** Though **beasts** (*[behemah]*, from which is derived the word 'behemoth' = 'brute beast') is singular, the term is used corporately to denote the entire class of beasts of burden, distinct from the cattle mentioned next. The prophet interprets their lowing in human terms as **groans.** Not only have the locusts devoured all vegetation, cutting off their source of food, but even more significantly, their drinking sources, the one thing left untouched by the locusts, have been evaporated by the drought (cf. 1:19, 20). And all of this, though they are innocent, because of man's waywardness! 'There is an implicit contrast between the response of brute animals and the people's insensitivity.'[122] The verb 'groans' is not used elsewhere as an activity carried out by cattle, causing some to follow the LXX rendering of the opening phrase: 'What shall we put in them?' *i.e.* into the storehouses and barns (v. 17) that are now standing empty. Bewer argues:

---

122. Allen, 62. Compare Jonah 3:7-8.

'This gives a very satisfactory conclusion to v. 17 and is most likely the correct reading.'[123]

However, it seems best to leave the text as written. Although the later Septuagint translation presents an alternative reading, the Masoretic Text gives no evidence of variants. The context fits as well, if not better, with the current rendering. As noted earlier, verse 17 shows characteristics of a self-contained chiasmus; following the LXX would disrupt the poetical sequence and the contextual flow of the passage. Furthermore, Joel's choice of 'groan' connects it with what follows, not with what precedes. 'Groan,' used sparingly in the Old Testament (12x) ties in closely with the verb employed in the following phrase 'wander aimlessly.' Both terms are used to describe Israel's activity while under the bondage of Egypt (cf. Exod. 2:23; 14:3). Consequently, there is no compelling reason to follow the lead of the LXX.

With continued compassion, the prophet observes that **The herds of cattle wander aimlessly because there is no pasture for them.** After noting the larger brute beasts, he turns his attention toward the smaller cattle.[124] Even they, accustomed to the grassy slopes of the wilderness hillsides, can no longer find food. Instead, they **wander aimlessly.** The word means 'to be confused, perplexed, to wander aimlessly.'[125] Again, Joel employs a term used only elsewhere of man, using poetic imagery to heighten the drama and raise the consciousness of the people. As Israel wandered aimlessly shortly after their departure from Egypt, to lure Pharaoh after them (Exod 14:3), so the cattle do not know where to turn for food.

Even the flocks of sheep suffer erects an intensive comparison with the previous two groups of animals. While the cattle and beasts might have difficulty finding suitable pastures, sheep generally can subsist on vegetation which the others would find uneatable. Yet **even** *they* experience the consequences of the plague.

---

123. Bewer, 91. The LXX reads: *ti apothesomen eautois.*

124. 'Cattle' can refer to draught animals; however, its use in comparison with 'beasts' suggests that the writer has domesticated cattle in view.

125. BDB, 100. Keil describes it as 'to be bewildered with fear' (188).

The exact nature of this suffering is of some debate. The term given in the text means 'to be (held) guilty, suffer punishment.'[126] Here again, Joel employs a word never used elsewhere with reference to animals. Innocent creatures are involved in the consequences of guilt incurred by the transgressions of man (cf. Exod. 12:29; Jonah 3:7-8).[127] The rendering of the LXX is 'to be desolate; to be appalled, stand aghast,' in which case the phrase would be rendered: 'Even the flocks of sheep are famished (Lam. 4:5) or appalled' (Jer. 4:9). Outside the Septuagint, however, there is no significant support for the alternate reading. While the alternate reading fits the context nicely, it seems best to leave the earlier reading stand, at least until more convincing evidence surfaces.

The Response to the Call (1:19-20)

Out of a concern for his people (1:8-12), out of a zeal for continuation of sacrifices and worship of Yahweh (1:13-16), and out of a compassion for the animals (who cannot pray) that were suffering innocently (1:17-18),[128] the prophet himself is impelled to be the first to respond to the call to lament, to wail, to beseech Yahweh for mercy and relief.

> To Thee, O LORD, I cry;
> For fire has devoured the pastures of the wilderness,
> And the flame has burned up all the trees of the field (1:19).

The prophet Joel was the first to issue the warning of a greater Day of Yahweh coming and, following His command, to call every level of society to lament, fast, and pray. Thus Joel too must be the first to take the warning seriously. He must demonstrate the veracity of his claims by his example, thereby motivating the people to respond as he has instructed. 'It is designed to act as a stimulus to the community, inciting the members to respond to his pleas and hold such a service.

---

126. BDB, 79-80. It is sometimes used to denote actual 'guiltiness,' while at other times it speaks of bearing the consequences of wrongdoing (Hosea 13:16; Isa. 24:6).

127. Keil, 188.

128. Cf. Ps. 36:6.

Like a teacher with a child, he guides them through the proper motions and encourages them to do likewise.'[129]

And so he leads the way, crying out in first person, **To Thee, O LORD, I cry.** Intercessory prayer was a marked characteristic of Yahweh's prophets. As they were the first to declare God's justice/judgment to the people, they were also the first to cry out to God for mercy and forgiveness (cf. Exod. 33; Jer. 42:1-4; Dan. 9; Amos 7:1-6). Since the plague and drought had come by divine prescription, only He could stay further devastation.

Each verse of the prayer begins with the address and petition, followed by two lines of lament describing the severe conditions. His appeal to the **LORD** (*Yahweh*), the covenant-keeping name for God, is in essence an appeal to remember the covenant made with Abraham (Gen. 12:1-3; 15:12-21) and to His promises made to Moses (Exod. 3:14; 6:3). The Eternally Existing One and Eternally Present One is personally beseeched by the prophet.

Owing to the first phrase of verse 20, some have argued that **I cry** should be rendered in the third person, 'they cry.'[130] There is no manuscript evidence or textual basis, however, for this alteration. Neither verse 20 nor the actions described in Jonah 3 provide justification for changing the text.

> The text has undoubtedly the 1st pers. sing.—and has at any rate had it ever since it was penned in writing. It is the prophet himself who intones the lament and prayer, either because he himself feels it necessary to turn to Yahweh, or because he wishes to show his audience and especially the priests the way Yahweh should be appealed to.[131]

Just as he repeatedly reminded the people of the devastating effects, so here too. Only this time, following in the tradition of many prophets before him, he rehearses for an omniscient God the debilitating effects of the plague and drought, doing so primarily from the perspective of its impact on the

---

129. Allen, 63.

130. So Bewer, who adds: 'It is not the prophet but the animals that cry to Yahweh, as the parall. in v. 2-0 shows' (92). He also points to Jonah 3:7-8 to substantiate this change.

131. Kapelrud, 68.

innocent animals. **For fire has devoured the pastures of the wilderness, and the flame has burned up all the trees of the field.** The prophet is crying out to Yahweh, praying that He would mercifully reverse the ominous situation, if not for the sake of the people, then at least for the sake of the animals who were not to blame.

The **fire** and **flame** most likely refer to the scorching drought that accompanied the locust plague. It is true that fire is used figuratively to depict the all-consuming nature of the locust plague in 2:3.[132] But the more immediate context of verse 20, including its parallelism of thought with verse 19, suggests that the former idea is intended here. This thought is supported by Amos 7:4, where fire 'consumed the great deep and began to consume the farm land.' The consummation of the great deep by fire is similar contextually to 1:19-20, where fire is mentioned together with the drying up of the water brooks. The type of fire and flame that would possibly be present in this text cannot literally consume water (*i.e.* the great deep); that is something more rightly relegated to the effects of a scorching drought.

Wilderness need not denote to a desert. While it can refer to a desert, it is a broad term used frequently to describe grazing lands (distinctive from cultivated areas), or extended regions where occasional towns may exist, with grazing areas interspersed. In light of the contrast drawn by the writer, it is obvious that lush grazing lands are in view. In 2:3, the pastures are described as **like the garden of Eden** prior to the locust invasion. Furthermore, **the trees of the field** have been burned up—drought has dehydrated the trees. Once the locusts have stripped their leaves (cf. 1:7), the trees have no ability to absorb moisture from the

---

132. So Pusey, 168-169. It is agreed that 'spontaneous combustion frequently follows'; however, the context does not seem to be making a reference to literal fire. As Theodore Laetsch notes: ' "Fire," "flame" (v. 19), does not refer to the locusts destroying the fields as thoroughly as fire, nor to the efforts of people to destroy the locusts by starting fires' (*The Minor Prophets*, St Louis: Concordia, 1970, 117-118). Henderson (101) disagrees, contending that the actual burning of the grass 'is more probably the meaning' (so also Watt, 22).

early morning dew, a process both common and necessary in dryer, semi-arid climates.

'Not only do I cry out for mercy to You,' says the prophet, 'but **Even the beasts of the field pant for Thee.**' The **beasts** (*behemoth*) are mentioned in 1:18 as one of three groups. Here, however, Joel adds that they are beasts **of the field,** possibly depicting them as wild beasts as distinct from the brute beasts of burden in verse 18. As wild beasts, they would probably have the least dependence upon the disappearing vegetation. But even they, owing certainly to the drought-exhausted water sources coupled with the lack of vegetation (cf. Jer. 14:5-6), cry to Yahweh.

In verse 18, the beasts are said to groan; here, the prophet describes their cry as a **pant**[133] for Yahweh. Echoing the words of Psalm 42:1 [42:2], Joel depicts their longing desire for water and food. Although the word occurs only three times in the Old Testament, twice in Psalm 42 and once here, its meaning is not obscure. Both contexts vividly convey the idea of looking upward with longing, with passionate desire. The Septuagint translates the verb in Psalm 42 with *epipothei*, meaning 'to intensely crave, to desire, lust after.' Here, the LXX translates it with *aneblexan*, which means 'to look upward.' The picture is clear; the animals are in dire need of food and water, and thus they are said to cry out to Yahweh. Although doing so unwittingly, they too seek their sustenance from the Lord (cf. Job 38:41; Ps. 104:21, 27-28; 147:9).[134]

As in verse 19, Joel follows the address with two lines of lament: **For the water brooks are dried up, And fire has devoured the pastures of the wilderness.** The water brooks, again following the psalmist (42:1), denotes the river channels and wadis that run through Israel, some

---

133. The plural subject ('beasts of the field') with a singular verb ('pant') is not uncommon in Hebrew. The beasts of the field are viewed corporately by the writer, as a single group crying out to the Creator for sustenance.

134. This tender scene should not be surprising, for Scripture frequently depicts God as lovingly caring for all His creatures (cf. Ps. 104:21-30; Jonah 4:11; Matt. 6:25; 10:29; Luke 12:24).

supplied by snow and rain runoff and others fed by mountain springs.

The prophet closes the section by rhetorically rounding it off with a refrain borrowed from verse 19. Its repetition does not diminish the symmetry with the preceding verse.[135] On the contrary,

> the repetition of important phrases is a part of Joel's style (cf. vv. 9a, 13b, 16) and is a means of intensification. The phrase repeated here is reminiscent of the devouring fire and the lapping flame in theophany descriptions, such as belong directly to the Day of Yahweh depictions in Zeph. 1:18 and Joel 2:3. To this extent even the concluding section still interprets the cry of terror about the approaching Day of Yahweh found in 1:15.[136]

---

135. G. W. Wade, *Micah, Obadiah, Joel and Jonah* (London:Methuen, 1925), 96.

136. Wolff, 35.

3.

The Impending Day
of Yahweh
(2:1-17)

In a transition to the eschatological Day of Yahweh (2:18–3:21 [4:21]), Joel employs the plague of locusts (1:2-20) as a backdrop from which to launch into the discussion and description of the eschatological Day of Yahweh, an elaboration of the prediction announced in 1:15. 'The imagery, under which the approach of the 'day' is depicted, is borrowed from the recent visitation of locusts.'[1] In preparation for its coming, the prophet implores the people to repent.

There are two questions facing the interpreter. First, is the chapter still discussing the advancing plague of locusts or has the prophet begun to depict an advancing army, using locust imagery? And second, if the description is now of an attacking military force, is it referring to a historical invasion or is it to occur eschatologically?[2]

---

1. Driver, S.R., *The Books of Joel and Amos* (Cambridge: Cambridge University Press, 1907), 47.

2. If it does occur eschatologically, at what point in the text is the transition made by the prophet? Does it occur at 2:28 [3:1], as many premillennialists contend, or does it transition earlier in the chapter? Ladd has expressed the feelings of many: 'It is practically impossible to determine where the description of the natural disaster ends and that of the eschatological enemies begins' (*The Presence of the Future* [Grand Rapids: Eerdmans, 1974], 68).

Regardless of how these questions are answered, it should be noted that commentators on both sides are agreed that there is a new level of description in chapter two[3] —that the prophet is either projecting something beyond the locust plague of chapter one or elevating the level of description to new heights and focusing increased intensity on the plague and the utter necessity for an immediate significant response.

Those who suggest that Joel is now describing a genuine military attack make a number of observations. First, since the use of locust plagues as figures for invading armies was common in the ancient world,[4] it would be a natural transition here, one that the hearers could make naturally. Second, the descriptions given within the chapter are certainly more vivid and amplified than in the previous chapter, confirming this heightened relationship. 'The impression given is that earlier motifs are taken up and transposed into a higher key, a more strident setting and a faster pace.'[5] Third, the description of their orderly advance (e.g. 2:7-8) and ubiquitous devastation (e.g. 2:3, 9) bespeaks of actual armies, not locusts.[6] Fourth, the reference to 'nations' (v. 17) and 'northern army' (v. 20) indicate that Joel is no longer portraying a locust invasion but an army invasion.[7]

On the other hand, it seems preferable to view the subject matter of 2:1-17 as an intensified reference to the locust invasion and not pointing to a near-but-future

---

3. Allen has rightly noted that 'the increase in momentum and tension renders unlikely Bewer's [93] view that 2:1-14 was delivered earlier than 1:2-20 and that the present placing represents only literary arrangement' (64).

4. In Solomon's dedicatory prayer reference is made to a locust plague along with the enemy besieging the land (1 Kings 8:37). Both locusts and armies were used by God as His instruments of chastening and judgment (e.g. Deut. 28:38-39; 1 Kings 8:35-39).

5. Allen, 64.

6. Patterson, 246.

7. Henderson contends that this presents 'insuperable obstacles' to the literal locust view. Rather, he maintains, 'in the first chapter, Joel describes a devastation of the country which had been effected by natural locusts; but predicts in the second, its devastation by political enemies, in highly-wrought metaphorical language, borrowed from the scene which he had just depicted' (95).

army invasion of Palestine.[8] First, while Joel does liken the locusts to horses (2:4), to marching orderliness (2:7-8), and to army-like methods of attack (2:9), the emphasis is not on some intermediate enemy nation invasion but on the coming of the Day of the Lord, a day when actual armies will invade, capture and devour (Zech. 12-14). Second, the language suggests something more final than the attacks by the Assyrians on Palestine in the eighth century BC. Chapter 2:10 speaks of cosmic events,[9] drawing one away from an eighth century event. Joel 2:19 promises that they will never again be made a reproach, a statement that could not be made if 2:1ff is referencing the Assyrian invasions of the eighth and seventh centuries BC.

Third, the verbs of chapter two point noticeably toward the more distant future, in distinction from chapter one. 'An analysis of the verbal usage shows that there is a distinction in time perspective between 1:2-20 and 2:1-27. Thus while only three prefix conjugation verbs occur in chapter one, none of which is distinctly future, twenty-nine occur in 2:1-27, all of which are futuristic.'[10] The language of 2:26c, 27c is difficult to place into any segment of Israel's later history; an eschatological picture must be in view.

Fourth, in light of the closeness of terminology and subject matter in Joel chapters one and two (cp. 1:2 with 2:1-2; 1:14 with 2:15; 1:8 with 2:16; 1:9 with 2:14; et al.), it seems best not to attach any particular historical army invasion to the descriptions of 2:1-17; rather, the prophet is using the platform of the locust plague in chapter one to launch his warning of the impending, imminent Day of the Lord. The caution expressed by Calkins is appropriate:

---

8. Patterson argues that 'the near historical situation is in view under a double figure' (246). As such, he views the events as depicting both a historical event as well as an eschatological one: 'Joel portrayed a coming army, in particular, that of the Assyrian armies of the eighth and seventh centuries B.C.... The judgment effected by the Assyrian armies was in turn to be a harbinger of a still greater eschatological judgment (2:28-3:21)' (245). So also Douglas Stuart, *Joel, Word Biblical Commentary* (Waco: Word, 1987), 250.

9. The cosmic occurrences depicted in 2:10 are difficult to corroborate with the invasion of an Assyrian army.

10. Patterson, 246.

It is true that the poetical imagination of the prophet here raises to a point beyond the limits of experience into the sphere of apocalyptical dreams. Yet, with this admitted, the description of the locusts in chapter 2 is truer to fact than might at first appear, and that these are to be identified with the locusts of chapter 1 appears from 2:25. Thus Joel's locusts are neither allegorical nor wholly apocalyptical, but real locusts. In both passages he is describing an actual calamity wrought by them on the land of Israel.[11]

In the apostle John's vision of the fifth trumpet judgment (Rev. 9:1-11), he describes in significantly similar terminology the locusts that come out of the abyss.

Thus, chapter 2:1-17 appears to be transitional, providing the transition from the historical plague that they were experiencing to the eschatological day of Yahweh. The locust plague was a precursor of a greater day to come. It is unnecessary to insert an eighth century BC Assyrian invasion into the text, thereby complicating the picture. As the locusts have done, operating providentially at the behest of the divine Commander, so the nations' armies, carrying out the will of the Sovereign One as well, will execute His will in that eschatological Day of Yahweh. 'The extraordinary contemporary event therefore points to the proclamation of a revolutionary final event. That is what Jerusalem's pious, worship-centered self-assurance must recognize. The cultic lamentation over the economic crisis (1:16-20) hence first of all induces an eschatological alarm (2:1-11).'[12]

The impassioned summons that Joel initiates with chapter two is not an overzealous cry; the locust plague is a harbinger of greater things to come—the Day of the Lord, with all its attendant elements (2:2-11). And thus he once again, in terms more resounding than before, urges them toward repentance (2:12-17),[13] assuring them that with true repentance

---

11. Raymond Calkins, *The Modern Message of the Minor Prophets* (New York: Harper, 1947), 154.

12. Wolff, 13. Feinberg adds that 'Joel starts with the situation then existing in the land after the havoc of the locust plague and then goes on to picture the dreadful Day of Jehovah yet future, but imminent' (75).

13. Note Jeremiah 4:5ff where these same three elements of (1) an invasion alarm sounds, (2) the enemy is described, and (3) a call to repentance are combined.

and humiliation God would grant mercy and restore to them magnificent blessings: material (2:21-27), spiritual (2:28-32 [3:1-5]), and national/political (3:1-21 [4:1-21]).

The whole passage is suffused with tones that heighten the locust plague to a macabre religious pitch. The armory of eschatological prophecy is ransacked in order that, under a barrage of its themes, the religiously insensitive community may be compelled to react aright to the seriousness of the present situation and its critical significance in terms of their relation to Yahweh.[14]

The Alarm Sounds (2:1)

As though Yahweh Himself was the watchman on the city wall (cf. Ezek. 33:2-4; Isa. 58:1; Jer. 6:17), He cries out for the priests to warn the citizens of the land. The appeal, delivered through the prophet Joel, is similar to those delivered earlier (1:8, 11, 13-15), but the injunction here contains a new level of pathos.

> *Blow a trumpet in Zion,*
> *And sound an alarm on My holy mountain!*
> *Let all the inhabitants of the land tremble,*
> *For the day of the LORD is coming;*
> *Surely it is near* (2:1).

Yahweh, as the Commander of Hosts, commands the officials to **Blow a trumpet in Zion.** In the ancient world, horns were common instruments used for calling the people together for special occasions or to warn them of impending danger. And so in Israel. It was used to signal attack in war (*e.g.* Job 39:24-25; Judg. 3:27; 2 Sam. 2:28), to announce joyous occasions, especially on the Day of Atonement (*e.g.* Lev. 25:9; 2 Sam. 6:15; 1 Kings 1:34ff), to gather troops for battle (*e.g.* Judg. 6:34), or to inspire one's troops and thereby discourage the enemy (Judg. 7:18).

The **trumpet** (*shofar*) described here should not be confused with another Hebrew instrument generally translated 'trumpet' (*hasoserah*). The latter denotes a long, straight instrument made of hammered silver (Num. 10:2), while the

---

14. Allen, 67.

former denotes a curved ram's horn.[15] To avoid the confusion, it is generally better to translate *shofar* as 'horn' and not 'trumpet.' Both were used in the Temple and later in the synagogues, although the *shofar* appears to have been used primarily in secular functions and the *hasoserah* generally reserved for religious functions.[16]

The blowing of the trumpet was not only for the purpose of announcing to the people the imminent danger but also to invoke the presence and blessing of God in wartime. Significantly, Moses mentions both 'trumpets' and 'sounding an alarm' in Numbers 10:9 when he exhorts Israel: 'When you go to war in your land against the adversary who attacks you, then you shall sound an alarm with trumpets, that you may be remembered before the Lord your God, and be saved from your enemies.'

The sounding of the horn is frequently mentioned as an integral part of God's presence and His special visitation on behalf of His people, both in judgment and in blessing.[17] At the giving of the Law on Mt Sinai, the trumpet sounded (Exod. 19:13, 16, 19; 20:18). At the second advent, the trumpet will sound (Zech. 9:14; Isa. 27:13).[18]

The *shofar* was usually used for special days, but now it was to **sound an alarm in my holy mountain.** In the face of dire consequences, the alarm is sounded. The imperative 'sound an alarm' does have the sense of shouting and is so used in Joshua 6, where the people were to shout a general war cry to consummate the fall of Jericho. Here, however, it suggests the long, continuous blast of the horn, as in

---

15. For an in-depth treatment on the various horns used in biblical history, cf. Gerhard Friedrich, *TDNT*, VII, 76ff.

16. This is evident both from a study of the incidents of its usage (the *hasoserah* is usually seen in the hands of priests only) and from explicit instructions in Num. 10:8 that only the priests were to blow them: 'The priestly sons of Aaron, moreover, shall blow the trumpets, and this shall be a perpetual statute throughout your generations.' Friedrich does add, however, that 'In the OT as a whole there is no discernible distinction in the use of the two instruments' (VII, 77).

17. Zephaniah 1:16 even calls the Day of Yahweh 'a day of trumpet and battle cry.'

18. Also cf. 1 Thess. 4:16.

Hosea 5:8. 'It characterizes the horn blowing as a prolonged, startling, and frightening fanfare....'[19]

The horn is to be blown and the alarm sounded **in Zion, in my holy mountain.** Normally, warnings of any approaching enemy would be sounded along the borders and from the highest hills, not in the capital. That the whole land was to be summoned to Jerusalem is obvious from the context. But the blowing from Mt. Zion, which is lower than the hills immediately surrounding it, suggests that this was not an outside enemy. Rather, Yahweh's reference to 'my holy mountain,' as the center of the divine government, stresses the spiritual basis of the situation.[20] This enemy (locusts) has penetrated the entire country. The Day of Yahweh is at hand, and therefore even the stronghold itself must heed the warning.[21] Even in Zion, the location of Yahweh's enthronement (Ps. 2:6) and visible dwelling place of His shekinah glory, would not be immune; she too must repent and return (2:12-13).[22]

Following Yahweh's command to blow the trumpet and sound the alarm, the seer decrees: **Let all the inhabitants of the land tremble.** All the inhabitants were affected by the locust plague and drought (1:5, 9, 11, 18, 20). And certainly, all would be affected by the Day of Yahweh judgment. This exhortation would include the whole land—both the northern and the southern tribes. Even after the division of the kingdom, there were times when the citizens of both were summoned to Jerusalem (2 Chron. 15:8-17; 30:1-31:6). The gravity of the impending Day of Yahweh demands that all the land respond, regardless of geographical residence or political affiliation.

Thus all will tremble—to demonstrate a righteous fear of the Lord as an appropriate response to His presence and

---

19. Wolff, 43; cf. S. R. Driver, 48.

20. Patterson, 246.

21. Cf. 1 Pet. 4:17.

22. The warning is not to be taken lightly, for Zechariah indicates that Jerusalem will fall and be devastated by the enemy just prior to the second advent and will be one of the final places in Israel to be delivered by the coming of Messiah (12:1ff).

holiness.[23] On Mt. Sinai, at the giving of the law, when the people heard a very loud trumpet blast, it is said that they 'trembled' (Exod. 19:16; 20:18). In fact, such a response was expected. 'If a trumpet is blown in a city will not the people tremble?' (Amos 3:6a).

The cause for alarm is given in the phrase, **for the day of the LORD is coming; surely it is near.** Introduced by the causative preposition **for,** the basis for the call to such drastic response is not the approach of just any enemy nor the calamity at hand—it is the coming of the Day of Yahweh! The verb 'is coming' is located at the head of the clause, literally rendering it 'because coming is the Day of Yahweh.' Its position stresses the indisputable certainty of its coming—it *will* come. The verb can be understood either as in the perfect tense, 'has come,'[24] or as a participle, 'is coming.'[25] If taken as a perfect, it must be viewed as a prophetic perfect, since it is obvious that that Day of Yahweh was still future. In this case, the action is deemed so certain that the future is treated as already completed. If the verb is participial, then the action is viewed as moving toward fulfillment, it is on its way. The same verb in 1:15 is in the imperfect tense, signifying action not yet completed. With the increased intensity of chapter two over chapter one, and with the emphatic position of the verb in this clause, the prophetic perfect understanding would provide greater emphasis and thus fit the intensity of the situation. Thus it is to be preferred. In either case, however, when coupled with the following phrase, it signifies that the day had not yet arrived, but that it will come.

The prophet adds that **surely it is near.** This phrase is not redundant, as some have argued,[26] but is an appropriate

---

23. Watts, 24.

24. So Keil, 189; Wade, 97.

25. So Kapelrud, 71; Wolff, 43. Wolff suggests that Ezekiel 7:7, where both time indicators ('come' and 'near') occur together, supports his conclusion here. However, as in Joel, Ezekiel's usage also allows 'come' to be understood either as a perfect tense or as a participle

26. Watts (24-25) considers the phrase to be a redundant addition, a result of a copyist's addition.

guard against the idea that it had already begun, especially if one understands the previous verb in the perfect tense—'has come.' Rather, it stresses imminency; the Day of Yahweh is near! Imminency is frequently stressed in Day of Yahweh contexts, both in Joel (1:15; 3:14 [4:14]) and elsewhere (Isa. 13:6; Ezek. 30:3; Obad. 15; Zeph. 1:14).

Nor is there any need to attach this phrase to the following verse.[27] In Day of Yahweh contexts, the close relationship of the two words 'has come' and 'near' and the stress on imminency make the alteration of verse division unnecessary.

The Army Invades (2:2-11)

With the blowing of the trumpet and the sounding of an alarm, the citizenry are to take special note of the enemy. The announcement of the adversary's approach is followed by a vivid, lucid description of it, including its appearance (2:2-5), its operation (2:6-8), and its effectiveness (2:9-11).

Its Appearance (2:2-5)

> A day of darkness and gloom,
> A day of clouds and thick darkness.
> As the dawn is spread over the mountains,
> So there is a great and mighty people;
> There has never been anything like it,
> Nor will there be again after it
> To the years of many generations (2:2).

Though elevated here to a new level of intensity, the prophet reiterates the appeal made in chapter one to consider the significance of the contemporary moment. After summoning all (cp. 1:2 with 2:1), he again rehearses for them the vastness of their numbers (cp. 1:4 with 2:2)[28] and the uniqueness of the present crisis (cp. 1:2 with 2:2). But he sets aside his focus on the devastation they bring and rivets his attention on a description of the locusts themselves.

---

27. Wade (97) suggests that it should be rendered, 'for nigh at hand is a day....'
    So also Allen, 64 and NASB
28. To follow Robinson's (32) suggestion that the four synonyms for darkness
    (2:2) are descriptive of the four locust stages delineated in 1:4 is too speculative and cannot be upheld hermeneutically.

Joel commences this colorful and picturesque journey by stressing the darkness of the day with four synonyms: **A day of darkness and gloom, A day of clouds and thick darkness.** Darkness is a common figure for misery and calamity in the Old Testament (Isa. 8:22; 60:2; Jer. 13:16), with a variety of terms employed to depict it. The first synonym, **darkness,** is the most common word for darkness. It denotes the absence/opposite of light (Gen. 1:2). The term can be used figuratively; here, however, it is likely that both the literal and figurative are in view. Figuratively, it is a day of great sorrow and misery (1:8, 11, 13, 16; Rev. 6:15ff). But it can also be viewed literally, for not only do huge swarms of locusts block out the light of the sun (Exod. 10:15), but the eschatological Day of Yahweh is also characterized by the luminaries losing their light (2:31 [3:4]; Rev. 6:12-13). It is also described as a day of **gloom.** It is closely related to 'darkness' and is frequently so translated (cf. Amos 5:20 where both are repeated).

The prophet adds that it is **a day of clouds and thick darkness. Clouds** is derived from a primitive root meaning 'to cover;' or 'to intervene/obstruct.'[29] It is found having both positive and negative uses, both of God's presence in blessing among His people (Ps. 97:2; 105:39) and of His judgment. Here, of course, the focus is on His judgment. Israel's enemies are elsewhere depicted as clouds that cover the land; Gog's advancing army is so described in Ezekiel 38:9, 16 (cf. Jer. 4:13). The etymology of **thick darkness** is even more nebulous, perhaps from a root meaning 'to drip, to drop,' as the dropping of rain from clouds.[30] If so, it could indicate a gloomy, darkening sky caused by a lowering, heavily overcast sky. Like 'cloud' above, it can include God's blessing and rescue of His people (Ps. 18:9 [18:10]). It is used to describe a veil to hide the glory of Yahweh (Exod. 20:21; Deut. 4:11). At the dedication of Solomon's temple, the glory of God filled it with thick darkness (1 Kings 8:12). In this case, however, it pictures His wrath (cf. Jer. 13:16; Ezek. 34:12), the calamity He has initiated so as to bring about repentance.

---

29. BDB, 777
30. BDB, 791.

'Because the same term is used of God's enveloped glory and his awesome judgments, the term is paradoxical: it bespeaks terror, wonder, fear, majesty, awe, and reverence.'[31]

In picturesque similitudes, the prophet enhances the description: **As the dawn is spread over the mountains, so there is a great and mighty people.** The term **dawn** shares the same root radicals with 'blackness,' making its rendering here uncertain. While most versions and commentators translate it 'dawn,' following the pointing of the Masoretic Text, an alter-native reading meaning 'blackness' is footnoted in the Hebrew text (BHS).[32] Since a translation of blackness would certainly fit the context better and would not violate the consonantal, unpointed text, it is to be preferred.[33] But regardless of which rendering one prefers, the meaning is evident; the swiftness and all-pervasiveness of the onslaught of the Day of Yahweh, depicted by the locust plague spreading a pall of darkness over the hills of Judah, should strike alarm in the hearts of people.[34]

The subject of **is spread** is also debated. Some suggest that it is to be left indefinite,[35] while others contend that the 'people,' noted in the next phrase, are spread over the mountains.[36] However, there is no compelling reason to leave the subject indefinite; to employ 'blackness' as the subject is quite appropriate grammatically and contextually.[37]

---

31. Ronald B. Allen, *TWOT*, II, 698. In Exodus 10:15 as well, the locusts are described as effecting darkness.

32. Also cf. notations in BDB, 1007.

33. So L. C. Allen, 64, 68; Wolff, 44; Bewer, 95-96.

34. Henderson (103) seeks to explain the abrupt contextual focus from darkness to dawn by noting that 'The obvious points of comparison are merely the *suddenness* and *extent* of the change produced by the diffusion of the rays of light, without any reference to the nature of the change itself.'

35. Keil (190) renders it: 'like morning dawn is it spread over the mountains.

36. Wolff, 44.

37. It seems even less likely to designate 'people' as the subject. The *athnach*, dividing the verse logically into two sections, appears under **mountains**. Consequently, it is evident that the Masoretes viewed 'blackness' as the subject of the verb, since it is doubtful they would place the verb in one section of the verse and the subject in the other.

As in 1:4, Joel focuses again on the vast quantity and strength of the invaders: **So there is a great and mighty people.** The two adjectives, **great** and **mighty**, are essentially synonyms. The former depicts their vast numbers while the latter describes the sheer strength that numbers generate.[38] The locusts are viewed as a people (*am*) or nation, similar to the prophet's description of them earlier in 1:6.

The verse closes with the seer's incomparable depiction: **There has never been anything like it, nor will there be again after it to the years of many generations.** The unique crisis sounded in 1:2 is reverberated here, but in terms elevated in intensity beyond the earlier description. The Day of Yahweh would have no parallel in history, nor would it for many generations.

Joel's description of the Day of Yahweh displays remarkable similarities to Israel's exodus out of Egypt and the giving of the law at Mount Sinai. In fact, Scripture frequently compares the time of the second advent of Christ with the exodus out of Egypt (Isa. 11:10-11, 16; *et al*). The eighth and ninth plagues directed at Pharaoh were locusts and darkness (Exod. 10:12ff)—two of the prominent elements here. In Moses' description of the ninth plague (Exod. 10:22), he employs 'darkness' and 'gloom,' the identical words found in 2:2a. Three of the four descriptions given by Joel (darkness, clouds, and thick darkness) are used by Moses to depict the scene at Mount Sinai (Deut. 4:11; 5:22-23). Also present at the imparting of the law were the blasting of horns, dark clouds, and people trembling (Exod. 19:16-19; 24:16); so here (2:1, 2). Moses describes events surrounding the exodus and Sinai as unique (Exod. 10:14; Deut. 4:32ff). Joel, latching on to the same terminology, describes the Day of Yahweh as a one-of-a-kind occurrence.

The imminent Day of Yahweh corresponds to His awesome appearances in the past.[39] Just as Yahweh's theophanies/appearances and involvement in human history (especially the exodus)

---

38. BDB, 782-783, 912-914.

39. Wolff, 44.

incorporated judgment on those who perpetrated evil and blessing/protection from judgment on those who were His,[40] so too, with these two special days so often correlated in Scripture, it can be expected in the eschatological Day of Yahweh.

Having described the ominous, unique nature of the invasion, Joel continues to paint it in picturesque terms. In detailed fashion the prophet depicts how the land that once flowed with milk and honey would become a land overflowing with destruction and devastation. Nothing would escape.

> *A fire consumes before them,*
> *And behind them a flame burns.*
> *The land is like the garden of Eden before them,*
> *But a desolate wilderness behind them.*
> *And nothing at all escapes them* (2:3).

Again, the prophet uses synonyms and poetic parallelism to remind the hearers of the dire circumstances of the present and the awesome nature of the future Day of Yahweh. The language is borrowed in part from 1:19, where reference is made to a drought accompanying the locust plague and the resultant devastation,[41] especially on the animals (1:20). The context of 2:1-11 contains no inferences to the drought of chapter one.[42] Rather, the exquisite recitation of calamitous effects appears to be more metaphorical than literal. Specifically, it is the locust invasion, viewed as a harbinger of the coming Day of Yahweh, that is the subject of the seer in 2:1-11. 'There can hardly be any doubt that it is the locusts Joel is thinking of in the present section, but the terms he uses for describing them are chosen from another realm of conceptions. The thought of Yahweh's Day stands vividly impressed on Joel's mind.'[43]

Fire is said to be an appropriate metaphor for the destruction wrought by the voracious locusts: 'Wherever they come,

---

40. After the third plague, the land of Goshen where Israel resided was exempted from the plagues (Exod. 8:22).

41. Cf. Feinberg, 20.

42. 'It is clear that Joel meant here the devastation caused by the locusts, and not the drought which acc. to chap. 1 accompanied and accentuated the plague' (Bewer, 97).

43. Kapelrud, 75.

the ground seems burned, as it were with fire. Wherever they pass, they burn and spoil everything.... The places they had browsed were as scorched, as if the fire had passed there.'[44] As a harbinger of the Day of Yahweh, there is a commonality of language that joins them together. Fire and thunder accompanied the plague of hail (Exod. 9:23-24) and is often seen in divine theophany passages (Exod. 24:17; Num. 9:15-16; Ps. 97:3) as well as the Day of Yahweh (Zeph. 1:18).[45] Wolff even contends that 'v 3a does not portray a natural event, but rather can only be understood in light of the theophanic tradition in the Day of Yahweh formulations.'[46] His exclusion of 'a natural event' goes too far, but it can certainly be said that 'the echo of these dynamic terms puts the locusts on the side of divine reality. Joel's daring application of the language of theophany interprets them as a manifestation of the destructive wrath of God.'[47]

Joel is imagining an all-consuming fire as preceding and following the invaders. Employing poetical license, the **before them—after them** interchange expresses loudly, in clarion redundancy, the universality of devastation. They devour everything on every side of them. The pronominal suffixes **them** throughout the verse are masculine singular and would be more accurately translated 'him' or 'it.' In both the preceding and following verses, the prophet pictures the locusts corporately as an invading army, leaving one to expect that he would have it in mind here as well.[48]

In the opening phrases, Joel uses parallelism to dramatize the situation. Now he erects a vivid contrast between the **Garden of Eden** and the **desolate wilderness.** The land

---

44. Quoted in Pusey, 172.

45. In light of the subsequent reference to the garden of Eden, it is interesting to note that the verb **burns** is of the same root as the word used in Gen. 3:24 with reference to the flaming sword which guarded the way of the tree of life.

46. Wolff, 45. Keil agrees: 'This burning heat is heightened here into devouring flames of fire, which accompany the appearing of God as He comes to judgment at the head of His army' (191).

47. Allen, 70.

48. Cf. Bewer, 96; Wolff, 45.

is like a **garden**, a protected place often surrounded by a stone wall. But not just any garden; it is the Garden of **Eden** that is here depicted by way of contrast. 'Eden' means 'luxury' or 'delight.' It is usually used with specific reference to the first home of Adam and Eve, but is also used to denote optimum productivity and fertility of the land (Jer. 51:3; Ezek. 36:35)[49] or to depict exceptionally luxuriant places (Ezek. 28:13; 31:9, 16, 18). The figurative contrast between the **desolate wilderness** and the Garden of Eden is not new to the listeners (Isa. 51:3; Ezek. 36:35). But here the situation is reversed; the Garden of Eden will become like the **desolate wilderness**. In the prophets, it is generally a part of Israel's future restoration and blessing; here Joel, in subtle yet dramatic fashion, reverses the reference to denote her destruction and judgment. 'Joel preaches as powerfully in his unspoken hints as in his plain speaking. A master in the craft of suggestion, he provokes the attentive mind to produce within itself conclusions more shattering than if he had voiced them openly.'[50]

With such a dramatic picture of total, all-pervasive devastation, a common theme among other prophets in Day of Yahweh contexts (Amos 5:9; Zeph. 1:2-3), Joel adds to the alarm and increases the urgency of the summons for the citizenry to repent. **And nothing at all escapes them.** The phrase is literally translated, 'And escape not there is/has been for him/it.'

But who or what cannot escape from whom or what? The word **escape** generally refers to those who have escaped in war, escaping either prison or death (Judg. 21:17; 2 Sam. 15:14; Ezra 9:13). However, it can be employed to denote the fruit of the land, or the land itself, which has not been destroyed (Exod. 10:5). The object **them** is masculine singular and therefore suggests a more accurate rendering of 'to/for him,' 'to/for it,' or 'with regard to it.' It is argued that **them** (or 'it') refers to the land. Though uncommon,

---

49. BDB, 726, 727.
50. Allen, 70.

the masculine singular **them** can have as its antecedent the feminine singular noun **land** (cp. Gen. 13:6). As such, the emphasis is on the fact that no part of the land escapes; the devastation is complete in geographical extent and applies to the entire land.[51] With this understanding the phrase would be rendered: 'And there is no escape for any part of the land.'

However, **them** most likely refers to the locust swarms. They are viewed throughout the verse as a corporate unity, thus the masculine singular suffix is employed. In each of the previous phrases, 'them' refers to the locust horde, making it doubtful that Joel is referring to the 'land,' which is feminine. Allen correctly notes: 'But this is set in a chain of suffixes referring to the locust horde of v. 2.'[52] This is confirmed in the following verse, where **their** [masculine, singular] **appearance** is most definitely a reference to the invaders of 2:3. The preceding parts of verse 3 point to an emphasis on the completeness and pervasiveness of the devastation rather than on its geographic extent. The locusts come to a land like the Garden of Eden and leave behind a desolate wilderness. No hint is surrendered contextually of geographic extent; the emphasis is on the severity of the destruction.

> *Their appearance is like the appearance of horses;*
> *And like war horses, so they run* (2:4).

Joel continues to draw a comparison between the locust assault and the invasion of a foreign army. In verse 2 he likens them to a great and mighty people infiltrating the land. Here he draws attention to their appearance; they look like horses. The resemblance of their heads is striking, so much so that the prophet reiterates the word **appearance** twice, calling attention to its unmistakable nature. The Italians call them *cavaletta* ('little horse'), the Germans speak of them as

51. Cf. Keil, 191-192; Wade, 98.
52. Allen, 65.

heupferde ('hay horses'), and the Arabs know them as *Djesh Allah* ('God's army').[53]

Horses were not used in ancient times for agricultural purposes. On the contrary, they were weapons of war. Horses and the arsenal of weaponry that accompanied them was the most feared military equipment of ancient times (Exod. 15:1, 19; Deut. 20:1; Josh. 11:4).[54] Thus the writer's mention of them provides a very striking metaphor, one that his listeners would readily understand.

He also takes note of their swiftness. In 2:2, 3, the prophet describes their vast numbers and voracious appetite; here he takes special note of their ability to run swiftly.[55] Both their appearance and swiftness of movement paints for the listener a picture of military invincibility.[56] Joel uses a different, somewhat ambiguous, term for **'horse'** in the second phrase, choosing one that seems to signify a horse in battle. Some have suggested that the proper translation 'is always 'horse' and if 'horsemen' is ever allowable, the reference is to those who were charged with managing the horses (as in a chariot)....'[57] In light of the following verse, where the themes of swiftness and chariots are commingled, this translation seems appropriate and probable.

---

53. Feinberg, 20; Robinson, 33. 'This is a metaphor which is still familiar to the Arabs. They say that in the locust, small as it is, there is the nature of ten of the larger animals. For the locust has the face of a horse, the eyes of an elephant, the neck of a bull, the horns of a deer, the chest of a lion, the belly of a scorpion, the wings of and eagle, the thighs of a camel, the feet of an ostrich, and the tail of a serpent' (Walter K. Price, *The Book of Joel and the Day of the Lord* [Chicago: Moody, 1976], 34).

Locusts are used figuratively in the Old Testament (1) as innumerable, powerful hordes (Judg. 6:5; 7:12; Jer. 46:23), (2) as horses (Joel 2:4; Job 39:20; Rev. 9:7), (3) as a personification of greed (Isa. 33:4), and (4) as representative of insignificance and weakness (Num. 13:33; Ps. 109:23; Isa. 40:22; Nahum 3:17).

54. Scripture also frequently employs the mention of horses in contexts related to the eschatological Day of Yahweh (Jer. 6:23; Ezek. 38:4; Zech. 1:8; 12:4; 14:15; Rev. 6:2, 4, 5, 8; 19:11, 19, 21).

55. Cp. Job 39:19-25.

56. Cf. Allen, 71.

57. Victor P. Hamilton, *TWOT*, II, 740.

Joel makes another change when moving from the first phrase to the second. The first line, continuing the masculine singular suffixes begun in verse 3, is literally rendered: 'As the appearance of horses its appearance.' In the second line, however, he switches to the masculine plural: 'And as horsemen in battle, so they run.' The shift is abrupt, but not atypical of Hebrew poetry. Bewer notes that **they run** (v. 4) and **they leap** (v. 5) 'are used purposely to bring out the whole weight and power of the attack, they deepen the impression of terror and awe.'[58]

The role that horses were *not* to play in ancient Israel should not be overlooked. As noted by Yahweh in Deuteronomy 17:16, Israel was not to multiply horses for herself; her protection was to come from Yahweh. And when He makes His appearance on His day of visitation, He will cut off the horses and the chariots (Hosea 14:3 [14:4]; Micah 5:10 [5:9]; Hag. 2:22; Zech. 9:10; 12:4). 'To the prophet horses were the symbol of war and armed power and of everything that was hostile to Israel and Yahweh.... It is in this connexion that the comparison between the locust-swarms and the horses must be seen.'[59]

The analogies given earlier continue here, with the prophet Joel utilizing three very prominent elements of war to draw his comparisons: chariots, fire, and soldiers.

With a noise as of chariots
They leap on the tops of the mountains,
Like the crackling of a flame of fire consuming the stubble,
Like a mighty people arranged for battle (2:5).

Each of the three comparisons begins with the preposition **like**, each standing at the head of the three lines in the Hebrew text. Through the senses of sound and sight, the seer enhances their description in cloaking the listener with a feel of reality, of actual occurrence. The apostle John alludes to this characterization in Revelation 9:9: '... the sound of their

---

58. Bewer, 98.
59. Kapelrud, 77.

wings was like the sound of chariots, of many horses rushing to battle.'

The emphasis, as introduced in verse 4, continues to focus on the speed of the invasion. Endowed with the finest of weaponry, the enemy moves through the land with unhindered rapidity. Before they are seen, they are heard. **With the noise of chariots, they leap on the tops of the mountains.** The **noise** or **sound of chariots** refers to the clattering of chariot wheels bounding over rough surfaces (Nahum 3:2). The sound of locusts 'has been compared to the dashing of water occasioned by a mill-wheel, to the roar of a cataract, to the noise of wind blowing through trees, and to the tramp of armed hosts.'[60] The text intimates that the noise is generated not so much by flying as by **leaping.** The term is used to refer to dancing (Job 21:11; Eccles. 3:4) and frolicking (Isa. 13:21). 'It is not improbable that the sound here referred to is that produced by the large hind legs of the locust in leaping.'[61] Mountains normally provide natural barriers, but not for this enemy. Nothing can stop their progress, not even the rough, remote terrain of mountain peaks and canyon walls. As one sent by the Commander of Hosts, no barrier could stay the hand of judgment from the Almighty.[62]

The Old Testament mention of **chariots** is predominantly in the context of warfare. But not incidentally, it is also used as a symbol of God's majesty and judgment (Ps. 68:17 [Heb. 68:18]) and personal intervention (2 Kings 2:11; 6:17).

In the first analogy, the noise of chariots is replicated in the locusts' jumping; in the second, **the crackling** [lit: 'noise'] **of a flame of fire** is replicated in the locusts' eating, in **consuming the stubble.** Swiftness and rapidity is again the focus. As fire

---

60. Wade, 99.

61. Henderson, 105.

62. It should be noted that the phrase cannot be rendered 'With a noise as of chariots on the tops of the mountains, they leap,' since chariots cannot be driven in such locales. On the contrary, it must be rendered 'With the noise as of chariots [when driven rapidly over level ground], they leap on the tops of the mountains.' This latter understanding is also attested to by the Hebrew accents (cf. J. P. Lange, *Joel* [Grand Rapids: Zondervan, n.d.] 17).

devours with lightning speed dry straw and chaff [63] after the
harvest, so the invaders overrun and consume the land.

The third comparison switches from sound and swiftness to sight and power. The first two comparisons employ
noise—it is the noise that is being compared. In the third
simile, **noise** is absent. It is the appearance that is the point
of comparison. They are **like a mighty people arranged for
battle**. As a well-disciplined army, they are orderly and in
rank and file, ready for battle. 'They prepare for the attack
like a mighty nation, seized to a man with martial ardor, and
arrayed in order for the fray.'[64]

The three similes in verse 5 maintain a close relationship, in reverse order, with the preceding descriptions. The
chariots are tied with verse 4; the **fire** is reiterated in verse 3;
the **mighty people** reverberates the nomenclature of verse
2. But in identifying them as **a mighty people**, Joel also
provides a smooth transition of thought to the following
stanza, where this final simile is graphically expanded.

Its Operation (2:6-8)

The prophet now turns his attention away from their appearance toward their method of operation.

> *Before them the people are in anguish;*
> *All faces turn pale* (2:6).

The analogies portrayed in 2:3-5 have carried the listener
from a focus on the destruction of their fields and crops
to an attack upon their stronghold—the city; from distant
sounds and sights to the invasion of their own houses. Even
within the stone walls of the city, the attack has left them
unprotected and vulnerable.

Even before they actually arrive, the rumbling sound of
their approach and the visual evidence of their awesome
weaponry and massive numbers leave the citizenry in a state

---

63. The term is used both of the dry stubble left standing in the fields after the
heads of grain have been cut off as well as for the chaff, the hull and stalk
of the grain after it has been threshed on the threshing floor.

64. Driver, 51.

of **anguish**. The picturesque term means 'to whirl, dance, writhe in pain.'[65] It is frequently used with reference to the giving of birth (Isa. 51:2; Job 39:1; Ps. 29:9) and occasionally to describe, as here, the agony of impending disaster in the terms of pain in child-bearing (Exod. 15:14; Jer. 6:24; 22:23; 50:43; Micah 4:9-10).

Coupled together with the anguish, **all faces turn pale. Turn** is literally 'to gather,' given in the intensive form of the verb. In other words, the faces are intensely gathering something. But that which is gathered is uncertain. The only other use of the term **pale** in the Old Testament (Nahum 2:11) provides no additional help in discerning the meaning here. Both the LXX and the Vulgate translate it as a 'cauldron' or 'cooking pot,' assigning the word to a derivative of 'pale.' Following this etymology, Calvin translates it 'blackness.'[66]

Keil, on the other hand, relates it etymologically to the Hebrew term 'to adorn, beautify, glorify,' referring it to the splendor or healthy ruddiness of the cheeks. Taken together with the preceding verb **turn** (lit, 'to gather intensively'), he believes it should be understood 'in the sense of drawing into oneself, or withdrawing, inasmuch as fear and anguish cause the blood to fly from the face and extremities to the inward parts of the body.'[67] This would require translating 'turn' with the less common rendering 'to take away, withdraw.'

Based upon the context, and on the similar circumstances described in Isaiah 13:8, Wolff maintains an interpretation of 'aglow.' Following the etymology suggested by the LXX, he notes that the Arabic and Syriac cognates have the meaning of 'to boil, to be excited, to be flush with passion.' 'The motif of faces aglow with intense anguish also belongs to the description of the Day of Yahweh in Is 13:8b, where it is used in the same connection as here.'[68]

---

65. BDB, 296-297.

66. John Calvin, *Commentaries on the Twelve Minor Prophets*, tr. by John Owen (Grand Rapids: Zondervan, 1979 rpt), II, 49.

67. Keil, 192-193.

68. Wolff, 46, 38.

Although the etymology is uncertain, the context makes
the meaning quite clear. A state of panic and fear is clearly
marked on their faces. 'The reaction of writhing and flushed
faces in hot panic on the part of entire nations conveys the
fear of seeing a conquering military horde led by Yahweh.'[69]

They run like mighty men;
They climb the wall like soldiers;
And they each march in line,
Nor do they deviate from their paths (2:7).

The invasion of the locust swarms, pictured as an advancing
army, is here developed further. In the previous stanzas of
the poem, the hordes were described in terms of the destruction they caused to the fields and pastures. The noise of their
approach is no longer a distant din; the army has arrived in
full view, attacking the very city itself.

The firsthand account of their remarkable assault is given
in two couplets. The first depicts their assault: **They run
like mighty men; they climb the wall like soldiers.** Like
an army of foot soldiers, they attack like warriors. Although
run is a general Old Testament term for various types and
modes of running, it is used here (and elsewhere—Job 15:26;
Ps. 18:29 [18:30]; Nahum 2:5) to signify the assault or attack
of the army. The term is also employed earlier in 2:4 with
reference to horses, tying the passages together thematically. The attackers are **mighty men** or 'warriors.' This term
is a reference to champions among the armed forces, to men
at the pinnacle of their strength, both of physical prowess
as well as of character and integrity. The character and
power of God Himself (Isa. 9:6 [9:5]) is the model for such
a warrior, a valiant one who does not trust his own power
but has 'made the Lord his trust' (Ps. 40:4 [40:5]).

The second line of the first couplet defines the mighty
men further, depicting them as **soldiers,** or literally **as men
of war/battle.**[70] As soldiers, **they climb the wall. Wall** is

---

69. Stuart, 251.

70. See 3:9 [4:9] for identical language depicting the enemy who is roused by
    God to invade Palestine in the eschatological Day of Yahweh.

rarely used figuratively[71] or with reference to the walls of other buildings; rather, it is usually employed to designate the walls of a city. Consequently, it probably depicts the arrival of the invaders to walls of the capital city itself. Jerusalem herself is being threatened.

The swift, unstoppable invasion of the 'mighty men' is the primary focus of the first couplet. The second couplet of verse 7 depicts the character of the 'mighty men,' men who are disci-plined, organized, unswerving in their pursuit of the conquest. **They each march in line.** In the first (v. 7a), the corporate, collective movement is specified; in the first half of the second (v. 7b), attention is directed on each of the individuals. The invading force enjoys success because of the disciplined char-acter of its individual members. **March** is a general term meaning 'to go, walk.' The designation 'march' is derived from the meaning of the words associated with it. Each one marches **in line.** Literally translated 'in his ways/paths,' the attackers are noted as each having their own designated highway or charted route.

Nor do they deviate from their paths. Attention is once again directed toward the collective actions of the invading force. Neither the massive numbers nor the swiftness of pursuit intrude upon their disciplined purpose and single-ness of focus.

The term **deviate** proves difficult for translators. Its rare use in the Old Testament (six times) contributes to the difficulty. The root meaning, 'to take or give a pledge,' in the sense of trespassing on a course or path intended for another, is virtu-ally impossible to fit into the context. Some have suggested a relation to the Arabic *'abata* ('to go off the middle of the road'), allowing the Masoretic Text to stand.[72] S. R. Driver connects it with a similar word 'which occurs in Mic. vii.3, and which, though the root is not otherwise known, may perhaps mean *twist together, intertwine.*'[73] Following this view, Keil translates it: 'They do not twist their path, i.e. do not diverge either to

71. Cf. Sol 8:9, 10; Zech. 2:5.

72. Patterson, 249. Cf. G. R. Driver, *JTS*, 1933 (34) 378.

73. S. R. Driver, 52.

the right hand or to the left, so as to hinder one another.'[74]
A third option is to render the term in the sense of 'to hold
to,' thereby slightly modifying the 'taking a pledge' idea. In
this view, taking the negative **nor,** which stands at the head
of the clause as an asseverative particle ('yea, indeed'), 'the
whole line would read "And each marches on his own way;
yea, they hold to their own paths." '[75]

For **paths,** the prophet selects a synonym of **line,** the two
being often used together as parallels (e.g. Ps. 27:11; Prov. 4:14).[76]
The invaders move forward in perfect order. They demonstrate
in their attack the characteristics of a regular, disciplined army
(Prov. 30:27). Moving forward at the behest of the Commander
of Hosts, nothing impedes their rapid advance.

> *They do not crowd each other;*
> *They march everyone in his path.*
> *When they burst through the defenses,*
> *They do not break ranks* (2:8).

The prophet continues his vivid description of their orderly
attack. They do not 'crowd' or press upon one another so as
to force another to deviate from his appointed place. In spite
of the vast numbers of locusts, their orderliness is inconceiv-
able, defying comprehension and striking a perfect balance
between cooperation and independence. They do not crowd
or break rank, but everyone marches in his **path.** The verb
means 'to lift up, to exalt,' signifying a 'highway' or 'elevated
roadway.' As a precisely charted[77] and engineered roadway,
the locusts follow their appointed paths.

---

74. Keil, 193-194.

75. Patterson, 249. He adds, 'That *lo'* [not] occurs in the next verse as the
regular negative particle is no argument against its being an asseverative
particle here; for in 2 Sam. 18:12 it occurs twice, once with asseverative
emphasis and once as a negative' (249). Also cf. Ahlstrom, 'JTCJ,' *Vetus
Testamentum,* XXI, 11-12.

76. The 'character' ingredient noted earlier in 'mighty men' is not to be overlooked in the use of these two synonyms. 'Path' is frequently employed
to denote 'lifestyle, character' (e.g. Gen. 6:12; Ps. 1:6). 'Line' is also used
figuratively, describing character of life (e.g. Ps. 16:11; 27:11; Prov. 2:8).

77. See Judg. 5:20 where it refers to the courses of the stars. It is also used metaphorically of the character of the righteous (Prov. 16:17), and is employed to
describe the highway traveled by the remnant returning to Israel (Isa. 11:16).

So disciplined are they that **when they burst through the defenses, they do not break ranks** (lit.: 'when the defenses they burst through...'). Numerous attempts have been made to provide the proper rendering of **defenses**. The noun means 'missile, weapon'[78] (cf. Neh. 4:17, 23) and, because of its verb means 'to send, cast forth,' it probably refers to any type of weapon that could be thrown at the enemy, such as a javelin. Keil prefers not a missile but a weapon extended or held in front, noting that it designates both offensive (2 Chron. 23:10; Neh. 4:11) and defensive weapons (2 Chron. 22:5).[79]

Observing that 'a missile or javelin, which the word strictly means, is hardly a likely deterrent to be tried against locusts nor is it supported in historical reports, Allen explains it as a reference to the Pool of Siloam. He notes that elsewhere the term does stand for Siloam (Neh. 3:15) or some type of aqueduct (Isa. 8:6).[80] Following this understanding, the rendering is: 'They press headlong through the aqueduct without halting their course.'[81]

During a time of prolonged drought (cf. 1:20), it is possible that the springs feeding the pools and aqueducts would be very low. However, the reference appears to be to some type of defensive weaponry, aimed at denying the locusts access into the city. What type of weapon that might be is unknown. But the following verse does not suggest an invasion via the aqueduct (cp. David's overthrow of Jerusalem). On the contrary, they rush the city from the outside and climb the walls rather than

---

78. BDB, 1019. In 2 Chron. 23:10 it replaces the ordinary term for weapon employed in the parallel passage of 2 Kings 11:11.

79. Keil, 194. Many interpreters see this word as pointing to a later period of Israel's history, since it is found primarily in the later writings. But the Assyrians employed both the verb *salu* 'to cast' and the noun *selu* 'javelin.' Kapelrud notes: 'Assyrians were the ruling nation in the Near East for such a long period that it is not surprising that words and terms taken from their language gained access to other nations, especially military technical terms, inasmuch as Assyrians were a war-like people' (77). Furthermore, this designation for javelin is found in Ras Shamra texts (1 Krt 20), proving its usage in Canaan as early as the fourteenth century BC. (Cf. Kapelrud, 77f).

80. Allen, 72-73

81. Allen, 66.

entering the city through the aqueduct. Furthermore, the verb **burst** can denote violent assaults, implying that 'the locusts fling themselves through (or between) the weapons with which men vainly try to oppose their march.'[82]

All attempts to stop the onward, overflowing destruction and to defend the city from these persistent invaders utterly fail. In fact, the impact of such defense mechanisms is hardly noticeable. Pusey observes that 'the locust seems armed as in a suit of armor.'[83] Passing seemingly unscathed through the defenses, they advance further without breaking rank or being cut off.[84] They just keep coming!

Joel's imagery has often suggested itself to observers: 'On they came like a disciplined army....' Like some infantry corps charging with high morale, like commandos assaulting some fortress, on they press with remorseless purpose. 'The roads were covered with them all marching in regular lines, like armies of soldiers.' 'They seemed to be impelled by one common instinct and moved in one body, which had the appearance of being organized by a leader.... They seemed to march in regular battalions, crawling over everything that lay in their passage, in one straight front.'[85]

Its Effectiveness (2:9-11)

The following verses continue to describe the locusts' method of operation, but bring to the reader the additional glimpse of their overpowering effectiveness. The results they enjoy are evidenced by their effect on the city and its inhabitants (v. 9), by their effect displayed in the cosmic arena (v. 10), and by the power upon which their effectiveness is based (v. 11).

---

82. Wade, 100.

83. Pusey, 177.

84. Bewer (103) agrees that 'evidently what is meant is that nothing can stop them in their march, neither weapons nor walls,' but doubts that the verbal phrase 'they do not break ranks' can express this in the absolute sense, and instead renders it 'they are not stopped.' However, there are no textual grounds to support such a doubt or for such an emendation. 'In our passage the word is used in the absolute sense of: to break off, to break away from one another' (Kapelrud, 78). See Amos 9:1 for a possible corresponding use of the word

85. Allen, 72.

In the City (2:9)

> They rush on the city,
> They run on the wall;
> They climb into the houses,
> They enter through the windows like a thief (2:9).

The inhabitants have already felt the impact of this mighty army with the lack of food (1:11-12, 17) and the necessities for grain offerings and libations (1:13, 16). The distant clamor of an invading horde (2:5) now gives way to the eyewitness accounts of their massive numbers and precise advance (2:6-8). Now the enemy has reached the city and their very own homes! Orchestrated magnificently by the prophet, the symphonic movement, with escalating emotion, reaches its final crescendo. The walls are scaled, the city falls, the houses are plundered.

They rush on the city, they run on the walls. The defenses (v. 8b) do not impede their onward march of destruction. They attack the city and its walls, seemingly impervious to the all-out assault against them by the citizens. The prophet reports how they '**rush** on the city, picturing again the massive numbers swarming the city and her walls with insatiable zeal.[86] The precision and orderliness, so descriptive of the invaders earlier (vv. 7, 8), here gives way to a portrait of innumerable hordes scrambling, almost chaotically, to lap up as much of the spoil as possible. The sense, using the same analogy and terminology, is given by Isaiah: 'And your spoil is gathered as the caterpillar gathers; as the locusts **rushing** about, men **rush** about on it' (33:4). Similarly, Nahum's colorful analysis enhances Joel's description here: 'The chariots race madly in the streets, they **rush** wildly in the squares, their appearance is like torches, they dash to and fro like lightning flashes' (3:4 [Heb, 3:5]).

The city, on which assault is carried out, is given the definite article, suggesting that the prophet has Jerusalem

---

86. Cf. Isa. 29:8 where the term is employed to depict a thirst that is not quenched.

in mind. As was common in those times, there were many cities in Palestine encircled by protective walls, allowing the phenomenon described here to be applicable to any of the walled towns of Judah. However, the definite article points to a specific city, one which would be the most familiar and which could be designated as **the** city.

They run on the wall depicts the total overthrow and domination of the city. Walls were the fortresses of the city; they provided vantage points from which to most effectively defend the citizens. But the opposite is intimated here; the enemy now has complete access to the last bastion of protection for the people — the city walls.

The first two phrases focus on the city and her walls; the second two phrases picture the infiltration of their homes. **They climb into the houses, they enter through the windows like a thief.** Typical of tropical areas, homes of that day had only a lattice or shutter-type covering for their windows. There were no glazed windows. Thus, access into the home by any type of flying insects, including locusts, would be quite easy. In an attempt to satiate their appetites, these voracious eaters did not restrict their feeding to the fields, pastures and trees. Human provisions were also sought (cf. Exod. 10:5-6). 'They loot and forage where they will, irresistible conquerors to whom every house in their path must surrender.'[87]

The simile **like a thief** has been difficult for some. The entrance of locusts through open, latticed windows would not normally be depicted in terms of stealth. Bewer, for example, asserts that 'the comparison is not appropriate here, and ... is to be regarded as a later gloss.'[88]

However, there are a number of considerations that make the metaphor pertinent. First, the word order emphasizes the place of entrance, not the stealth factor. Scripture describes anyone who enters through anything other than the door as a thief (John 10:1, 2, 10). Thus the locusts' entrance through the window would logically engender the idea of a thief.

---

87. Allen, 73
88. Bewer, 103.

Second, anything (or anyone) that enters the home unin-
vited and pilfers the contents, whether it be food or anything
else, could be classified as a thief. The locusts, in this situation, would certainly fall into this category.

Third, when the comparison is seen in the larger light of its
portrait of the coming Day of Yahweh, its presence is quite germane.
The same analogy is often repeated in other Day of Yahweh
passages throughout Scripture (1 Thess. 5:2; 2 Pet. 3:10; Rev. 16:15).

Fourth, the prophet obviously intends to portray the
eschatological Day of Yahweh by means of this contemporary Day of Yahweh.[89] The locusts are meant to picture
a coming, more severe invasion of Palestine, during which
time actual soldiers will capture the city, plunder the houses,
and ravish the women (Isa. 13:16; Zech. 14:2). Consequently,
the 'thief' simile is more than appropriate; it is thematically
germane to Joel's portrayal of the Day of Yahweh.

In the Cosmos (2:10)

> *Before them the earth quakes,*
> *The heavens tremble,*
> *The sun and the moon grow dark,*
> *And the stars lose their brightness* (2:10).

The watchman's cry increases with intensity and grows more
ominous. This is Yahweh's day, a day when the Creator and
Sustainer of the universe will cause the earth to quake, the
heavens to tremble, and the celestial bodies to withhold their
light.[90] The entire universe is in a state of commotion and
turmoil. Something more than just locusts is in view.[91] The
mention of the sun, moon, and stars retracting their light
intimates a greater day. The verbs of verses 10-11, once again
in the perfect tense, 'substantiate the acts as weighty in their
own right.'[92] Both of these factors indicate that the prophet

---

89. Note the proximity of this phrase with the following two verses and the
     Day of Yahweh theme they so emphatically herald

90. Chapter 3:15-16 [4:15-16] describes the same phenomena, only in reverse
     order from that found here. Note also the inclusion (3:16a [4:16a]) of
     Yahweh uttering his voice in the same context as found here (2:11a).

91. S. R. Driver, 53; Henderson, 106; Kapelrud, 79.

92. Wolff, 47.

is moving beyond the literal obscuration of the heavenly bodies by the locust swarms to also depict the extraordinary, awe-inspiring cataclysms of the future Day of Yahweh.[93]

Contrary to the usual order in Scripture, Joel, transitioning to the description of heavenly phenomena, begins by mentioning the earth. He states: **Before them the earth quakes. Before them** is literally 'Before it/Him.' Once again, the prophet has switched to the masculine singular suffix (cf. 2:3, 6), viewing this invader in a unified, corporate fashion.[94] But the suffix may also allow for a reference to the presence of Yahweh Himself. Before the Commander of this great army (2:11, 25), the whole cosmos is shaken (cf. Hab. 3:10a). The cosmic disruptions expressed by the prophet are well-attested elsewhere as concomitant signs of theophany and the Day of Yahweh. There is shaking and quaking (Judg. 5:4; Ps. 18:7 [18:8]; 68:8 [68:9]; 77:18 [77:19]; Isa. 13:13; Ezek. 38:19-20), trembling (Jer. 4:23-26; Nahum 1:5-6), and darkness (2:2, 31 [3:4]; 3:15 [4:15]; Isa. 13:10; Ezek. 32:7-8; Matt. 24:29; Mark 13:24-25; Rev. 6:12).

The verbs in the first couplet focus on the shaking and turmoil of the physical universe, while the latter couplet centers on the withdrawal of light. The synonyms **quake** and **tremble** are often used as poetic expressions to denote God's sovereign rule over the physical world.

Not only do the earth and heavens shake before Yahweh's army, but **the sun and moon grow dark, and the stars lose their brightness.** The phenomenon, typical of that which is associated with the Day of Yahweh elsewhere (cf. above), gives an indication that something more than just a locust plague is being pictured here. The verb **grow dark** signifies 'blackness' or 'darkness,' but is occasionally translated 'turbid' or 'murky' (*e.g.* Job 6:16). It is used

---

93. 'Hitherto he has been mixing factual description with metaphysical comment, but now he drops the role of observer of the locusts' movements and concentrates on their religious significance' (Allen, 73).

94. Although the locust infestation does not exhaust the essence of 2:10-11, neither should it be excluded. The use of the preposition with its suffix ('before them') in 2:3, 6 argues strongly for a similar understanding here. Cf. Keil, 195.

primarily in contexts of judgment, where celestial bodies will be darkened. But the concept of mourning is closely attached (cf. Jer. 4:28a) and the term is sometimes so translated (Ps. 42:9 [42:10]; Jer. 14:2). Its relationship to mourning is more than an allusion to the dark colored sackcloth worn by mourners (cf. Rev. 6:12). In the ancient Near East light and brightness depicted life and good, while darkness represented death and evil.[95] As such, the darkening of the heavenly light-bearers not only speaks of the judgment of God, but also intimates their active role in mourning the state of affairs (cf. 1:10; Jer. 12:11).

In addition, **the stars lose their brightness.** The verb **lose** means 'to gather in, to withdraw' (cf. Job 34:14; Ps. 85:3 [Heb. 85:4]; 104:29). Instead of emitting their rays of light, they pull them back in, no longer sending forth their brightness (cf. 3:15 [4:15]; Amos 5:20). The noun **brightness** denotes light generated by the stars. It is also used figuratively of the glory of God (Ezek. 1:4; 10:4; Hab. 3:4).

Its Power Base (2:11)
The effectiveness of the invasion, as evidenced by the ease with which the city was overrun and demonstrated by the concomitant phenomena displayed in the cosmos, was due solely to the omnipotent power of the Creator and Sustainer of the universe.

> And the LORD utters His voice before His army;
> Surely His camp is very great,
> For strong is He who carries out His word.
> The day of the LORD is indeed great and very awesome,
> And who can endure it? (2:11).

Although the language of the passage takes one beyond the locust invasion, the concept of an armed invasion fits even the winged creatures. They too are Yahweh's army (cf. 2:25). The picture is familiar. The Old Testament portrayal of Yahweh leading His people into battle, going before them, fighting on their behalf, is a common one (e.g. Exod. 14:25; Num. 10:35-36; 14:42-45).

---

95. Conzelmann, *TDNT*, VII, 427.

But here He is not leading them into battle against the enemy; rather, He is directing an army against them! Israel's enemies are now His sanctified ones (Isa. 13:3; cf. Matt. 22:1-14). The watchman, Joel, heralds the shocking news: **And the Lord utters His voice before His army.** Introducing the verse with **and,** the prophet ties the descriptions of verse 11 closely to the preceding. The locusts are His soldiers. The celestial bodies are also His 'hosts,' doing His bidding. The One who orchestrates the cosmic disruptions also leads this army.

Yahweh **uttering His voice** is frequently noted as 'thunder' in Scripture (Job 37:4; Ps. 18:13 [Heb. 18:14]; 29:3; 104:7; also cf. Exod. 19:16, 19), leading some to assert that Joel is describing an actual thunderstorm occurring in connection with the coming of the locusts.[96] However, this need not be inferred or the prophet's meaning so limited. In both the Old and New Testaments, thunder is generally a prominent feature when describing awe-inspiring scenes, theophanies, and divine visitations (*e.g.* Exod. 9:23ff; 19:16ff; 1 Sam. 2:10; Isa. 29:6; Rev. 6:1; 14:2; 16:18).

The precise manner in which He utters His voice is not revealed, only that with it He leads **His army.** On the contemporary scene, the locusts were Yahweh's agents of vengeance, retribution and judgment (cf. 2:25). Historically, many nations were viewed as His military ambassadors (Isa. 13:3; 44:28-45:1). Eschatologically, they will be also (Zech. 14:2). The message shouts with clarion succinctness; the locust plague is indeed the judgment of Yahweh! He had spoken to them, but they had not listened; therefore, He is now uttering His voice before another army against them.

The following three clauses are coordinate, building toward the climax of the third one. Each begins with the preposition **because** or **for,** establishing why Yahweh utters His voice before His army. The first reason is because His army is vast; **surely His camp is very great.** He has the armies/ resources of the universe at His disposal. The **camp,** used here as a synonym for an army on the march (cf. Exod. 14:24;

---

96. So Lange, 19.

Josh. 8:13; 10:5; 11:4), is exceedingly **great** or **numerous**. The second reason is because of His strength: **For strong is He who carries out His word.** The text is unclear as to whether the antecedent of 'He' is Yahweh or Yahweh's army. Pointing to Jeremiah 1:12, Wolff suggests that it 'probably means here performance of the 'word' which had come to the prophets in earlier times.'[97] The alternative suggests that the reference is to the obedience of the army to the command actually being issued by a commander (as in v. 11a). The use of the two adjectives **great** and **strong** in 2:2 ('great and mighty people') with reference to the invaders and not their commander supports the latter perspective. Those carrying out Yahweh's word enjoy Yahweh's power. Their strength is derived from their obedience to His word.

The third reason is because of the exceptional character of the Day of Yahweh: 'The day of the Lord is indeed great and very awesome.' The prophet has been building toward this climax, having introduced it in 2:1 and having dropped some hints throughout as he carried the listeners toward this point.

> The prophet has slowly but surely increased the feeling of gruesomeness on the part of the audience by a detailed description of the might and inexorable advance of the locust-swarm. Almost imperceptibly the description in verses 10 and 11 has passed on to point to Yahweh's Day, the dread catastrophe announced by the arrival of the locusts. In a few glowing phrases this day is portrayed before the eyes of the hearers.[98]

Lest anyone should fail to make the inevitable association of the locust plague with the Day of Yahweh, Joel makes mention of the two adjectives, **great** and **very awesome,** so often connected with it (cf. Joel 2:31 [3:4]; Mal. 4:5 [3:23]). It is a day that will strike terror and dread into the heart (cp. Hab. 1:7) and evoke great fear. Generally, these are associated with Yahweh's mighty deeds on behalf of Israel (Exod. 23:27; Deut. 2:25; Josh. 2:9ff; 9:9-10). But now, as recipients of the judgment of that great and awesome day, the people are helpless. And thus the prophet asks rhetorically, **and who**

---

97. Wolff, 48.
98. Kapelrud, 81.

can endure it? The implied answer is 'none!' None is able to withstand the outpouring of the wrath of Almighty God (cf. Jer. 10:10; Mal. 3:2; Luke 21:26; Rev. 6:12-17). His camp is great, His army, as obedient instruments, is powerful, and His day is great and awesome. His judgment is irresistible — who can endure it?

The Admonition to Repent (2:12-17)

In chapter one, the prophet follows the description of the calamitous conditions brought about by the unprecedented locust plague (1:4-12) with a call to personal humiliation and mourning (1:8, 11, 13) and then a public fast and solemn assembly (1:14). The pattern is similar in chapter two. Having graphically depicted the locust hordes in terms of a military invasion (2:4-11), Joel once again summons the people to personal repentance (2:12-14) and then reiterates his plea for a corporate display of fasting and weeping (2:15-17). Apart from the drunkards (1:5) and the farmers (1:11), the constituency whom he addresses in 2:16-17 is the same as that found in the first chapter: elders (1:2, 14), children (1:3), bride and bridegroom (1:8), priests (1:9, 13), ministers (1:13), people (1:14). Raised to a new level, the prophet renews his impassioned plea for both a personal and corporate response to Yahweh. Perhaps He will withhold further devastation and 'leave a blessing behind' (2:14).

Personal Repentance (2:12-14)

> *Yet even now, declares the LORD,*
> *Return to Me with all your heart,*
> *And with fasting, weeping, and mourning* (2:12).

The call for genuine repentance is given in the first person. Yahweh is the speaker, strengthening the urgency of the summons for immediate action. With the invincibility of Yahweh's army ('who can endure it?' [2:11]), the people's task is not to prepare themselves militarily, but through repentance to throw themselves on His mercy. Since none can stand or endure, then let all pray that God may stay His hand of judgment. With verbal industry, Joel seeks to demonstrate to his people that the plague is more than a mere coincidence of history. God is at work through the locusts and famine.

> Joel seeks to rip away the veil of normal perception and reveal a new dimension of divine power at work in the locusts. His aim has been gradually to arouse in his hearers' insensitive minds and consciences a sense of utter foreboding and a state of intolerable tension. Having strung his hearers to the pitch of feverish excitement warranted by the occasion, he is ready to channel their emotions to a point of spiritual release.[99]

The prophet begins with the adversative conjunction **yet,** connecting the urgent summons with that which preceded. On the basis of the preceding—terrible devastation and destruction—the conjunction must be seen as adversative, urging the people to make amends and to repent. As such, the conjunction marks a turning point in the message of the seer. Up to this point, the prophet's message has been one of darkness and gloom; but now there appears a ray of hope, a glimmer of light shining on the black clouds of calamity. **Yet even now,** in spite of all that has gone before, there is hope of divine mercy and blessing.

The adverb **now** injects an element of urgency, designating the immediate attention which this divine oracle requires. Although the hour is advanced and time to stay further devastation is expiring, it is not too late for total disaster to be averted. Verse 12a can be rendered as an independent nominal clause: 'But even now Yahweh's oracle (is valid).'[100] However, the phrase 'yet even now' should be attached to the following imperative 'return.'[101] The urgency of the prophet's summons throughout the prophecy serves to corroborate this understanding. Also, the absence of any previous invitation to repent makes the other rendering doubtful. The offer of pardon is initiated by Yahweh Himself.

The invitation is something He alone can offer. **Declares** is used only of divine speaking, calling special attention to

---

99. Allen, 76.

100. Wolff, 44.

101. Henderson, 107.

the origin and authority of the gracious offer. Not only is He the commander of the locust army, but He is also the One to whom they must turn for mercy and rescue.

The invitation of Yahweh, **return to me,** is expressed in terms of an imperative. The verb **return** is a most common one employed by the prophets and denotes a change of direction, a turning from evil, a renouncing of evil, and a turning away from God (Ezek. 14:6; Hosea 14:2). The terminology is strong and clear; yet the specific sin from which they are to turn is not stated. This absence is unusual when compared with other texts using the same terms (cf. Isa. 30:15; Jer. 4:1; Ezek. 33:9, 15; Amos 4:6ff). The prepositional phrase **to me** is specific, denoting the idea of 'as far as.' It speaks of going all the way, not just part way. Only a complete return could usher in a day of mercy and blessing.

This 'return' is to be characterized in two ways: inwardly and outwardly. Inwardly, they were to return **with all your heart.** The heart is viewed in the Old Testament as the seat of the intellect and will, not the organ of affections. It depicts 'the organ of moral purpose and resolve.'[102] If they would return to Yahweh with the entire force of their moral purpose, with a genuine, unreservedly repentant heart, then He would hear and forgive (Deut. 4:29-30; 30:2; 1 Sam. 7:3; 1 Kings 8:48ff; Ps. 51:17 [51:19]; cf. Jer. 3:10 where Yahweh chides Israel because she 'did not return to Me with all her heart, but rather in deception'). Outwardly, they were to return **with fasting, weeping, and mourning.** Weeping and mourning are often associated with fasting in the Old Testament (Judg. 20:26; Ps. 69:10 [69:11]; Zech. 7:3). These are the outward signs of repentance. While a genuine change of heart must always be thoroughly and profoundly inward (and thus it is mentioned first), it will have outward expressions.[103]

---

102. S. R. Driver, 54

103. Cf. Matt. 3:8. On the nature of fasting, weeping, and mourning, see 1:14, 1:5, and 1:13 respectively. The same trio, occurring together in Esther 4:3, are used to describe the response of the Jews to the decree of King Ahasuerus and Haman.

And rend your hearts and not your garments.
Now return to the LORD your God,
For He is gracious and compassionate,
Slow to anger, abounding in lovingkindness,
And relenting of evil (2:13).

The thought of a thoroughly repentant people continues to be the thrust. The repetition of thought in the first phrase of verse 13 makes it obvious that inward repentance is the emphasis of Yahweh's invitation, not the outward manifestations of verse 12c. Lest the public expressions of fasting, weeping, and mourning be motivated from selfishness (cf. Zech. 7:5ff; Matt. 6:16-18) and predominate the essence of their repentance, the prophet reminds them of the pre-eminent need for a repentance of the heart—to **rend your hearts and not your garments.** The urgency of Yahweh's call for a change of heart is evident from the continued use of imperatives. The command is to **rend** the heart, an obvious allusion to the practice of tearing apart one's clothing in demonstration of great sorrow and grief. It is similar to instructions elsewhere to circumcise the heart (Lev. 26:41; Deut. 10:16; Jer. 4:4) or to break or crush the heart (Ps. 51:17 [51:19]).

Tearing one's garment was a common expression of sorrow and grief (e.g. Gen. 37:29, 34; Josh. 7:6), a ritual generally performed prior to the donning of sackcloth (2 Sam. 3:31). The tearing of garments is not here proscribed.[104] But the idea is that such is not to be done without the resolve of the heart leading the way.

Now return to the LORD your God is generally thought to be the point at which Joel takes up the task of explaining the inviting words of Yahweh given in 2:12-13a.[105] The hope for returning to the Lord is introduced by **for,** thereby explaining the reason why the prophet can confidently proclaim the

---

104. An exception would be the priests, who were prohibited from engaging in certain mourning rituals, including the tearing of clothing (Lev. 10:6; 19:28; 21:5, 10).

105. Bewer, 106.

possibility of mercy.[106] Israel's God is a God of mercy, One who responds to human contrition (Jonah 4:2; *et. al.*).

Four of the five characteristics mentioned here are taken from Exodus 34:6, where Yahweh reveals His nature to Moses on Mount Sinai: 'Then the LORD passed by in front of him and proclaimed, "The LORD, the LORD God, compassionate and gracious, slow to anger, and abounding in lovingkindness and truth." ' These same characteristics are set forth elsewhere (*e.g.* Neh. 9:17; Ps. 86:15; 103:8; 145:8), but only Jonah 4:2 reiterates all five character qualities noted here.

The adjective **gracious** is used only as an attribute of God[107] and describes His gracious acts and goodwill toward mankind. In all but two cases, it is always used with **compassionate.** With only one exception (Ps. 112:4), this adjective is employed exclusively with reference to God as well. It denotes care, tenderness,[108] and speaks of the intense love and compassion of a parent for a child (cf. Ps. 103:13; Micah 7:17). **Slow to anger** is literally 'long of nostrils' or 'long of anger,' picturing one who takes long, deep breaths to keep from getting angry. Proverbs 25:15 describes a patient man as one who is long of breath. **Lovingkindness** 'refers to an attitude as well as to actions. This attitude is parallel to love, goodness, etc. It is a kind of love, including mercy, when the object is in a pitiful state.'[109]

The final characteristic is that Yahweh is **relenting of evil.** It would appear that such a description of God's character is contradictory to other statements regarding His immutability (*e.g.* 1 Sam. 15:29; Ps. 110:4). However, when used of God, 'relent' (or 'repent' as it is often translated) is to be viewed as an anthropopathic expression, eliminating any sense of contradiction. From man's finite perspective, it only

---

106. Watts, 28.

107. BDB, 337.

108. BDB, 933

109. R. Laird Harris, *TWOT*, I, 307. The exact meaning of this term has been discussed voluminously for the past half century. Harris presents an excellent overview of the principals involved and the ramifications of their conclusions in *TWOT*, I, 305-307.

appears that God has changed His mind and purpose. It must be understood that God's stern warnings of judgment are not inflexible; rather they are

> subordinate to the higher purpose of his people's welfare. This divine relenting is not to be regarded as fickleness or an irresolute retraction of a formerly absolute decree, as if God dillydallies or cannot make up his mind. The emphasis here is on the personal relationship of God with his people and his varying attitude toward them according to their sensitivity to his will.[110]

The **evil** noted here is not a specific reference to the locust plague or any military invasion (past or future). Rather, the phrase is a general statement regarding any circumstance or calamity which God brings about for the purpose of judging sin. When it states that He is One who relents of evil, it is merely describing His character—that He is One who relents of evil when the response of the people is right and when He deems it is appropriate and in concert with His plan and will.

> Since the promise of judgment is conditioned on man's failure to meet God's standards, for man to repent and meet God in his gracious provision for him is to avert the just judgment of God. From man's point of view, God would seem to have 'changed his mind' or 'feelings' or 'repented concerning the evil.'[111]

> *Who knows whether He will not turn and relent,*
> *And leave a blessing behind Him,*
> *Even a grain offering and a libation*
> *For the Lord your God* (2:14)

The opening words **who knows** is not an expression of doubt or unbelief concerning Yahweh's character. That He is a God who, when the people repent, chooses not to bring judgment upon them has been definitively established in verse 13—it is part of His character. Verse 14, however, is no longer a description of His character; rather, it is a statement of uncertainty, from man's point of view. Yahweh's character

---

110. Allen, 81
111. Patterson, 251.

is beyond doubt, but whether He will choose to withhold judgment in the present circumstance is not so certain. The phrase, carrying the idea of 'perhaps' (cf. 2 Sam. 12:22; Jonah 3:9), underscores the freedom and sovereignty of God.

> Human repentance does not control God. People cannot force God to show them his forgiveness. They can only appeal to him for mercy in not meting out against them what they very well deserve. They may hope for his compassion, but they cannot command it (Zeph. 2:3; Lam. 3:29).[112]

Perhaps, if the people demonstrate a genuine change of heart, Yahweh may withhold further judgment **and leave a blessing behind.** The **blessing,** though often thought of in the abstract, here denotes a physical blessing, something concrete left behind (i.e. food, grain, fruit), as the mention of offerings and libations mandates. The picture is one of harvest time in Israel. The Mosaic Law had instructed them to leave sheaves of grain in the fields, to not cut the corners, and to leave behind olives and grapes, so that the poor, the widow and the orphan might have food (Lev. 19:9-10; 23:22; Deut. 24:19-21). Yahweh's army of locusts has 'harvested' the grains, pastures, fruit trees, and vines. The prophet expresses the hope that, upon repentance, He might command his reapers to leave some grain and fruit behind. The **after Him** would be better translated 'after it,' referring to a blessing left after the locust invasion. The same prepositional phrase is used in 2:3 with reference to the locusts.

The continual concern of Joel for the sacrifices and offerings is reiterated here (cf. 1:9, 13, 16). There is a need to maintain the requirements of the covenant, for how else is judgment to be averted if the stipulations of the Levitical law are not carried out? God does not delight in sacrifices and burnt offerings in and of themselves,[113] but delights in righteous sacrifices when performed from a pure heart (cf.

---

112. Stuart, 252

113. Passages which attack the sacrificial system (e.g. 1 Sam. 15:22; Prov. 15:8; Isa. 1:11-16; Amos 5:21-24) must be seen in light of their fuller contexts. The disdain was not for the sacrifices themselves but for their pursuit apart from inward piety and holiness.

Ps. 51:17-19 [51:19-21]). And thus the prophet hopes that some grain and wine will be left for a grain offering and libation, all the while cognizant of the realization that they can give back only what He has first given them. As David acknowledges: 'But who am I and who are my people that we should be able to offer as generously as this? For all things come from Thee, and from Thy hand we have given Thee' (1 Chron. 29:14).

Corporate Repentance (2:15-17)

The prophet, now turning his attention toward Israel as a covenant people, as a group belonging to Yahweh, summons them once again (cf. 1:14) to engage in corporate, uninhibited fasting and prayer.

> *Blow a trumpet in Zion,*
> *Consecrate a fast, proclaim a solemn assembly* (2:15).

The command given in 2:1 is here reiterated and expanded. Earlier the blast of the trumpet was for the purpose of sounding an alarm to warn of the approaching enemy. Here, however, the trumpet was to be sounded to gather the people together to fast, pray, and lament. For that purpose, the theme has greater similarities to 1:14 than to 2:1. The invitation to genuine repentance had opened the door to the possibility of restored blessing, and therefore the priests and leaders were to gather the people for a national demonstration of contrition and repentance.[114] All three verbs are imperatives, highlighting the passion with which the prophet's message is expounded and reinforcing the need to act with expedition.

> *Gather the people, sanctify the congregation,*
> *Assemble the elders,*
> *Gather the children and the nursing infants.*
> *Let the bridegroom come out of his room*
> *And the bride out of her bridal chamber* (2:16).

---

114. Note further discussion in 1:14 and 2:1.

The elaboration of chapter 1:14 is continued in 2:16, with a series of tersely worded imperatives briskly pointing the way. The depth demanded in 2:12-13 is here to be matched with breadth. The mourning was to be universal. From the oldest to the very youngest, all were to gather for this solemn assembly. Having gathered, they were commanded to **sanctify the congregation.** Solemn occasions called for a full ritual purification. The devastation of the locusts and famine was unparalleled; Yahweh's army had invaded. Therefore, preparations for the solemn gathering and time of fasting and praying were to be meticulously and fully carried out. Generally, purification rites included bathing, washing clothing, dressing with clean apparel, and abstaining from conjugal activity (Gen. 35:2; Exod. 19:14-15; 1 Sam. 21:4-5 [5-6]).

From the oldest to the youngest they were to come. Because of the comparison drawn with infants, the **elders** probably makes reference to the aged and not to the office of elder, as specified in 1:2, 14. With the mention of **children** and **nursing infants,** the terms of corporate prayer and mourning are expanded beyond the exhortations of the earlier chapter, where the younger members of society were not mentioned. The two terms can be used as virtual synonyms, both speaking of children who are still nursing.[115]

The situation is so grave that even the bride and groom are exhorted to assemble—consummation of the marriage will have to wait.[116] Under normal circumstances, Israelite law exempted the newly married from public duties for a period of one year (Deut. 20:7; 24:5).[117] The three imperatives with which Joel begins 2:16 are followed by the jussive **let come out,** which carries the force of a command. Although the term **bride** specifically refers to a woman who is sworn to a man and therefore may designate a woman married for

---

115. The former term may, on occasion, refer to a child or young man (cf. Job 21:11). Even children are not spared in the Day of Yahweh (Isa. 13:16).

116. Later, the prophet Jeremiah notes that because of judgment, the festal scenes of marriage will be stopped (7:34; 16:9; 25:10).

117. According to the Mishnah, the groom was even provided an exemption from reciting the Shema (Deut. 6:4) each evening (Berakot 2.5).

some time (cf. Gen. 38:11; Ruth 1:6), the reference here is to a bride, as the context clearly indicates.

The groom is enjoined to come out of his **room** and the bride out of her **chamber**. The bride and groom are not in different rooms, but are together. The terms are poetical synonyms used interchangeably for the bridal bedroom (cf. Judg. 15:1; 2 Sam. 16:22; Ps. 19:5 [6]), the place of consummation of one's marriage. Originally referring to a special nuptial tent, it later came to designate the bridal bed, richly adorned with canopy and curtains.

The briskly shouted commands of 2:15-16 to 'stop everything!', enunciated by Yahweh's spokesman in terse, staccato fashion, is followed by two jussives in 2:17, specifically delineating the appropriate actions and words for the priests.

> *Let the priests, the* LORD's *ministers,*
> *Weep between the porch and the altar,*
> *And let them say, 'Spare Thy people, O* LORD,
> *And do not make Thine inheritance a reproach,*
> *A byword among the nations.*
> *Why should they among the peoples say,*
> *'Where is their God?'* (2:17).

The prophet does not begin with the jussive Let as the English text reads. Rather, the Hebrew text places emphasis on the location of the weeping and praying, commencing with the phrase Between the porch and the altar of Solomon's temple. Thirty feet wide and fifteen feet deep, the space provided an entry way to the Holy Place from the east. The location, also known as the 'inner court' or 'court of the priests' (1 Kings 6:3, 36; 7:19), was distinct from the 'outer court' or 'great court' (2 Chron. 4:9) to which the laity were restricted. Though not often mentioned in Scripture, there are two negative events which occurred here. Prior to Nebuchadnezzar's final siege of Jerusalem, Ezekiel, in a vision, observes a group of about twenty-five men prostrating themselves with their backs toward the Holy Place, worshiping the rising sun (Ezek. 8:16). Matthew (23:35) records this as the place of the murder of Zechariah. Joel, however, prescribes its traditional function—a place where priests were to call upon Yahweh (1 Kings 8:22), and to weep and pray. In their approach to Yahweh and the physical residence of the Shekinah Glory above the Mercy Seat, the priests would have moved—empty-handed—past the altar of burnt offering, the locust plague and drought having prevented them from offering anything. It is here, with their backs toward the altar, they were to weep and to make supplication. With nothing to offer Yahweh by way of sacrifice and libation, their only recourse was to entreat their God with contrition of heart and beg for mercy.

The seer's instructions were two-fold: they were **to weep** and **to pray** (lit, **to say**). The weeping that is here called for is not so much a sorrow for the punishment already inflicted, although the term can be so used elsewhere (*e.g.* Judg. 21:2). Rather, as the context of 2:12ff indicates, it is a weeping of repentance, a bitter sense of sorrow over having offended Yahweh (*e.g.* 2 Kings 22:19; Neh. 8:9).

As Moses had done on various occasions (Exod. 32:11-12; Num. 14:17) and as Daniel would do (Dan. 9:4-19), they also were to do.[118] First of all, they were to pray for deliverance, that Yahweh would **spare** them. With the idea of **spare**, the term includes the concept of feeling **pity** toward another or **looking on with compassion**[119] (*e.g.* Deut. 19: 12, 13, 21; Ezek. 16:5). Yahweh is appealed to on the basis of compassion; He is petitioned for mercy, to feel pity for them (cf. Tit 3:5).

Second, they were to pray that He would not make His **inheritance a reproach**. Israel is frequently described as Yahweh's inheritance (Deut. 4:20; 9:26, 29) or His special treasure (Exod. 19:5; Deut. 7:6; Ps. 135:4; cf. Tit 2:14).[120] They were to appeal on the basis of that special bond, that special relationship forged as His adopted children (cf. Ezek. 16).

---

118. Also cf similarities with the lament over the destruction of Jerusalem in Ps. 79.

119. BDB, 299.

120. Even the land of Canaan is often noted as being the mountain of Yahweh's inheritance, the place into which His people were planted (Exod. 15:17; 1 Sam. 26:19; Ps. 2:6; 78:54). Also cf. 1 Pet. 2:9.

Reproach means 'to say sharp things against, to taunt.'[121]
The negative particle **not** suggests the idea of stopping
something that was already occurring—that scorn was
already being directed toward them. As with Moses before
(Deut. 9:29), the basis of the appeal is that they belonged to
Yahweh, as **Thy** people and **Thine** inheritance denotes.

A **byword among the nations** has been repeatedly debated,
with specific attention focused on **byword**. When employed
elsewhere as a verb, this Hebrew infinitive followed by the
preposition '**among**' is never used in the sense of *derision* or
scorn; rather, it is always utilized in the sense of *exercising rule*
or *dominion*.[122] Following this rendering, if the locust plague
and famine were to continue unabated, then the nation would
be impoverished and unable to defend itself, making it an
easy mark for subjugation by other nations.

The aforementioned reasons not withstanding, it appears
best to let the translation **byword** stand.

1) The context both before and after is riveted on the
   thought of scorn and derisive taunting. The element
   of foreign subjugation is absent.[123]

2) The Hebrew words for **reproach** and **byword** are
   employed together in Jeremiah 24:9, suggesting
   a close relationship in the context of judgment.

3) In Deuteronomy 28:37, Israel is warned of becoming
   a byword within the context of a locust devastation to
   crops and lands (cp. Deut. 28:38, 40-42).

4) While the verb when followed by the preposition elsewhere always refers to *exercising authority*, the noun
   form followed by the same preposition is used to
   mean *byword* or *parable* (Ezek. 12:23; 18:3).

5) In 2:19, Yahweh promises to send grain, new wine,
   and oil to take away the **reproach among the nations**,

---

121. BDB, 357.

122. So Henderson, 108; Laetsch, 121; Stuart, 248.

123. This, of course, is based on the conclusion that the historical invasion of
Assyria is not in view in 2:1-11. Those who subscribe to the alternative
view understand the text to be describing a military invasion.

indicating that it was not some foreign domination that led the nations to scorn Israel, but the unparalleled locust plague and drought.[124]

6) Finally, the translation **to exercise authority** or **to rule** is rendered incompatible with the immediate context.[125] Both before and after, the theme is one of derision and dishonor.

The prayer of the priests ends with a plea for Yahweh to intervene for the purpose of protecting His honor. For His possession to be scorned and taunted is one thing, but for His honor to be attacked is another. Yahweh's reputation is at stake, providing the strongest reason why He should act to avert the judgment,[126] and thereby vindicate both Himself and His people.

124. BDB, 199.

125. So Allen, 83-84; Bewer, 107-108; Keil, 198; Wade, 103.

126. Beseeching God on the basis of protecting His reputation is an approach found frequently in the Old Testament. 'For Thy name's sake' is often employed by those earnestly seeking His face (*e.g.* Ps. 25:11; 79:9; Jer. 14:7, 21).

4.
The Eschatological
Day of Yahweh
(2:18–3:21)

Beginning with the opening stanza of the book, the reader's attention has been constantly drawn toward the future. The present circumstances, as grave as they were, were signposts of something greater yet to come. The prophet's instructions to rehearse the present events to subsequent generations (1:2-3), the call to set aside age old traditions and engage in unprecedented mourning rites (1:9; 2:16), and the comparison of the current devastation with the unparalleled Day of Yahweh (1:15; 2:2) compel one to realize that the plague of locusts and the accompanying drought serve as a backdrop from which the prophet could launch into a discussion and description of the eschatological Day of Yahweh.

After describing the contemporary Day of Yahweh brought on by the onslaught of locusts and after depicting the impending Day of Yahweh by means of an intensified description of the locusts' indefensible attack, Joel launches into a three-fold description of the eschatological Day of Yahweh. The text assumes an interval of time between 2:17 and 2:18, during which Israel repents, allowing the Lord to 'relent' (2:13). As a result of her repentance, the three major concerns confronting Israel in the former section (1:1–2:17) are answered by the Lord in three corresponding parts in the latter section (2:18–3:21 [4:21]). It will be a day of material restoration (2:21-27), spiritual restoration (2:28-32 [3:1-5]), and national restoration (3:1-21 [4:1-21]). The need for the restoration of each of these was touched upon earlier by the prophet, though not to the same degree.[1] But now, following a brief introduction (2:18-20), they are given his full attention.

1. Introduction (2:18-20)

With the advent of 2:18, the book makes a dramatic and decisive transition, devoting the remainder of its message to the restoration of material, spiritual, and national prosperity. Moving from lamentation to salvation,[2] Yahweh reminds His people that, based on their genuine repentance, He is pursuing them with a jealous love (2:18) and that they will enjoy safety from their enemies (2:19f, 27; 3:1ff [4:1ff]). The catastrophic upheavals which will come (2:30 [3:3]), of which they had experienced a foretaste, would no longer signal Yahweh's judgment on them but His retributive wrath on His enemies. Instead of cries of lament and pleas for mercy, in hopes that He might relent (2:14), there are now assurances of a welcomed response and a divine blessing, with the goal that 'you will know that I am the Lord your God' (3:17 [4:17]). 'From here on only oracles pertaining to the future are collected, oracles that promise new and salutary life for Jerusalem and Judah, as well as the warding off of all their opponents.'[3]

> *Then the LORD will be zealous for His land,*
> *And will have pity on His people* (2:18).

---

1. Cf. Wolff, 7. The symmetry of these topics on each side of this transition point should not be overlooked. 1:4-2:17 is replete with examples of the material devastation. The spiritual and religious aspects are noted in 1:9, 13-14, 16; 2:12-13. The nation is referenced in 2:1-11, 17.

2. The movement from lamentation to divine assurances (through a prophet) is seen elsewhere in lament psalms (cf. Ps. 12:5 [6]; 60:6-8 [8-10]) and in the prophets (cf. 2 Chron. 20; Isa. 33:10ff; Jer. 4:1f) (cf. Allen, 85).

3. Wolff, 57. Cf. Watts, 32.

Similar to the role which 1:4 plays in the first section, 2:18 is the thesis statement upon which the final section of the book hinges. Because of Israel's repentance, the zeal and pity for His land and people will eventuate in personal bounty, spiritual blessing, and national prosperity. The tenses of verbs through 2:24 are employed in a proleptic sense. Like prophetic perfects, they are used to depict future events with such certainty that the action is expressed in terms of history—as though it had already occurred. A glimpse of the future has been revealed to the seer, and he is now reporting on what he has seen.[4]

Yahweh is described as being **zealous** and having **pity**. The former term depicts someone who becomes red or flushed with passion or deep emotion.[5] As a husband for his wife, so Yahweh feels strongly for His people. Because He has an exclusive claim in His people and loves them with a great love, He is aflame with a jealous zeal for them.[6] Thus, when this special relationship is fractured by idolatry, His jealous wrath is aroused against them (Exod. 20:5; 34:14; Deut. 4:24; 32:21; Josh. 24:19). When they have suffered enough at the hands of their enemies and have repented, then His jealousy is said to be aroused against the enemy on their behalf (Isa. 42:13).

He also has **pity** on them. The verb encapsulates the idea of sparing one from difficulty,[7] generally motivated out of a heart of compassion or emotion (Exod. 2:6; Ezek. 16:5). Frequently, His pity is said to be aroused when the 'apple of His eye' (Zech. 2:8; Deut. 32:10) has suffered greatly at the hands of His enemies (Isa. 9:7; 37:32; Ezek. 36:5; 39:25-29; Zeph. 3:8; Zech. 1:14; 8:2). Together, these two verbs here depict Yahweh's intensely passionate action on behalf of His people to spare them further harm and suffering.[8]

---

4. Kaiser suggests that the past tense verbs indicate an historical restoration of material blessings (2:19-27), while the spiritual and material restoration (2:28-3:21 [3:1-4:21]) have their fulfillment in the end times (Kaiser, *The Messiah in the Old Testament* [Grand Rapids: Zondervan, 1995], 139-140).

5. BDB, 888.

6. Cf. Watts, 32.

7. BDB, 328.

8. Although different words are used, Ps. 103:13f connotes a similar idea.

The focus of Yahweh's jealous actions is **His land** and **His people**. As Israel's husband, He is the passionate guardian of His wife and the purity of their relationship. As Israel's guardian/suzerain, He is the jealous protector of their land, eager to deliver the promises stipulated in the tenets of the covenant treaty. The land concept had more significance to Israel than merely the designation of a territory. The Old Testament speaks of the land as the place of God's revelation and of His special influence (cf. Gen. 4:16; Jonah 1:3, 10). Though all the earth belongs to Him and although He rules in all the world, there is a unique sense of relationship and influence which God has with His land. There is a close connection between His people and the land He gave to them through Abraham (Gen. 13:14-18; 17:6-8). Thus He is zealous to defend not only His own rights but also the rights and privileges of His people and His land into which He has planted them.

> *And the* LORD *will answer and say to His people,*
> *Behold, I am going to send you grain, new wine, and oil,*
> *And you will be satisfied in full with them;*
> *And I will never again make you a reproach*
> *among the nations* (2:19).

This is the third action attributed to Yahweh and introduces the narrative portion which follows. Not only will He be zealous for His land and have pity on His people, but He will also **answer** them. The first half of Joel is an appeal to Yahweh; now He responds to their cries, specifying how He will 'relent of evil' (2:13) and restore the fortunes of Israel.

The passion, intensity, and resoluteness of Yahweh's actions are exposed and highlighted by the use of the first person. Undoubtedly the message is delivered through the mouth of the prophet, but it is heralded in first person. Yahweh Himself speaks, lending power and authority to the contents. The introductory formula, **Behold I**, is literally '**Behold [it is] I who is sending,'** drawing riveting attention to the source of these good and comforting words (cf. Zech. 1:13). Just as 2:11 specifically identifies Yahweh as the ultimate source of the calamitous judgment, so too He is the fountainhead of unprecedented prosperity, blessing, and security.

The promise is two-fold and the order in which they are presented is not without significance. The prayer of 2:17 specifically appealed for two things: to spare His people and to not make the nation a reproach. The response follows the same order. Understanding the trauma which a lack of food for both man (1:10-12) and beast (1:18-20) entails, He announces that the basic necessities of life are restored first, then the national reproach is lifted. He is sending[9] **grain, new wine, and oil**. These products are the same as those mentioned in 1:10, though there without the article. Here, the article is planted before each (lit. *the* grain, *the* new wine, and *the* oil), thereby denoting their prominence both for food and for livelihood in an agrarian society. These were the principal objects of destruction by the locusts and drought; now restoration is promised.

With ample grain, new wine, and oil, Yahweh states that they **will be satisfied in full with them**. The verb has the sense of being fully satisfied, of being satiated.[10] Food would not be scarce; there would be plenty. The language is reminiscent of Yahweh's promises to Israel upon her entry into Canaan, that if she would honor Him in obedience, then she would enjoy food in abundance (Deut. 6:10-11; 8:7-10; 11:13-15).

In chapter one, the absence of grain, wine, and oil was bemoaned because it meant not only a loss of food but also the inability to present libations and grain offerings (1:9, 13, 16). An important part of their appeal to Yahweh for mercy was the need to continue carrying out the tenets of the covenant by offering their divinely prescribed sacrifices and libations. In their restoration here, no mention is made of the renewal of grain offerings and libations in the house of Yahweh. Although the reason for the absence can not be known with certainty, it is possible that the offerings and libations of chapter one were nothing more than mere tokens and did not truly reflect a heart totally devoted to Him (cf. 1 Sam. 15:22; Ps. 50:7-15; 51:16-17; 69:30-32; Prov. 15:8). With

---

9. Literally, 'am sending' (present participle).
10. BDB, 959.

the increasing severity of the locust plague and drought
(2:1ff), nothing more is said of the need for grain offerings
and libations, only of the need to 'rend your heart and not
your garments' (2:13), to 'spare Thy people and do not
make Thine inheritance a reproach' (2:17). Yahweh did not
need their offerings and libations (Ps. 50:7ff); He wanted
them. And when they came to Him in true repentance, then
restoration of the necessities of life were granted in return.[11]

The second part of Yahweh's response was His promise
that **I will never again make you a reproach among the
nations**. As a result of their dire condition, they were being
scorned among the nations. As with the locusts and drought,
their reproach was also under Yahweh's direction. As in
verse 17, the verb **make** is literally 'give;' He had given them
over to that condition. But while the negative **not** [*al*] in 2:17
suggests that they were already being made a reproach and
were praying that it would stop, here the negative **never**
[*lo'*] intimates that Yahweh would never allow it to happen
again. The negative coupled with the adverb **again** indicates a finality which goes beyond Israel's return from the
Babylonian Captivity. Although many blessings did come
to the returning remnant, they were again dispersed among
the nations. The strong language here seems to point beyond
a sixth-century BC fulfillment.

> But I will remove the northern army far from you,
> And I will drive it into a parched and desolate land,
> And its vanguard into the eastern sea,
> And its rear guard into the western sea,
> And its stench will arise and its foul smell will come up,
> For it has done great things (2:20).

Following the promise of ample food supplies and the
promise never again to allow His people to suffer reproach-
ment, Yahweh adds a third promise—the removal of the
northern army from their midst. A magnificent reversal
takes place; judgments promised to a disobedient Israel
(Deut. 28:20-26) are here applied to her enemies.

---

11. Cf. Mal. 3:11-12.

The identification of the **northern army** has been long debated. Some have argued that the reference is to the locust invasion. They propound that there is not the slightest trace of a hostile invasion of Judah by literal armies.[12] Since the context speaks only of locusts, only locusts can be here designated.

Others contend, however, that the specific designation should be translated 'northerner.' With the Hebrew letter *yodh* suffixed to the term, it strongly intimates that it is not referring to the direction from which they come but to the location of their origin.[13] Such is probably the sense here. First, since locusts are not native to countries north of Palestine, it becomes doubtful that the name is intended as a reference to locusts. Rather, it is more likely referring to a country that invades from the north. Second, the closing phrase of the verse, 'For it has done great things,' is logically more attributable to human pride which had exceeded its bounds than to an irrational locust scourge brought about by the hand of God.[14]

Third, the **never again** finality of 2:19 suggests that the time period in view encompasses the era of millennial prosperity, blessing, and security. Any fulfillment prior to that time would reduce the impact of those words. Fourth, the Hebrew text places the term **northern army** first in the verse, so that it could be rendered, 'And the northerner, I will ....' There is no evidence that locusts were ever known as such. Fifth, later prophets take up the topic of a northern power invading and subjugating Israel (Isa. 5:26-30; 13; Ezek. 38-39). Sixth, of the two other occurrences of the noun **stench** in the Old Testament, it is employed both times with reference to corpses killed in battle (Isa. 34:3; Amos 4:10).

---

12. Lange, 25. Cf. Von Orelli, 89; Keil, 202.

13. This is similar to the 'i' suffixed to the name of a country, such as Israel, to designate someone who originates from Israel, *i.e.* an Israeli. Keil (202) argues that 'it cannot be philologically proved that *tsephoni* can only denote one whose home is in the north' but fails to provide evidence.

14. Pusey, 150-154. Also cf. Feinberg, 24-25; Wade, 104.

Consequently, it appears that Yahweh, utilizing the imagery of a locust invasion, is describing the attack of an actual army invading from the north.

Joel sees in the natural event of the locust catastrophe a pledge that the prophetic eschatology of disaster will not become void. He can describe its fulfillment only in the form of locust-like apocalyptic creatures, however, and he similarly uses the cryptic term 'the northerner'...for the 'last enemy.'[15]

The promise is that the northern army will be **removed** from them. The Hebrew verb is causative, emphasizing the activity and responsibility of the one doing the removing. Distance is also emphasized, denoting that it will be removed far away (cf. Isa. 49:19).[16] Yahweh will cause it to be removed, to be lifted **from upon you**, depicting a heavy burden being lifted.[17]

As locusts are subject to being driven by the prevailing winds, so the enemy will be **driven** out. This term speaks of pursuing and casting down with the intent to do harm (cf. Ps. 118:13; 140:4 [140:5]).[18] In a violent manner, they will be divided and conquered, with the vanguard driven into the eastern sea and the rearguard into the western sea. The **eastern sea** denotes the Dead Sea[19] which lies in the south-eastern portion of Israel, and the **western sea** quite certainly has reference to the Mediterranean Sea. Literally, the two seas are noted as being the 'in front of' sea and the 'after/behind' sea. For ancient Orientals, the east with the rising of the sun was regarded as the primary point of the compass, causing the four points of the compass to so referenced.[20]

---

15. Wolff, 62.

16. BDB, 934-935. Cp. Isa. 59:9, 11; Jer. 2:5.

17. Cp. Zech. 12:3 where, instead of the nations being a heavy burden on Israel, Jerusalem will be made like a heavy stone for the surrounding nations, causing severe injury for those who attempt to lift her.

18. BDB, 190-191.

19. Deviating from majority opinion, Watts (33) suggests that the eastern sea denotes the Persian Gulf, concluding that 'the scene is very broad. It fits the great drama of "the day" better....'

20. In keeping with this orientation, one of the Hebrew words for South is designated by 'on the right.'

The stench and foul smell that will come up does not appear to be due only to the enemy's violent demise. Rather it seems the writer wishes to link the phrase with the final notation. Because of the great (evil) things which the enemy has done, a putrid smell arises before God (Exod. 3:9). Acting out of pride and hatred and for their own purposes, the northern army had subjugated Yahweh's people (Zech. 1:15; also cf. Isa. 10:7-15; 37:28-29; Amos 1:11; Nahum; Dan. 8:4, 8, 11; 11:36-37). The phrase depicts the haughtiness of man, elevating himself to positions of greatness through the selfish subjugation of Yahweh's people. But Yahweh is greater, as the next verse attests.[21]

Material Restoration (2:21-27)

In the previous three verses, Yahweh was the speaker. Here the prophet Joel resumes the role of spokesman, taking up the theme established by Yahweh in 2:18-20 in more elaborate and defining tones. The specifics are unfolded in a progressive fashion, beginning first with the land (v. 21), and then the animals (v. 22), before moving on to the inhabitants (v. 23). In each, the prophet begins with the command, followed by the reasons why they are to rejoice. With each admonition, the reasons become increasingly comprehensive and detailed.

The topics addressed are significantly reminiscent of chapter one. The terminology so prominent in lament earlier is here repeated, but with a reversed effect. Mourning has turned to gladness, famine has given way to abundance, and drought has been washed away with rain.[22] Von Orelli rightly asserts: 'Repentance has made such a revolution possible, divine grace made it actual.'[23]

---

21. The phrase need not be seen as an 'accidental dittograph, which should be omitted' (Wade, 105) nor need one alter the text to read (as in verse 21a), 'I have done great things' (Bewer, 113). On the contrary, the writer has drawn a contrast between the actions of the enemy and those of Yahweh (cp. Ps. 35:26c with 35:27a).

22. Wolff (63) notes: 'Thus 2:21-24 shows itself to be an assurance oracle answering a plea which corresponds exactly to the laments in 1:16-20; neither passage mentions the locust plague.'

23. Von Orelli, 90.

> *Do not fear, O land, rejoice and be glad,*
> *For the LORD has done great things* (2:21).

In chapter one, the land was said to be in a state of mourning (1:10) because it could not deliver grain, fruit, wine, and oil (1:10-12). But a reversal of circumstances has brought a change. Joel begins with the command, **Do not fear**. As noted in 2:17, the Hebrew negative employed here connotes the admonition to terminate an action already in progress, i.e. 'stop being afraid.' The **land**, as in 1:10, is more properly translated 'ground.' Its mourning was to end, its fear was to be stopped; rather, it is to **rejoice and be glad**. The former verb most often denotes rejoicing at the works of God (cf. Ps. 9:14 [9:15]; 31:7-8; 118:24; Isa. 49:13). The latter imperative 'denotes being glad or joyful with the whole disposition as indicated by its association with the heart (cf. Exod. 4:14; Ps. 19:8 [19:9]; 104:15; 105:3), the soul (Ps. 86:4); and with the lighting up of the eyes (Prov. 15:30).'[24] The conditions of 1:6-7, 10-12, 19-20 have been reversed. The gladness and joy which had been cut off (same root words as in 1:16) are here commanded.

How could this come about? **For the LORD has done great things.**[25] The Hebrew verb **done** is an infinitive, highlighting the nature of the action rather than the time of the action. The phrase makes an obvious, contrasting reference back to verse 20. Vaunting itself, the enemy had 'done great things.' But Yahweh, with omnipotent power, destroys the enemy. No longer would the invading force be allowed to tread His land underfoot. The **great things** also introduces what follows, where the prophet spells out the material blessings restored to the land, the beasts, and the inhabitants.

> *Do not fear, beasts of the field,*
> *For the pastures of the wilderness have turned green,*
> *For the tree has borne its fruit,*
> *The fig tree and the vine have yielded in full* (2:22).

---

24. Waltke, *TWOT*, II, 879.

25. Cf. Ps. 126:2ff.

In the same manner as the ground (v. 21), the **beasts of the field** are issued the imperative to **not fear**. The Hebrew command is constructed identically to verse 21, admonishing the animals to stop being afraid. That they felt the brunt of the locust devastation and drought is abundantly clear in 1:18-20, where its designation is the same.

Although there is no exhortation for them to rejoice and be glad, it is implied. As recipients of the great things Yahweh has done, they too have much cause for which to rejoice, **for the pastures of the wilderness have turned green**. Again reminiscent of 1:19, the former situation has been reversed. The verb[26] **turned green** is literally 'to sprout, grow green,' the verb being cognate with the word for new, tender shoots of grass (cf. Deut. 32:2; 2 Sam. 23;4; Ps. 23:2). Yahweh's great acts will permit the ground/soil once again to fulfill its purpose (Gen. 1:11f; Hosea 2:21-22).

With the phrase, **the tree has borne its fruit**, the writer moves away from the beasts and toward the opening of verse 23, where man is mentioned. Historically, the **fig tree and the vine** are symbolic of prosperity, peace and security in Israel (I Kings 4:25; Micah 4:4; Zech. 3:10).[27] In 1:7, 12, the locusts strip the tree bare; here it once again **yields in full**. Literally rendered 'gives their strength,'[28] Joel employs the noun as a metaphor in which the cause is exchanged for the effect, as a synonym for 'fruit' (cf. Ps. 1:4).

After addressing the land (ground/soil) and the beasts of the field, the prophet now focuses direct attention on the people, the inhabitants of the land.

> *So rejoice, O sons of Zion,*
> *And be glad in the LORD your God;*

---

26. As in 2:18ff, it seems preferable to interpret the verbs proleptically, as prophetic perfects. Although the final realization of these promises is in the eschaton, the certainty of their fulfillment compels the writer to express them in the completed tense.

27. Jesus also used the analogy of the fig tree as a symbol of His restored relationship with Israel (Luke 13:6ff; 21:29ff).

28. Cf. Gen. 4:12.

For He has given you the early rain for your vindication.
And He has poured down for you the rain,
The early and latter rain as before (2:23).

The land and the beasts of 2:21-22 were admonished first to stop being afraid. But there is no such admonition here. Rather, the prophet exhorts the people to rejoice and be glad, employing the same terminology as in 1:16 and 2:21. When the material blessings were previously cut off (1:16), their absence became the basis for prayer and fasting, mourning and lamentation. Now they will be restored and thus become the cause for celebration.

The verse begins with reference to the **sons of Zion**, giving the designation the prominent position at the head of the verse. Zion specifically refers to Jerusalem, which was located on Mt Zion. Here, however, it has a broader reference, designating all of the land of Israel (cf. Ps. 149:2 where 'Israel' and 'sons of Zion' are combined in poetic parallelism). The plague engulfed all the land and every level of society (1:5, 11, 13-14), not just its capital city, and thus the call to rejoicing is extended to all the people of Israel as well. The phrase also carries a covenantal theme. Yahweh dwelt in Zion (Ps. 9:11; 48:2; 74:2; 76:2). Her inhabitants were the recipients of His special covenantal love and choosing (Ps. 78:68; 87:2ff; 132:13ff; Zech. 1:14, 17). To this covenantal designation is added the object of the rejoicing: **in the LORD your God**. The choice of the name **Yahweh** (1:1) again reiterates the special covenantal bond between Him and His people.

The reason for this call to joy and happiness is introduced, as in 2:21, 22, with **for** and continues the theme initiated in the previous verses. The material blessings, of which they had been deprived, were now to be restored without restraint. Noting the specifics, Joel elaborates: **For He has given you the early rain for your vindication**. Consensus on the meaning of this phrase has been lacking.[29] The primary difficulty revolves around the term **the early rain** (*hammoreh*).

---

29. Keil (205) says it well: 'From time immemorial there has been a diversity of opinion as to the meaning of these words.'

Should it be translated 'the teacher' or does it refer to 'the early rain?'[30] It is derived from *yarah* which means 'to throw, shoot.' In the causative stem, as it is found here, the meaning is broader, including 'to throw; to shoot arrows; to throw water; to point out, show; to direct, teach.'[31]

When occurring in the causative stem, the term generally designates one who teaches or instructs another (*e.g.* Prov. 5:13; Isa. 30:20; Hab. 2:18).[32] As a result, the phrase has from earliest times been translated 'the teacher,' with specific reference to the Messiah.[33] A number of reasons have been presented in support of this translation. First, the article prefixed to *moreh* specifies a reference to that Prophet foretold in Deut. 18:15-18. There is no reason for the article if the reference is to 'rain.'[34] Second, instruction/teaching is given in the context of sending rain in 1 Kings 8:36 and 2 Chronicles 6:27. There the answer to prayer for rain must be preceded by divine instruction respecting the good way. Third, the subsequent verb **and He has poured down**, with its conjunction, denotes an action which is a consequence or result of the previous action **He has given**. That which follows explains that which precedes. In other words, because of/for the sake of the Teacher of Righteousness (the Messiah), the Lord sends the rain described in the latter part of the verse. Fourth, to interpret it as 'early rain' would be repetitious, and thus meaningless, since the latter part of the

---

30. Other less suitable translations have been given, the most notable of which is that of 'food' in the LXX. While food is more natural to the context, it is not based on good grammatical grounds. Most recent commentators have not endorsed it. For a concise discussion of this and other views, see Laetsch, 125f and Wade, 106f.

31. BDB, 434-435.

32. But cf. Ps. 84:6 [84:7], where it may refer to rain.

33. The standard early Jewish interpretation, including the 'Teacher of Righteousness' in Qumran writings, understood Messiah as the teacher, with others in more recent times following (cf. Laetsch, 125f), noting Deut. 18:15-18 as being here fulfilled (so also the Targum, Vulgate, and church fathers). Others have suggested that Joel is being referenced (Von Orelli, 90) or that all teachers/prophets from Moses to Messiah are being noted in a collective sense (Keil, 206-207).

34. Cf. Laetsch, 125; Keil, 206.

verse again speaks of the early rain. If one did have the 'early rain' being spoken of in both parts of the verse, it would be expected that the first word would be a more general term. Yet the term *moreh* is a specific term.[35]

A second view understands the term with reference to rain. First, the context speaks of temporal, material blessings, with discussions concerning spiritual blessings relegated to 2:28ff [3:1ff]. It would be contextually out of place to insert so briefly a mention of a teacher of righteousness, whether with reference to Messiah or one of the prophets. Second, the repetition of *moreh* (though without the article) immediately following essentially compels one to translate them identically. Since interpreters agree that the latter usage of *moreh* means 'rain,' the former should also. It is more difficult to render them so very differently when in such close proximity.[36] Third, the emphasis given to *moreh* by the article and the particle (*'eth*) indicates that the prophet had some immediate and definite object in view, namely, the autumn rains. So indispensable after an extensive drought, they provide moisture for soil preparation and planting. Its anticipation would be considerable, and thus the writer gives it a position of prominence in the text.[37] Fourth, when *moreh* is rendered 'teacher,' it is usually followed by the Hebrew preposition *in, with,* or *by,* or more rarely by *unto* or *from*.[38] Fifth, 'it is significant that in both of the two Pentateuchal passages whose data this piece takes up with remarkable consistency, *ntn,* "give," is used with rain as object (Lev. 26:4; Deut. 11:14). This fact strongly suggests that here the object of *natan* has to do with rain.'[39]

A third alternative views the first *moreh* (*hammoreh* when accompanied by the definite article) impersonally as a participle rather than as a noun.[40] The verse would

35. Wade, 106.

36. Henderson, 111; Driver, 61.

37. Henderson, 111. Cf. Ps. 65:9-10 [69:10-11].

38. Lange, 25.

39. Allen, 93.

40. So Patterson, 254.

then be rendered: 'For He will give to you that which gives instruction in righteousness, that is, He will send down to you the early and latter rain, as before.' First of all, this understanding would focus attention on the word play between the first *moreh* and the second *moreh*, which is written as *yoreh* in over thirty MSS and is the more common word for 'early rain' (*e.g.* Deut. 11:14). Secondly, the conjunction that follows the first *moreh* is an explanatory conjunction meaning **'that is.'** The subsequent phrases identify that which gives instruction in righteousness, namely, the renewed sending of the early and latter rains. The renewal of the rains would give indication of Yahweh's forgiveness, restored fellowship with His people, and restoration of the covenant privileges. This view would remove any allegations of tautology.

For vindication has also been translated variously, but requires a rendering of 'righteousness' or 'faithfulness.' The term is an ethical one and must be rendered accordingly.[41] Together with its prefixed preposition, it most probably denotes a relationship—Yahweh would provide rain in relationship to and in accordance with His righteousness (cf. Isa. 51:5-6). This righteousness would be 'Yahweh's own, meaning, that Yahweh will provide rain in agreement with His "justice," to wit, His loyalty to the people in harmony with the Covenant contracted.'[42]

As a token of the restored relationship (Lev. 26:3-5), Yahweh **has poured down for you the rain**. This term for **rain** (*geshem*) is more common, designating showers or rain in general, with the more specific words following to provide further explanation. The **early rains** fell during the months of October–December and helped with the preparation of the soil, planting of the seeds, and germination. **Latter rains** means 'to gather, to collect' and speaks of harvest-time. Coming primarily during the months of March and April, these crucial rains provided ample moisture for the heads of

---

41. This makes the translations 'moderately' (AV) or 'in just measure' (RSV) unlikely.
42. Kapelrud, 116. Cf. Kirkpatrick, 77-78; Wade, 106.

grain to fill out properly (cf. Deut. 11:14; Job 29:23; Jer. 5:24; Amos 4:7; James 5:7).

The final phrase of the verse, **as before**, has also proved difficult for translators. Various options have been followed. Some render it 'as the first,' describing the rains as the first of all the gifts enumerated in 2:24-26.[43] Others translate it 'in the first month,' noting that the first month of the religious calendar (Nisan) corresponds to March/April when the latter rains fall. In this case, the term would refer only to the **latter rains**, and not to the entire phrase.[44] This would be somewhat redundant, since everyone would know when the latter rains normally came. Still others suggest 'first' in order of time, corresponding to the 'after this' of 2:28. In other words, Yahweh will first send the plentiful rains, then the spiritual blessings.[45] However, the position of the word within the construction of the verse does not correspond to the construction of 2:28 [3:1].[46] Following the LXX and the Vulgate, probably the best rendering is 'as before,' referring to previous happier conditions which are now restored (cf. Deut. 9:18; Isa. 1:26; Jer. 33:11; Dan. 11:29).[47]

> *And the threshing floors will be full of grain,*
> *And the vats will overflow with the*
> *new wine and oil* (2:24).

In the previous three verses, Joel calls upon the land, the beasts, and the people to celebrate the end of the plague and the restoration of their fellowship with Yahweh. In verses 24-27 he elaborates on the effects of the abundant, seasonal rains described in verse 23.

---

43. So Laetsch, 126, drawing upon Deut. 17:7; 1 Kings 17:13; Isa. 60:9; and Zech. 12:7 for support.
44. So Wade, 106. He points to Gen. 8:13, Num. 9:5, Ezek. 29:17; 45:18 for justification. Wolff (64) also notes that the term, in the form found here, always means 'in the first month.'
45. Keil, 208.
46. Wolff, 64.
47. So Henderson, 112, and S. R. Driver, 62. Even this rendering requires one to attach the preposition 'as.' Henderson (112) observes that one of Kennicott's MSS does include the particle of comparison, noting that its ellipsis is not infrequent in the Hebrew Scriptures.

As the prophet so often does, he denotes the specific blessings by explicating promises previously, though briefly, introduced. The reference to grain,[48] new wine, and oil draws upon the theme broached in verse 19a, where Yahweh promised to send these food staples. The terminology is not new; the destruction of these staples tearfully lamented in 1:10ff is here similarly described in bold reversal. In contrast to the utter lack of food and grain for man, beast, and offerings to the Lord, Joel begins the verse with the verb **will be full**, thereby placing emphasis on the total reversal of circumstances. Literally, it reads, 'And full will be the threshing floors of grain.'

In ancient times, the threshing floor encompassed a small, generally round, area of hard-packed ground upon which the ears or heads of grain were laid. Depending on the circumstances or the type of grain being harvested, removal of the grain occurred in one of at least three ways: a) by beating the grain with clubs or rods (Isa. 28:27); b) by oxen stomping on it, often while pulling a cart (Deut. 25:4; Hosea 10:11; Micah 6:15; 1 Cor. 9:9); or c) by dragging over the grain a heavy piece of wood, called a sledge, usually with sharp stones attached to cut the straw into pieces (Deut. 28:27-28).

Harking back to the productive trees and vines (2:22), the vats will overflow with new wine and oil. The latter phrase also begins with the verb **will overflow**, emphasizing the overwhelming abundance. The plentiful rains, coming at the appropriate times, have made the grapes and olives extremely juicy. As a result, when they are crushed in the winepress, the vat overflows. The **vat** consisted of a small basin hewn into the top of a flat stone. A narrow trough would then be cut from the vat to an area of the rock that was slightly higher in elevation, where another basin (the wine-press) would be hewn into the rock. For harvesting, grapes or olives would then be placed into the wine-press and trodden upon, with the juice flowing downward into the vat (cf. Isa. 5:2; Jer. 48:33; Micah 6:15).

---

48. The word for **grain** here is different from 1:10 and 2:19. Though both can be translated 'grain,' the former is frequently employed to denote wheat and the latter corn.

Then I will make up to you for the years
That the swarming locust has eaten,
The creeping locust, the stripping locust,
*   and the gnawing locust,*
My great army which I sent among you (2:25)

The speaker, as in 2:19-20, is once again Yahweh. As spokesmen for God, the prophets often moved with relative ease from first person to third person, and back to first person (*e.g.* Isa. 56:6-8; 20-21). But the use of the first person here, with Yahweh as the speaker, presents a more vivid image of His intimate presence and involvement.

The actions of Yahweh—His grace, His blessing, His restoration—are the focal point of the text. Thus the text, as with both phrases in 2:24, begins with the verb describing His actions toward His people. The verb **I will make up** is a legal term depicting restitution for damages paid to the party wronged or suffering loss (cf. Exod. 22:3-5 [22:2-4]; Lev. 24:18).[49] Yahweh here promises to provide full compensation to Israel for all the losses suffered, even though she herself was the guilty party and therefore could make no formal claim.[50]

The years is a poetical metonym for the crops destroyed during the course of time that the locusts and drought enveloped the land (cp. Ps. 90:15; Prov. 5:9). The plural could indicate that the plague and drought were not limited to a single year, but extended over a longer period of time,[51] or that the results of a single invasion were felt for several years.[52] Regardless of the invasion's

---

49. The verb also provides the root for the noun **peace** (*shalom*). Peace is restored through the restitution or payment to the one wronged. Once recompense for sin has been made, then peace is restored. The theological implications are both picturesque and far-reaching (cf. Judg. 6:24; Rom. 5:1).

50. A magnificent portrait of God's grace, Allen (95) recalls the similarity of Paul's offer to Philemon concerning his runaway slave (Philemon 18-19).

51. Allen, 95.

52. Lange, 26. Keil (208), citing Gen. 21:7, argues that the word is used with indefinite generality, or as a poetical expression denoting the greatness and violence of the devastation. Robinson (32) points to Rev. 9:10 to corroborate his contention that a locust visitation seldom exceeds five months.

duration, the residual effects of the locusts' devastation on fruit orchards and vineyards would undoubtedly extend beyond only one year.[53]

The locusts mentioned are the same as those described in 1:4, but in a different order. Here **the swarming locust** is given first. They are Yahweh's great **army**. Intimated in 1:6 and verified in 1:ll, they belonged to Him; they take their orders from Him as their Commander.[54] The adjective **great** is added, accentuating the overwhelming nature of this formidable foe, one **sent** by the Almighty (cf. 1:15). The verb **I have sent**, written in the intensive stem, depicts an army dispatched with fervor and great fury to carry out the Commander's orders.[55]

> *And you shall have plenty to eat and be satisfied,*
> *And praise the name of the LORD your God,*
> *Who has dealt wondrously with you;*
> *Then My people will never be put to shame* (2:26).

The effects of the abundant rain (2:23) are further enumerated here. In contrast to the years of a lack of food, years in which the locusts had eaten everything, now they will do the eating; they will **have plenty to eat**. The Hebrew infinite absolute verb depicts eating in continual abundance, to the extent that they will **be satisfied**. Again using the infinite absolute, the writer emphasizes the continual satisfaction of abundant food.

The lack of food had caused the people to weep and mourn, to cry out to the Lord. With food in abundance, their lamentation has turned into praise to the Giver. In response to His bountiful blessings, they praise **the name**, placing special emphasis on the character and reputation of Yahweh. Full enjoyment of the gifts of God requires

---

53. Stuart (260), following the possible reading noted in BHS, suggests the translation 'double' instead of 'years.' In this case, Jerusalem, having paid double for all her sins (Isa. 40:2; Jer. 16:18; 17:18), will receive a double reward/repayment (Isa. 61:7; Zech. 9:12).

54. Cf. discussions on 1:6; 2:11.

55. Contrast with 2:19, where the same root word is used to describe the sending of gifts.

appropriate thanksgiving and praise to the Author.[56] The designation is often substituted for God Himself (e.g. Dan. 98:18-19; Amos 2:7),[57] and signifies ownership and authority (cf. Isa. 63:19; Amos 9:12). For Yahweh had **dealt wondrously**. The adverb underscores the greatness of all His actions (2:21b; cf. Exod. 15:11; Ps. 77:14 [15]; 126:1ff), in judgment and now even more in His complete deliverance and restoration (cf. Isa. 28:23-29).

> *Thus you will know that I am in the midst of Israel,*
> *And that I am the LORD your God*
> *And there is no other;*
> *And My people will never be put to shame* (2:27).

Scripture often links the Exodus out of Egypt with the time of the second advent (cf. Isa. 11:16). Quite noticeably, 2:27 takes up certain elements that reflect those early days of the nation of Israel and the giving of the covenant. The first is noted by Yahweh's announcement **that I am in the midst of Israel**.[58] As a result of His wonderful acts, Israel's physical needs will be met, eating and being satisfied (2:26a), they will engage in genuine worship, directing praise toward their Benefactor (2:26b), and **they will know that Yahweh is in their midst** (2:27a). Through the experience of the drought and subsequent restoration, they would answer the mocking challenge in 2:17: 'Where is their God?' The remarkable and magnificent restoration would provide most effective, visible retort to the heathen detractors. In the midst of trials, Moses records how the people would question whether or not God was with them (Exod. 17:7; Deut. 31:17). Joshua reiterates this, noting that victory over the enemy was Israel's means of knowing if Yahweh was in their midst (Josh. 3:10). Yahweh's presence was a matter of security and protection (Deut. 7:21; Hosea 11:9; Micah 3:11; Zeph. 3:15-17) and was verified through objective evidence.

---

56. Cf. Jas 1:17. The sequence described here (eat, satisfied, praise) is to be carefully guarded, lest the source of the gift be forgotten (cf. Deut. 8:10-11).

57. This designation also carried over into the New Testament (cf. Acts 4:12; 5:41; 3 John 7).

58. Cf. Num. 11:20; 14:4; Deut. 7:21.

Similarly, the world also would come to know the same fact (cf. Num. 14:14; Ps. 22:26-31 [22:27-32]). They would also know **that I am the Lord your God**. The experience of the locust plague and drought, coupled with the awesome act of deliverance, would lead them to the conviction that Yahweh truly was their God, and that **there is no other**. Recurring frequently in the Pentateuch (*e.g.* Exod. 6:7; 16:12; Lev. 18:2), the phrase draws immediate attention to the opening words of the ten commandments in Exodus 20: 'I am the Lord your God.... You shall have no other gods before Me' (20:2-3). 'This is both a comforting assurance and a stern reminder. God does not relinquish his claim to his people to any other god, nor does he allow them to look to any other. God can have no rival in his people's loyalty.'[59]

As if to make the point unequivocally clear, the text repeats the closing refrain of 2:26, **and My people will never be put to shame**.[60] The jealousy of Yahweh for His people (cf. 2:18) can be observed not only in His demand that there be no other, but also in the more intimate designation of them as **my people**. Heretofore, it has been 'His people' (2:18, 19) and 'His land' (2:18). Now, with His blessings poured out and genuine worship restored, it is **My people**—depicting His great love for Israel as His wife.[61]

There will be no more shame due to the lack of harvest (1:11). No longer, nor ever again, will they have to suffer humiliation and reproach among the nations (2:19; cf. Isa. 49:23; 50:7-10;). The prayer (2:17) has been answered. 'Other nations had mocked Judah, believing their gods to be superior to Yahweh; but Israel would learn from her rescue the lesson of a convinced faith in her God, which none could shatter.'[62] Yahweh's dwelling in their midst and

---

59. Watts, 37. Cf. Isa. 45:5, 6, 14; 46:9.

60. Many scholars (Wade, 108; Wolff, 65) have unnecessarily removed the repetition. Believing it to be an accidental duplicate, they have deleted it in either 2:26 or 2:27.

61. Cf. Hosea 1:9-2:1, 14-23 where this special relationship is depicted, accompanied by the restoration of similar material blessings.

62. Allen, 96. Cf. Deut. 4:35.

the absence of being put to shame are dependent upon their obedience and faithfulness to the covenant and to the one true God of that covenant, Yahweh. If they will truly be His covenant people, then they will be able to enjoy His power among them and protection over them. His presence in the midst of them and their embracing Him as the one true God together dictate that they will never be put to shame.

Spiritual Restoration (2:28-32 [3:1-5])
The previous section ends with Yahweh's promise that He will dwell in the midst of His people, a reality attested by the abundance of fruit, grain, new wine, and oil. The outpouring of rain and the concomitant material blessings will give proof of His presence and they will know that He is Yahweh. In addition to the material blessings, Yahweh will shower down upon Israel spiritual blessings on a grand and unprecedented scale.

As noted earlier (2:19-20), blessing and judgment go hand in hand. In bringing blessing to His people, Yahweh must also hand out judgment to those who oppose Him and seek to thwart His will. The spiritual blessings to be poured out will be accompanied by judgment and the destruction of the opposition.

Pouring Out of the Spirit (2:28-29 [3:1-2])

> *And it will come about after this*
> *That I will pour out My Spirit on all mankind;*
> *And your sons and daughters will prophesy,*
> *Your old men will dream dreams,*
> *Your young men will see visions.*
> *And even on the male and female servants*
> *I will pour out My Spirit in those days* (2:28-29 [3:1-2]).

Joel's opening phrase forms a temporal transition from the material blessings to the spiritual and national blessings which follow. **After this** points back to the previous. Yahweh's presence would be manifested by the abundance of rain and the absence of physical needs (2:21-27), followed by another manifestation of His presence: the outpouring of the Spirit. In other words, the spiritual and national restoration would follow, in time, the effusion of material blessings. A second act of blessing would follow the first—the outpouring of rain would be followed by another outpouring.

Although the expression **after this** does not specifically connote any eschatological timeframe,[63] there are two other temporal phrases within the passage which do—namely, **in those days** (2:29 [3:2]) and **before the great and awesome day of the Lord comes** (2:31 [3:4]). The unprecedented supernatural activity described in the passage, and the superlative language of the preceding section ('I will never again make you a reproach among the nations' [2:19] and 'My people will never be put to shame' [2:26, 27]) points to a second advent fulfillment timeframe. In addition, Joel's use of **your sons and daughters** (2:28 [3:1]) reinforces the conclusion that he is speaking of a future generation, not the present one.

Not only is the effusion of material blessing a sign that Yahweh was in the midst of Israel (2:27), but the outpouring of the Holy Spirit also demonstrates His presence.[64] The gift of the Spirit is described in terms of an effusion. He says: **I will pour out My Spirit.** That this is the focal point of 2:28-29 is evident by the fact that they are bracketed with the same phrase. It will be a remarkable, unprecedented event. As the rain poured down on His people, so they would be the recipients of a profusion of the Holy Spirit. In contrast to the scarcity or rain and lack of food, there would be a pouring out of the Spirit in great abundance.[65] Following

---

63. But cf. Hosea 3:5 where 'after this' is coupled 'in the last days.'

64. Both Rom. 8:16 and Eph 1:13-14 describe a similar role of the Holy Spirit, providing proof of His presence. Natural phenomena, such as rain, can demonstrate His presence and blessing, but not with the clarity that the giving of the Spirit will do.

65. Kaiser (*Essays*, 118) relates the terminology here with 'rivers of living water' (John 7:38f) and the baptism of the Holy Spirit (e.g. Matt. 3:11; Acts 1:5; 11:16), explaining that 'there is something additional and unique abut this ministry of the Holy Spirit that first occurred at Pentecost, Samaria and Caesarea. Now a believer was not only regenerated and indwelt to some degree by the Holy Spirit but, beginning at Pentecost and following, all who believed were simultaneously baptized by the Holy Spirit and made part of the one body (1 Cor. 12:13).'

Joel, other prophets affirmed the same concept using the same word (Isa. 32:15; 44:3; Ezek. 39:28-29; Zech. 12:10).[66] It would be a great, supernatural outpouring.

The giving of the Holy Spirit in the Old Testament was not unusual. It is repeatedly noted how individuals were given the Holy Spirit for the purpose of carrying out various responsibilities (*e.g.* Exod. 31:3ff; 35:31ff). But this does not suggest that Old Testament believers were without the work and aid of the Holy Spirit (cf. John 3:8-10; 14:17). Similar to His role today, He was working in many ways, including initiating and preserving faith (Ps. 51:11-12; 143:10; Isa. 63:10). Kaiser summarizes it well:

> In no way must this special profusion of the ministry of the Holy Spirit that operates much in accordance with the blessing found in the new covenant be interpreted in such a way as to suggest that the individual OT saints and believers were unaware of any ministry of the Holy Spirit in their lives apart from temporary endowments of the Spirit for special tasks at special times. On the contrary, the Holy Spirit was the author of new life for all who believed in the coming man of promise (=regeneration), and he also indwelt these same OT redeemed men, at least to some degree, even as David testified in Ps. 51:11.... This judgment is strongly supported by Jesus' pre-cross affirmation in John 14:17: '[The Holy Spirit] lives with you and is [now] in you.'[67]

Joel records that the Spirit will be poured out **on all mankind**. Literally rendered **flesh**, the term **mankind** draws immediate attention to the contrast between 'flesh' and 'spirit,' the former depicting weakness and frailty and the latter strength and vitality (cf. Ps. 56:4 [56:5]; Isa. 31:3; 40:6).

---

66. Elsewhere, Ezekiel continues the theme with a different verb (11:19; 36:26, 27; 37:14).

67. Kaiser, *Essays*, 122. Although Kaiser embraces the less-supported translation, "and is [now] in you," his arguement remains valid. Noting the many passages that say Spirit must yet come, he answers: 'Had the Holy Spirit not come visibly at Pentecost with all its evidential value, then the previous ministry of the Holy Spirit in the lives of individuals would also have been in vain.... He must come visibly as an exhibition that all who had previously depended on the ministry of the Holy Spirit were totally vindicated just as those [OT saints] who had depended on the future death of Christ' (117-118).

It also designates the extent of the profusion. The phrase does at times refer to all mankind, exclusive of race or ethnic distinctions (Gen. 6:12; Deut. 5:26; Isa. 49:26; also cf. Acts 2:39).[68] On other occasions the phrase is even broader, referring to all living creatures (Gen. 6:17; Lev. 17:14; Num. 18:15). Consequently, its extent in each case must be determined by the context. Here the phrase is limited to Jews only, as a number of factors indicate.[69] First, the subsequent reference to your sons and your daughters suggests that reference is being made to their descendants only, not to Gentiles. Second, the context (3:2, 9ff [4:2, 9ff]) depicts the Gentiles as receiving God's wrath, not His blessing. In fact, nowhere in the prophecy are the Gentiles promised any type of blessing. Third, the oracle belongs to His land and His people (2:19). Fourth, Ezekiel 39:29, referring to the same second advent time period, promises: ' "And I will not hide My face from them any longer, for I shall have poured out My Spirit on the house of Israel," declares the Lord GOD.' Fifth, while many have pointed to Peter's promise of the Holy Spirit to 'all who are far off' (Acts 2:39)[70] in support of the broader understanding, it should be remembered that even Peter was surprised when the Spirit was poured out on the Gentiles (Acts 10:45). There can be little doubt that the gift of the Spirit has been given to those of the present age, but that is not the message of Joel's prophecy,[71] nor can one transplant its broader usage in the New Testament into the text here. The wish of Moses is finally realized: 'Would that

---

68. So Kaiser, *Essays*, 119ff. While Acts 2:9ff speaks of different people from various nations, it is doubtful that they were Gentiles—probably only Jews (and proselytes [Acts 2:10]).

69. Most commentators espouse this restricted view.

70. Also Paul in Ephesians 2:13, 17.

71. Kirkpatrick remarks: 'Universal as the promise to *all flesh* seems at first sight to be, the context and the explanation...shew that in its first and original intention it is limited to Israel. The words admit of the larger meaning which was given them on the day of Pentecost, but it does not appear to be as yet explicitly present to the prophet's mind' (74). So Allen: 'Those commentators who scan it for universalistic hints are in danger of misrepresenting its primary meaning' (104).

all the Lord's people were prophets, that the Lord would put His Spirit upon them' (Num. 11:29; also cf. Exod. 19:6f).

The **all flesh** is given further delineation, being defined by **sons and daughters, old men, young men, male and female servants**. The giving of the Spirit would be without distinction of sex, age or social status. Traditional or social boundaries will have no bearing on privilege. The aged, who held positions of power and respect in Israel (cf. Lev. 19:32; Prov. 20:29), will not be ranked above the young.[72] The term **young men** specifically means 'chosen one' and is often used to signify young men who are old enough to go to war (cf. Jer. 11:22; 18:21). Nor will sons and daughters enjoy privileges not given to the male and female servants of the house;[73] all will share the blessing.[74]

The **and even**, with which the verse begins, focuses special attention on this group and designates something extraordinary and unexpected. Though their rights and privileges were few, God had made special provisions for them, that they would not be totally excluded from the religious life and worship of Yahweh. They were counted as part of the religious community and took part in Israel's festivals (Deut. 5:14; 16:9-11). Yet there is no recorded case in the Old Testament where the gift of prophecy was granted to a slave.[75] In the future, however, that will change. They too will be given the outpouring of the Spirit, just as the others. 'The prophetic privilege of standing, as it were, among Yahweh's council and hearing his word at first hand (Jer. 23:18) would be the personal experience of every member of the religious community.'[76]

As a result of this outpouring, the recipients will **prophesy, dream dreams**, and **see visions**. There is no word about

---

72. Even God Himself is sometimes depicted as old (Dan. 7:9, 13, 32). See 1:2 for discussions on the meaning of this term.

73. Kaiser claims that the mention of slaves 'forces the interpreter to acknowledge that Joel had 'all mankind' in mind here. Even the Gentiles slaves in the Jewish households would benefit in this outpouring' (*Essays*, 119). However, there is no indication that the slaves are of Gentile extraction.

74. Cf. Jer. 31:34: 'from the least of them to the greatest of them.'

75. It is doubtful that the messengers of Saul (1 Sam. 19:20-23) can be so classified.

76. Allen, 99.

the contents of their prophecies, the nature of the dreams or visions seen, only that they would occur. In fact, the emphasis appears to be on the evidence or proof that such a manifestation would provide for Israel herself, not on what it would do for others. It is doubtful that this outpouring would totally exclude an influential role toward the nations, since the benefit of divinely given prophecies, dreams and visions were generally not restricted to the recipients only. Prophets were to speak God's revealed message, not harbor it. But the context suggests that the primary purpose is to visibly demonstrate that Yahweh was dwelling in their midst and to depict Israel's new relationship toward Him. Wolff concludes that 'it is the relationship to God, then, which has become completely new in the new creation through the pouring out of the spirit.... Thus [Joel] expects the new relationship to God in a form similar to Jer. 31:33-34: everyone will stand in a relationship of immediacy to God.'[77]

Dream dreams can represent either ordinary dreams or revelatory dreams, as there is no other Old Testament word for a dream. Preceded with **prophesy** and followed by **see visions**,[78] it appears that revelatory dreams are in view. Both dreams and visions were often, though not exclusively, employed as modes of divine communication in the Old Testament (cf. Num. 12:6-8).

Displaying of Wonders (2:30-32 [3:3-5])

Proof of Yahweh's presence in their midst would extend beyond the material blessings of abundant rain and harvests, beyond the outpouring of the Holy Spirit upon all ages and

---

77. Wolff, 66-67. Kaiser (*Essays*, 120) agrees: 'Everyone would immediately and personally know the Lord.... Heretofore it took the mediation of a prophet to have God revealed to the people (Num. 12:6) or a priest to have the people represented to God (8:15-19). But now everyone, regardless of age, sex or social status, would be able to prophesy, dream dreams and see visions.'

This also appears to be the emphasis of Ezek. 39:29, where the same verb is employed. Although Ezek. 36:26-27 and Isa. 32:15, 44:3 highlight the gift of the Spirit for the purpose of new obedience, they use different verbs and connote a different emphasis.

78. For the close relationship between one who prophesies and one who sees visions, cf. 2 Kings 17:13; 1 Chron. 29:29; Amos 7:12.

social distinctions. It would also include the supernatural display of terrestrial and celestial wonders.

> *And I will display wonders in the sky and on the earth,*
> *Blood, fire, and columns of smoke.*
> *The sun will be turned to darkness,*
> *And the moon to blood,*
> *Before the great and awesome day of the LORD comes*
>   (2:30-31 [3:3-4]).

The timely rains, bountiful harvests, and the abundant out-pouring of the Spirit all speak of blessings. Now the tone changes abruptly, with descriptions of Yahweh's super-natural power and cataclysmic judgment. His presence will mean deliverance for the righteous and judgment for the wicked. The text does not specify which of the events described in 2:28-32 [3:1-5] comes first or if they occur con-temporaneously. While the conjunction and verb with which verse 3 opens may indicate a temporal priority, this is not required. Without any specific time distinctions between verse 29 and verse 30, it is most likely that the verb intro-ducing verse 30 denotes a simple continuation from verse 29, leading one to conclude that the events of 2:30ff occur simultaneously or in close temporal proximity.

The demonstration of Yahweh's awesome power is des-cribed as a display[79] of **wonders** in the heavens and in the earth. Often used in tandem with 'sign,' the term denotes phenomena that are extraordinary and out of the character of normal activity. It frequently depicts the deliverance/judgment plagues of Egypt (Exod. 7:3; Deut. 6:22; 1 Chron. 16:12; Neh. 9:10; Jer. 32:20), reinforcing Scripture's frequent com-parison between the Exodus from Egypt and the Second Advent of Messiah. In the midst of that great act of judgment, the deliverance and blessing of Yahweh was demonstrably evident. So it will be in that great and terrible Day of Yahweh.

The eschatological display of wonders will be both celes-tial and terrestrial, both **in the sky and on the earth**.[80] There

---

79. The Hebrew verb 'display' is literally 'give, put, set' (cf. Gen. 1:17).

80. Cf. Mark 13:24-25.

is a chiastic order here. The signs in the sky are mentioned first and enumerated last (3:31 [4:4]), while those of the earth are mentioned last but expounded first (3:30b [4:3b]). **Fire and smoke**[81] are frequent in descriptions of theophanies and Yahweh's involvement in human activities (*e.g.* Exod. 3:2; 19:18; 24:7; Deut. 5:4; Ps. 18:8 [18:9]; 144:5; Isa. 4:4-5; Rev. 15:8). **Blood, fire** and **smoke** were present during the events surrounding the Exodus (Exod. 7:17-27; 9:23-29; 13:21-22; 19:16-18). Here, the immanent Yahweh displays His power over the enemy in a superlative, awe-inspiring fashion,[82] utilizing these same terms to depict war and destruction (cf. Ps. 78:63; Judg. 20:38; Isa. 10:16; 26:11; Zech. 11:1). But this will be more than just another war. The nature of this event is unprecedented, suggested by the 'wonders' designation (cf. Zeph. 1:14-18; Zech. 12:2ff; 14:2-3, 12-15).

The display of supernatural power on earth will be conjoined with the unveiling of wonders in the heavens. **The sun will be turned to darkness, and the moon into blood**. Descriptions of celestial catastrophes are a recurring theme in Joel and are often rehearsed by later prophets (cf. 2:10; 3:15 [4:15]; Isa. 13:10; Ezek. 32:7-8; Amos 8:9). Just how the moon will turn to blood is not made known, but something more than an eclipse is intimated.[83] Frequently, the

---

81. 'Columns of smoke' found elsewhere only in Song of Solomon 3:6 and is unrelated contextually.

82. Limiting the reference to 'abnormal atmospheric phenomena' (Driver, 65) is unnecessary, in light of the terminology's specific usage elsewhere as well as the emphasis of the extended context (cf. 3:1ff [4:1ff]).

83. Suggestions have been many, from solar and lunar eclipses to atmospheric upheavals to 'reddish obscuring of the moon through sandstorms and the like, whose color ominously suggested bloodshed' (Allen, 101). Volcanic ash is also known to obscure the sun and create a reddish glow of moonlight. Smoke and ash from the fire noted in 2:30 [3:3] could be a factor as well.

   The one verb **turned** governs both the solar and lunar action and means 'to turn, overturn.' In the Niphal stem, the verb could possibly have a reflexive idea, i.e. 'will turn itself.' However, it is difficult to imagine how these actions could be self-induced. Consequently, it is best to translate it with the passive idea—'will be turned.'

   Though not specified here, the actions depicted are almost certainly to be taken figuratively, as Rev. 6:12 makes clear.

characteristics described here are coupled elsewhere with the presence of earthquakes (Jer. 4:23-24; Rev. 6:12; also cf. Isa. 13:9-13). The Day of Yahweh is described with the same adjectives used by the prophet earlier (cf. 2:11) to portray the dread and astonishment which will accompany that day.

The text adds that these events will occur **before the great and awesome day of the Lord comes**.[84] Many have emphasized the preposition **before**, thereby seeking to underscore a specific time sequence within the passage. The preposition, they conclude, dictates that the pouring out of the Spirit and the cosmic cataclysms occur *prior to* the Day of Yahweh.[85] However, caution should be taken to not read too much into the preposition. Literally translated 'to/ at the face of, in the presence of,' the term is most commonly used to designate 'before' in the sense of presence or priority status rather than connoting the idea of time priority.[86] Consequently, parallel passages must be consulted when determining the sequence of eschatological tribulation events; the preposition is incapable of bearing the time/sequence burden with which some have laden it.

> *And it will come about that whoever calls on the name of*
> *the Lord will be delivered;*
> *For on Mount Zion and in Jerusalem*
> *There will be those who escape,*
> *As the Lord has said,*
> *Even among the survivors whom the Lord calls*
>   (2:32 [3:5]).

The prophet changes once again from first person to third person. In 2:11, noting that the Day of Yahweh is great and awesome, Joel follows with the rhetorical query: 'And who can endure it?' Here, following the same description of that day, he posits the answer. Endurance and deliverance will come to **whoever calls on the name of the Lord**. In 2:28 [3:1], the breadth of the Spirit's effusion is emphasized; the

---

84. Cf. Mal. 4:5 [3:23].

85. Cf. Richard D. Israel, 'Joel 2:28-32 (3:1-5MT): Prism for Pentecost,' *Charismatic Experiences in History*, ed. by Cecil M. Robeck, Jr. (Peabody, MA: Hendrickson, 1985), 7.

86. BDB, 816-817. Stuart (257) suggests a translation of 'in the presence of.'

Spirit will be poured out irrespective of age, sex or position in society. In 2:32 [3:5], a narrower, more exclusive, perspective is presented. The emphasis turns from the anthropological and sociological (2:28) to the theological (2:32). All those who call on the name of Yahweh will be delivered. Out of the broad anthropological and sociological categories noted in 2:28, there will be those who escape,[87] namely, those who call on the name of Yahweh, **even among the survivors whom the LORD calls**. The first and last phrases provide a subtle play on words and illustrate the human responsibility/divine sovereignty aspects of God's election.[88] The last phrase, introduced by the explanatory conjunction, provides further definition to the first. It is the chosen elect who call on the name of Yahweh that will be delivered.[89]

To call **on the name of Yahweh** does not denote some magical formula for invoking divine assistance. Rather, it speaks of entering into intensive personal contact or interaction with Yahweh for the purpose of worshiping Him (Gen. 12:8; 13:4; 1 Kings 18:24; Ps. 116:17) and confessing Him among hostile nations (Ps. 105:1; Isa. 12:4; 41:25; 44:5).[90] **Will be delivered**, meaning 'to slip away, to escape,' is synonymous with the nouns **escape** and **survivors**, the latter noun often used to describe deliverance from death or great danger and destruction (Deut. 2:34; Josh. 10:20, 28ff).

Escape or deliverance is not found in the power of horses (Ps. 33:17), allies (Isa. 21) or one's physical heritage with Abraham; it is found in Yahweh. 'The name of the Lord is a strong tower; the righteous runs into it and is safe' (Prov. 18:10).

---

87. The 'all' of verse 28 [3:1] need not be restricted by the 'whoever calls' of 2:32 [3:5]. As indicated by Zech. 13:8-9 and 14:2, considerable numbers in Israel will not escape, many of whom may have had the Spirit poured out on them.

88. Cf. Acts 16:14; 13:48; Phil 1:29; John 6:44; Exod. 33:19; Zeph. 3:9.

89. As noted earlier, the context would limit this passage specifically to Israel. In Rom. 10:13, however, Paul utilizes the phrase in a broadened sense to include all peoples who call on the Lord, regardless of nationality (so also Acts 2:21). His use of it there is heavily dependent on the theological framework erected in Romans 4.

90. Wolff, 56, 68.

He is residing in their midst, **on Mount Zion and in Jerusalem** (cf. 3:17 [4:17]), and therefore it is a safe haven. The survivors whom the Lord calls are the escaped ones in Jerusalem and Mt Zion, making it doubtful that there is a reference to those of the Diaspora.[91] Rather, it appears more likely that the reference is to those regathered to the land of Israel at the time of the second advent of Messiah. 'Its focus is eschatological, yet as a prediction of what will someday happen to Israel, viewed as a continuum, it would have constituted a great encouragement to the believers among Joel's audience.[92]

As the LORD has said points to a prophetic word already known. The phrase is repeated in Obadiah 17; however, if an early date of writing for Joel is correct, then Obadiah's reference would be a quotation from Joel, making it unknown as to where Joel is referring.

Relationship to Acts 2

The apostle Peter, on the day of Pentecost, quotes from Joel 2:28-32 [3:1-5], introducing it with the phrase: 'this is what was spoken of through the prophet Joel' (Acts 2:16). This has troubled commentators, since the events describing the day of Pentecost did not fully encompass the details set forth by Joel. In fact, very little of Joel 2 happened in Acts 2. The cosmic signs of Joel 2:30-31 [3:3-4] are significantly absent in Luke's account of Pentecost. The sun was not darkened; the moon did not turn to blood. There is no blood, fire, or columns of smoke. Joel mentions nothing of speaking in supernaturally generated foreign languages nor does Acts give evidence of supernatural dreams.[93] Only

---

91. Wolff, 68. S. R. Driver (67) suggests the escapees will be from among the dispersion. Henderson (116) concludes that Joel is speaking of those who fled from the Romans (AD 70) to Pella, while Laetsch (130) argues that these refer to the Church of God, the heavenly Jerusalem. Stuart (261) contends that the reference is to those who survive either the Assyrian or Babylonian exile.

92. Stuart, 261.

93. Charles Ryrie remarks that 'the events prophesied by Joel simply did not come to pass' ('The Significance of Pentecost,' *Bibliotheca Sacra* [1955] 112:334).

two points of contact are found: God's Spirit was poured out, and those who called upon the name of the Lord were saved. But it is these two elements of Joel's prophecy—the Spirit poured out and salvation for those who call on the Lord—that provide the connecting link to Pentecost. They lead logically to the central focus of Peter's sermon.[94]

Consequently, it appears best to view Joel's prophecy as fulfilled in a preliminary fashion at the time of Pentecost, with a complete fulfillment reserved for the time surrounding the second advent. A couple of factors suggest this conclusion. First, the outpouring of the Spirit and the salvation of all who call upon the name of the Lord, both of which are central to the Pentecost event, are a preview of the outpouring promised at Christ's second advent. 'These events and the subsequent baptisms of the Holy Spirit that take place whenever anyone receives Christ as Lord and Savior and is thereby ushered into the family of God are all mere harbingers and samples of that final downpour that will come in that complex of events with Christ's second return.'[95]

Second, Peter specifically notes that the events of Acts 2 inaugurate 'the last days' (Acts 2:17a), a time period which begins with the first advent of Christ (Heb. 1:2) and extends out to incorporate the second advent.

> The NT writers made it clear that both Israel's future age and the church age are designated by the same terms: 'The Last Days'(1 Tim. 4:1; 2 Tim. 3:1-8; Heb. 1:1-2; James 5:3; 1 Peter 1:5, 20; 4:7; 2 Peter 3:1-9; 1 John 2:18; Jude 18). Accordingly, the point of Peter's remark in Acts 2:16 must be that Pentecost, as the initial day of that period known as 'The Last Days,' which will culminate in those events surrounding the return of Jesus the Messiah, partakes of the character of those final events and so is a herald and earnest of what must surely come. Pentecost, then, forms a corroborative pledge in the series of fulfillments that will culminate in the ultimate fulfillment of Joel's prophecy in the eschatological complex.[96]

94. Richard N. Longenecker, *The Acts of the Apostles, The Expositor's Bible Commentary* (Grand Rapids: Zondervan, 1981), 276.

95. Kaiser, *Essays*, 122.

96. Patterson, 258.

Thus, while Peter does say 'this is what,' indicating at least some aspect of fulfillment,[97] the phrase does not necessarily exhaust the fulfillment. That which was prayed for by Moses (Num. 11:29) and inaugurated at Pentecost is to be fully realized in the Day of Yahweh. Finley adds insightfully that Peter 'took the event Joel foresaw and linked it with the beginning of the new age of the Spirit. In other words, Joel saw the end point of the whole process, while Peter fixed his eyes on the onset.'[98]

Finally, Peter's inclusion of Joel 2:30-31 in his Pentecost sermon need not suggest that he was necessarily ignorant of God's plan for the church. It could very well have been a deliberate attempt by Peter

> to bring before his hearers a proper respect for the God who could right then and there deliver them from threatened judgments to come. For that was exactly the connection made by Joel. Thus while there has not yet been any fulfillment of verses 30-31 in that they await our Lord's second advent, nevertheless Peter used this truth in the same way that Joel used it in his day: It was an incentive to call on the name of the Lord.[99]

National Restoration (3:1-21 [4:1-21])

Judgment on the Unrighteous (3:1-16a [4:1-16a])

> *For behold, in those days and at that time,*
> *When I restore the fortunes of Judah and Jerusalem* (3:1).

The text closely relates to the context preceding it. But the focus changes. The fortunes of Israel are still in view, but now it is the foreign nations who are brought to the fore. The reiteration of the time indicators, **in those days** and **at that time**, emphasizes the closeness with the events described from 2:18 onward.[100]

---

97. Kirkpatrick, 75. Though Peter's introduction is not a commonly used formula to indicate a fulfillment of an Old Testament prophecy, it can be so used. Kaiser (*Essays*, 113) notes: 'There is no single formula used consistently in Acts or elsewhere in the NT for that matter.'

98. Thomas J. Finley, *Joel, Wycliffe Bible Commentary* (Chicago: Moody, 1990), 80.

99. Kaiser, *Essays*, 121. Cf. E. W. Hengstenberg, *Christology of the Old Testament* (Grand Rapids: Kregel, 1970 rpt), 533.

100. These phrases also occur in combination in Jer. 33:15; 50:4, 20. Stuart adds that 'in all their Old Testament contexts, the phrases are associated with future blessings promised as consolation for God's people' (266).

Yahweh is zealous for His people and His land. **In those days** is repeated from 2:29 [3:2], indicating that the judgment of the nations is an integral part of the outpouring of the Spirit on Israel and the restoration of her national fortunes.

While the temporal phrases are the key chronological links with the preceding context, the preposition **for**, with which the text begins, is the key topical link. In 2:32 [3:5], the deliverance of those who call on the name of Yahweh is further explained in the latter half of the verse, being introduced by the preposition **for**. Here the same preposition is employed to shift from an emphasis on spiritual restoration to that of national restoration. The focus in 2:32 [3:5] surrounds those in Israel who escape the deadly attack of the enemy. Here the spotlight is focused on Yahweh's attack on the enemy and His protection of His people. The deliverance and blessing of His people goes hand in hand with the judgment of the nations.

The tone of Yahweh's resolve is strengthened by the fact that He Himself is once again the speaker. His course of action is revealed firsthand. The importance of the announcement and the remarkable, extraordinary character of His actions are underscored by the interjection **behold**, demanding immediate attention and emphasizing the startling nature of the proclamation. What follows is not to be taken lightly!

When I restore the fortunes of Judah and Jerusalem is a continuation of the events described in 2:32 [3:5], but from a new perspective. In the previous passage, the emphasis is on the escape of a select group of Israel; here a decidedly more positive picture emerges. The restoration of the nation is in view. As noted by its usage in Job 42:10, the term **fortunes** need not be restricted in meaning to 'captivity.'[101] While the context (2:32 [3:5]) suggests some type of subjugation or captivity of Israel during this time, the restoration of national fortunes extends beyond the removal of the yoke of bondage (cf. 3:17ff).

---

101. Harris (*TWOT*, II, 896) notes that the term is not a derivative of *shaba*, 'to take captive,' but that it is a cognate accusative of *shub* 'restore.'

I will gather all the nations,
And bring them down to the valley of Jehoshaphat.
Then I will enter into judgment with them there
On behalf of My people and My inheritance, Israel,
Whom they have scattered among the nations;
And they have divided up My land (3:2 [4:2]).

Restoring the fortunes of Judah and Jerusalem will entail the worldwide summons of the nations. They will be brought[102] before Yahweh's to answer for their offenses against His people. Like a subpoena, the presence of all nations[103] will be demanded by the Commander of Hosts.

The place to which they will be summoned is the **valley of Jehoshaphat**. The name means 'Yahweh judges' and forms a play on words with the following phrase. The location of this valley is unknown.[104] The term for **valley** designates a broad depression, not a steep, gorge-like valley.[105] Other prophets speak of this battle as occurring near Jerusalem (Ezek. 38-39; Dan. 11:45; Zech 9:14ff; 12:1ff; 14:1ff). History records a battle fought by King Jehoshaphat against the Moabites and Ammonites, but this engagement occurred in the Valley of Beracah (2 Chron. 20:20ff), near En-gedi. According to Eusebius, the Kidron Valley was so called later, but this nomenclature was probably due to the Joel reference. Also, the broad, open valley noted here would not fit the narrow Kidron Valley.

Future events described by Jeremiah as occurring in the Valley of Slaughter suggest that the valley of Hinnom may be the location (Jer. 7:32-33; 19:1-7). Joel's mention of this place with yet another name—**valley of decision** (3:14)—suggests that the designation given is probably intended to be a new,

---

102. The intensive stem (Piel) is used, rendering the verb 'to gather.'

103. Cf. Ezek. 38-39; Zeph. 3:8; Zech. 12:3, 9; 14:2, 14.

104. Cf. Feinberg, 'The Nations in the Valley of Decision,' *Prophecy and the Seventies* (Chicago: Moody, 1971), 218.

105. In contrast, the other Hebrew term for **valley** designates a deep, narrow ravine. Such would not be suitable for a battle of such magnitude.

descriptive title given to the place of final judgment, a literal valley where Yahweh judges the nations.[106]

I will enter into judgment with them there introduces the legal aspect of this event. When coupled with the preposition **with**, the verb **I will enter into judgment** denotes a case of governmental litigation against a defendant (cf. Jer. 2:35; Ezek. 17:20; 20:35f; 38:22). God as Judge has issued subpoenas to the nations of the world; He has brought them to His courtroom in the Valley of Judgment to judge them.

The indictment is rendered **on behalf of My people and My inheritance**. The phrase harkens back to 2:17, where the priests pray that Yahweh would spare His people and His inheritance, and to 2:18, where Yahweh responds with zeal for His people and His land. The preposition **on behalf of** could be translated **over the matter of** or **because of**. The judicial action taken by Yahweh is certainly on behalf of Israel, i.e. He is prosecuting the case for them. But it is also because of them—because of the manner in which they have been treated—that He is zealously pursuing this course of action. Yahweh is here fulfilling one of the tenets of the Abrahamic Covenant, which emphatically assures blessing to those who bless Abraham and his posterity but which also emphatically promises annihilation to those who speak lightly of her (Gen. 12:3).[107] To touch His people is to touch the apple of His eye (Zech. 2:8 [2:12]; cf. Ps. 105:15).

The summons to the courtroom in the Valley of Jehoshaphat is followed by an indictment. The charges against the defendant are entered into the record. The first charge: **they have scattered My people among the nations**. There were numerous times when Israel was exiled or deported. The northern tribes were carried away by Assyria (2 Kings 17:6)

---

106. References to ancient mythological concepts of a deity slaughtering his enemies in a valley notwithstanding, there is no need to restrict the title to a symbolic designation only. Most ancient battles were fought in valleys and there is no reason to think that this one will not be fought in one as well. Joel's play on words can still have their intended effect without denying that a literal valley will be the location in that future battle.

107. Also cf. Matt. 25:31-46 where judgment of the nations is rendered on the basis of their treatment of 'one of these brothers of Mine.'

in 722 BC, while the southern tribes were later transplanted
by Babylon (Jer. 50:17; Ezek. 34:6). She was dispersed among
the nations by the Romans in the first century AD and has
been scattered and persecuted repeatedly down through
the centuries (cf. Ezek. 11:17; 20:34, 41; 22:15; 36:19). The text
gives no indication as to which period is in view, making the
exact historical event uncertain. The reference is probably to
history in general. The fact that all nations are summoned
before Yahweh to be judged for this crime suggests that all
enemies of His people throughout history could be in view.

They have divided up My land is the second charge
leveled against them. Though Israel had been deported and
exiled as a result of disobedience to Yahweh (Amos 7:17;
2 Chron. 36:20-21), He has not relinquished His claim to His
land. He is still zealous for it (2:18). The issue of ownership
is very strongly rooted in this verse: **My people, My inheritance**, and **My land** (cf. 2:27; 1:6).

The third charge is that they have sold His people into slavery.

> *They have also cast lots for My people,*
> *Traded a boy for a harlot,*
> *And sold a girl for wine that they may drink* (3:3 [4:3]).

Following the ancient custom of dividing the spoils of war,
the nations had cast lots for the prisoners themselves (cf.
Nahum 3:10; Obad. 11). The Mosaic Covenant stipulates that
prisoners of war were not to be sold into slavery (Deut. 21:14)
and to kidnap someone to sell into slavery was a capital
offense, punishable by death (Exod. 21:16).[108] Further insult
was added by the minuscule price with which they were
valued. A boy was given in payment for a night with a prosti-
tute; a girl was sold for a drink of wine. In violation of God's
law, they had no intention of keeping the slaves. Rather, they
made a mockery of them and their God (cf. 2:17) by trading
them for momentary and sensual gratification.[109]

---

108. Cf. the sale of Joseph by his brothers in Gen. 37:36. Treated as a com-
     modity in ancient times, captives were often sold to foreigners.
109. Cf. Amos 2:6 where this charge is brought against Israel herself.
     Elsewhere, the prophet Hosea (4:11) couples these two vices as indica-
     tive of excessive dissipation and debauchery.

Moreover, what are you to Me, O Tyre, Sidon, and all the regions of Philistia? Are you rendering Me a recompense? But if you do recompense Me, swiftly and speedily I will return your recompense on your head (3:4 [4:4]).

Drawing upon and expanding the motif developed in 3:1-3 [4:1-3], this section (3:4-8 [4:4-8]) singles out the nations of Phoenicia and Philistia for special attention before returning to the theme of judgment on the nations in 3:9 [4:9].[110] Tyre and Sidon were the two major cities of Phoenicia. Situated on the Mediterranean seacoast, Sidon was located approximately 25 miles north of Tyre. Phoenicia was an early ally of Israel, assisting her in the building of Solomon's temple (1 Kings 7:13f) and ratifying treaties with her through marriage (1 Kings 11:1; 16:31). But in later years, Phoenicia joined with Philistia to harass Israel (2 Chron. 21:10, 16-17; Amos 1:6, 9; Obad. 10-16). The **regions of Philistia** consisted of five separate 'city-states' or provinces—Gaza, Gath, Ashdod, Ashkelon, and Ekron[111] — each governed by its own prince or overlord.

The use of **moreover** in the text signifies that something of remarkable note is being introduced, that special attention is to be given, both to the identification of the defendants and to the elucidation of the charges announced in the previous verse.[112] Both the Phoenicians and the Philistines are to be included with the 'nations.' Not only are they equally culpable, but they also provide an excellent historical example.[113] With Yahweh Himself taking the role of the plaintiff, the opening arguments of the lawsuit are presented in the form of a series of lively, rhetorical questions.

---

110. Because verses 4-8 seem to interrupt the flow, both in terms of style (from poetry to prose) and in terms content (from the general 'all nations' to the specific reference to two specific nations), some have concluded that the section is a later addition (*e.g.* Bewer, 130; Wolff, 78). However, this is unwarranted. The subject of slavery in 3:2-3 [4:2-3] is embellished quite naturally in vv. 4ff and the movement between poetry and prose is not uncommon (*e.g.* Isa. 6; 9; Hosea 1; Amos 7).

111. Cf. Joshua 13:2-3.

112. And so throughout the prophecy (cf. 2:3d; 2:12a; 2:29a [3:2a]).

113. This is typical of Joel, who employs the historical as a harbinger of the future.

The opening question, **what are you to Me**, is literally, 'what you to me.' With the pronoun 'you' in the emphatic position together with the absence of a verb, the phrase becomes a terse, emotion-packed query that accentuates the disproportion between the plaintiff and the defendants, thereby introducing the absurdity of their attempt to recompense Yahweh. The meaning of **what are you to Me** is explained by the subsequent phrase **Are you rendering Me a recompense?** The verb **recompense** signifies something done for or to another, either good or evil.[114] Its participial form here denotes an ongoing characteristic; an act of premeditated aggression that was being carried out repeatedly.

In essence, the rhetorical question asks: 'Is there any injustice which I have done to you through Israel that you should avenge with evil? The obvious answer is no! Their attempts to impoverish Yahweh by raiding His people lack justifiable provocation. On the contrary, it is they who deserve retribution, and therefore He promises, **swiftly and speedily**[115] **I will return your recompense on your head**. The law of retaliation (*lex talionis*) is here carried out with expedition on the very perpetrators themselves. In an accelerated fashion, these actions will ricochet back **on your head**.[116]

> *Since you have taken My silver and My gold, brought My precious treasures to your temples, and sold the sons of Judah and Jerusalem to the Greeks in order to remove them far from their territory* (3:5-6 [4:5-6]).

The rhetoric of the previous verse is here explained. The charges are two-fold. They are guilty of theft (v. 5) and slave trade (v. 6). Although the **silver and gold and precious treasures**[117] is designated as belonging to Yahweh, it is possible that the reference here is to the personal property of royalty

---

114. *E.g.* 1 Sam. 24:17, 18; Gen. 50:15, 17.

115. Cf. Isa. 5:26 where the same two words are used in reverse order.

116. Cf. Ps. 7:16 [7:17].

117. **Precious treasures** speaks of anything that is pleasant, beautiful or desirable, whether of persons, such as Ezekiel's wife (Ezek. 24:16) or of things, such as the temple (Isa. 64:11; Ezek. 24:21, 25).

and the wealthy (cf. Hosea 13:15) and not to the treasury of the temple. The charge is one of thievery, not desecration. Just as the people, the inheritance (2:26-27; 3:2-3 [4:2-3]) and the land (2:18) belong to Yahweh, so the silver and the gold of the people themselves are also His (1 Chron. 29:14; Hosea 2:8; Hag. 2:8). In addition, the absence of any record of Phoenicia or Philistia having plundered the Jerusalem temple,[118] except for Philistia's participation in a raid on the palace of King Jehoram (2 Chron. 21:17), establishes this possibility. Furthermore, **into your temples**, where these items were taken, need not refer exclusively to the temples of religious worship but can refer to a palace or the palatial home of the wealthy (cf. Amos 8:3).

At the same time, it should be remembered that it was not uncommon for warriors to donate to the gods certain items taken as spoils of war, in which case the reference here would not be to personal homes, but to cultic temples (cf. 2 Sam. 8:11; Dan. 1:2). Such actions would imply the supremacy of their gods over Yahweh, thereby making Him appear weak. Though the former view need not exclude the latter, the recompense motif so prominent within the context suggests that this understanding is primarily in view.[119]

The second charge is that they have **sold the sons of Judah and Jerusalem**. Here the prophet resumes the theme of slave trading introduced in verse 3. The reference to **sons** includes children of both sexes, as verse 8 specifies. Phoenicia's worldwide commerce included slave trading (Ezek. 27:13; cf. Amos 1:9; 1 Macc. 3:4, 41; 2 Macc. 7:11) and, according to Herodotus, even kidnapping.[120] The Phoenicians then sold them to the **Greeks** (literally: 'to the sons of the Ionians').

---

118. Bewer (131) notes that Joel's choice of the phrase 'you have taken' instead of a stronger, more militaristic one may have been intentional. 'It supports the view that the Phoenicians and Philistines were not the conquerors but the merchants who had come to profit by exchanging wares, selling wine, furnishing harlots, etc., for the spoil and the captives.'

119. This would also focus on the third of three things that are of great importance to Joel: the people and the land (v. 3) and the temple (v. 5).

120. *Persian Wars*, 1:1; 2:54.

The Greeks were descendants of Javan or the Ionians (cf. Gen. 10:2, 4; 1 Chron. 1:5, 7; Isa. 66:19; Dan. 8:21), a name which was used by the Hebrews and other eastern nations for the inhabitants of the Ionian colonies along the western coast of Asia Minor and the islands of the Aegean Sea. Greece apparently became a central clearinghouse for the slave trade: 'So famous did the island of Delos become as a slave mart, that sometimes 10,000 were bought and sold in a single day.'[121]

The magnitude of the crime is reflected in their motive: **in order to remove them far from their territory**. Not only did they sell the slaves, they also did so with the express purpose of sending them to a far country, making it impossible to return to their native country. Their motive, introduced by the purpose clause **in order to**, was obviously more than monetary gain—they were attempting to reduce their power, influence and numbers. Though Yahweh often used foreign powers to execute divine judgment on His people and His land, they were often motivated by their own insatiable greed, going beyond the divine dictates and endorsements (cf. Zech. 1:15; Amos 1:11). Consequently, it would now be their turn to receive divine retribution.

> *Behold, I am going to arouse them from the place where you*
> *have sold them, and return your recompense on your head.*
> *Also I will sell your sons and your daughters into the*
> *hand of the sons of Judah, and they will sell them to the*
> *Sabeans, to a distant nation, for the LORD has spoken*
>   (3:7-8 [4:7-8]).

The law of retribution (*lex talionis*)[122] is here introduced with the interjection **behold!** This remarkable turn of events demands the attention of the defendants. The reversal of fortunes will be startling, both in its manner of execution as well as in its extent. As for its manner of execution, the thought inaugurated in verse 4 is revisited and explained. Yahweh will **arouse** His people, the very ones He has

---

121. Henderson, 119.
122. Cf. Exod. 21:23-25; Lev. 24:19-20.

punished, 'activating' or 'setting in motion' (cf. 3:9 [4:9]) those who have been victimized. The victims themselves will be called upon to be the avengers of Yahweh's wrath. The recipients of oppression and suffering will now become His instruments of inflicting punishment upon the heads of the perpetrators (cf. Zech. 12:8; Isa. 11:12-14).

Instead of the Phoenicians, the Judeans will now take on the role of middlemen, buying the Grecian sons and daughters and then selling them. **I will sell your sons and your daughters into the hand of the sons of Judah** may denote an actual sale or, more likely, may depict the figurative idea 'I will deliver your...' The verb **sell** is often employed elsewhere with the idea of giving a person or people into the power of another, apart from any actual monetary exchange (*e.g.* Deut. 32:30; Judg. 2:14; 3:8; 1 Sam. 12:9). The fact that Yahweh Himself is said to be the one selling them to the Judeans implies a non-literal understanding here.

The second occurrence of the verb **sell** is most likely literal. Once delivered into the hands of their former slaves, **they will sell them to the Sabeans, to a distant nation.** The Sabeans came from southern Arabia, an area populated by the descendants of Abraham's marriage with Keturah (Gen. 25:3; cf. Gen. 10:28). Occupying a land of great wealth, including spices, gold and precious stones (1 Kings 10:2, 10; Ezek. 27:22), the Sabeans were well known for their proficiency in commerce and worldwide trading (Job 6:19; Ezek. 27:22).[123] The addition of the phrase **to a distant land** underscores the distance between the countries bordering the Mediterranean and the land of the Sabeans. As Phoenicia and Philistia sold Jewish slaves toward the west (Greece and beyond), so the sons of Judah will return the favor, selling the sons and daughters of Greece to a land far to the east, in the opposite direction.[124] As if to underline the certainty of the proclamation, the prose section concludes with an assertive **for the LORD has spoken!** Confined to the earlier

---

123. No trade connections are known to have existed between Judah and the Sabeans after the fifth century BC, intimating an earlier date of writing.

124. Jer. 6:20 describes Sheba as 'a distant land.'

prophets,[125] the phrase attests to the divine authority of the oracle and His commitment to carry it out.

The time of fulfillment of these five verses has been debated, with numerous attempts to find historical concurrence. The more prominent suggestions include the time when King Jehoram's palace was raided by the Philistines and Arabs (2 Chron. 21:16-17),[126] the invasion of Alexander the Great (333 BC),[127] and the time of the Maccabees, when the Jewish state flourished and the Phoenician and Philistine influence was reduced.[128]

While each of these possibilities possesses merits, neither the biblical text nor historical and archaeological data permits certainty. However, owing to the context and Joel's method of unfolding his message, the eschatological must remain a strong possibility. Repeatedly, the book uses the current situation as a platform from which to launch into a description of that eschatological Day of Yahweh.

> '[The] powers of Joel's day stood as representative of that great socio-religio-political system that would oppose God's people in a future day (cf. Dan. 2:44-45; 7:9-14; 8:23-27; 11:36-45; 2 Thess. 2:3-4; Rev. 13; 14:8-11; 17-18).... Joel's prophecy, though intended for the eschatological situation, is also made historically applicable by being based on the current situation of his day.'[129]

> *Proclaim this among the nations:*
> *Prepare a war; rouse the mighty men!*
> *Let all the soldiers draw near, let them come up!* (3:9 [4:9]).

With the opening of verse 9, Yahweh resumes the theme of 3:1-3 [4:1-3], reiterating the gathering of the defendants to the earthly courtroom, the valley of Jehoshaphat (cf. 3:2, 12 [4:2, 12]). There

---

125. Isa. 1:2; 22:25; 25:8; Obad. 18. Cf. the similar expression 'for the mouth of the LORD has spoken it' in Isa. 1:20; 40:5; 58:14; Micah 4:4.

126. Feinberg, *Joel*, 83.

127. Wade, 114; Allen, 114.

128. Henderson, 120. He concludes that since Alexander the Great was so favorable toward the Jews, he certainly would have freed them from their Grecian captors.

129. Patterson, 261.

is no restatement of the charges brought against them; those have been made clear in 3:1-8 [4:1-8].[130] The charges have been announced, the corroborating evidence has been presented, the sentence has been handed down. With the sound of the gavel, the Judge now orders His agents to hurriedly ready the scene of the execution and gather the defendants.

The text begins with the command to **proclaim this among the nations**. While Yahweh continues as the speaker (cf. verse 12), the identity of those ordered to carry out His proclamation is not given. The reference is most likely a rhetorical one (cf. Amos 3:9), but it is possible that His agents of judgment (cf. v. 13) or His angelic heralds (1 Kings 22:19-21; Obad. 1) may be in view. All the nations (3:2 [4:2]) are to be recipients of the divine mandate.

The battle centered in the Valley of Jehoshaphat is no mere skirmish. The day of the battle that will culminate the earth's present history (cf. Isa. 24:21ff; Micah 4:11-13; Zech. 12; 14; Rev. 16:14ff; 19:17ff) has now arrived and consequently every preparation is to be undertaken. With terse precision and staccato-like rhythm injecting strength and adrenaline into the text and stirring the emotions to a fevered pitch, the specifics of preparation are shouted out for all the nations to hear.

First, they are to **prepare a war**.[131] Literally translated **consecrate**, the nations are commanded to prepare for battle by making sacrifices and perform religious observances. In the Old Testament, the phrase is used both of Israel, who is called upon to so engage in preparation for wars against her enemies (cf. 1 Sam. 7:8-9; 13:9) and of the nations who are divinely summoned to mete out judgment on Israel (cf. Jer. 6:4; 51:27).[132] Here Yahweh is instigating the heathen nations to gather for war against Him. It is a divine holy war in which the nations are compelled to fight but which they cannot win. Their defeat and destruction are assured.

---

130. A brief allusion is given later in verse 13.

131. Cf. similar summons to battle (Isa. 8:9-10; Jer. 46:3ff; Ezek. 38:7-9). Cp. similar language in 1:14; 2:15.

132. Soldiers are also called 'consecrated ones' (Isa. 13:3). Even in Israel, the Ark of the Covenant accompanied them in battle (Num. 10:35f).

Second, they are to **rouse the mighty men**. As if in a sleep (cf. Zech. 4:1), the warriors and men of might are commanded to awaken from the lethargy of peace and prosperity (cf. Zech. 1:11f). Military endeavors make frequent use of **rouse** to depict a spirit that has been awakened from inertia or apathy and incited to action (*e.g.* Judg. 5:12; Isa. 64:7; Jer. 6:22; Dan. 11:2, 25). When employed with Yahweh as the subject, it depicts His active, sovereign involvement in the affairs of mankind (cf. 1 Chron. 5:26; Isa. 13:17; Jer. 50:9; Ezek. 23:22). He rouses His people (v. 7) as well as the nations (verses 9, 12) for His own purposes. The battle is His; He is in control.[133]

Let all the soldiers draw near, let them come up is an expression used of battle confrontations (*e.g.* Judg. 20:23; 2 Sam. 10:13). **Come up** is also employed by Joel (1:6) with reference to the invasion of the locust hordes. The phrase traditionally refers to the ascent into the hill country of Judea and the region of Mt Zion on which Jerusalem is situated. However, with a context focused on military engagement and the exact location of the valley of Jehoshaphat shrouded in uncertainty, it is best not to restrict the reference here to a topographical designation (cf. Ezek. 38:9, 11, 16, 18).

The rapid transition from the imperatives to the jussives (*i.e.* **'let...'** in verses 9c, 10c, 12a) is not uncommon among the prophets (cf. Isa. 34:1; 41:1). Grammatically, it adds liveliness to the description and summons.

> *Beat your plowshares into swords,*
> *And your pruning hooks into spears;*
> *Let the weak say, 'I am a mighty man'* (3:10 [4:10]).

The instructions for battle preparations continue with forthrightness. This decisive battle will be a terrible one. All the nations will be assembled. The massive nature and intense character demand full preparation and full participation. Every available instrument is to be transformed into suitable weaponry; there can be no deficiency in military equipment (cf. Jer. 46:3-4; 51:11). Thus, opposite to Isaiah 2:4

---

133. After the battle is over and the enemy destroyed, He will speak peace to the nations (cf. Ps. 46:9 [46:10]; Zech. 9:10).

and Micah 4:3,[134] the plowshares are to be hammered into swords and the pruning hooks into spears.

Not only should farming implements be transformed into instruments of war, but every available individual is to be enlisted for military duty. Even the weak get caught up in the frenzy of the war-cry, the incitement by Yahweh generating a Samson-like feeling of invincibility and camaraderie with the other 'mighty men' (v. 9). So great is the eagerness to fight against Yahweh and His people that even the weak volunteer for active duty, imbued with a false sense of power.[135] None are to be excluded; all are incited to come.[136]

> Hasten and come, all you surrounding nations,
> And gather yourselves there.
> Bring down, O LORD, Thy mighty ones (3:11 [4:11]).

To the summarization of the previous instructions, Yahweh injects a sense of urgency. The nations are bidden to **hasten**, to 'lend aid, come to help.'[137] As though Yahweh was enticing any remaining nations who might not yet be in attendance, He urges them to hurry and come help those already present. Their coming has been divinely ordained and even incited, yet the phrase **gather yourselves** indicates that they have come of their own accord.

Although the final clause of verse 11 is a terse, abrupt insertion into the context, it adds significantly to the drama of the moment. The excitement and anticipation of Yahweh's vindication of His people compels Joel to burst into the text of the divine oracle and exclaim, **Bring down, O LORD, Thy mighty ones!** Historically, the Israelites were accustomed to seeing Yahweh intervene on their behalf (*e.g.* Gen. 22:11ff;

---

134. Both Isaiah and Micah use a different term for 'spear.' While the two are similar, the Joel reference can designate a lance as well. Both words are relatively early, with Joel utilizing a word found in Judg. 5:8 and 1 Kings 18:28.

135. Contrast Deut. 20:5-9; Judg. 7:3. When Yahweh empowers His people, then even the feeble will be truly mighty (cf. Zech. 12:8; Isa. 60:22).

136. Stuart (269) suggests that 'This synecdochic formulation is a way of saying that all the enemy population will be judged.'

137. BDB, 736.

28:10ff; 31:11ff; Exod. 3:2ff; 14:19; 23:20), and thus the prayerful cry of the prophet is quite natural. The nations have gathered, and now the time for judgment to fall has arrived. The **mighty ones** almost certainly refers to those divine, angelic agents endowed with the responsibility of summoning the nations (v. 9a) and carrying out the Judge's sentence (v. 13).[138] The contrast with the nation's mighty men of verses 9 and 10 must not be missed. The nations have their warriors, but they cannot compare with those who wait upon the Sovereign of the universe. The agents of the Almighty One will not be thwarted from completing His will. **Bring down** should also be contrasted with **come up** (vv. 2, 9, 12).

> *Let the nations be aroused*
> *And come up to the valley of Jehoshaphat,*
> *For there I will sit to judge*
> *All the surrounding nations* (3:12 [4:12]).

Again, the nations' call to the valley of Jehoshaphat is reiterated (cf. verse 2). Of their own volition and yet compelled, in obedience to His providential control they assemble in the valley of 'Yahweh judges,'[139] **for there I will sit to judge**. The obvious play on words ('Jehoshaphat' means 'Yahweh judges') signifies a change of Yahweh's role. Earlier, He was portrayed as the prosecutor, presenting irrefutable evidence to support the charges brought against the defendants. Now He is the Judge. In verse 2ff, He stands to set forth the accusations against the defendants;[140] here He sits to judge.[141] The

---

138. Cf. Deut. 33:2-3; Ps. 68:17 [68:18]; 103:19-20; Zech. 14:5. The divine title 'Lord of hosts' connotes that Yahweh is surrounded by an angelic 'mighty ones' who are 'mighty' in strength and carry out His commands (Ps. 103:20), including the protection of those who are His (Ps. 91:11-12; 34:7 [34:8]).

139. Introduced by the preposition **'for,'** the phrase **'for there I will sit to judge'** provides the reason why the location of the judgment is so named. It is the valley of 'Yahweh judges' because 'there I will sit to judge.'

140. Standing to the right of the accused was the normal position taken by the plaintiff/prosecutor (cf. Zech. 3:1; Ps. 109:6; Isa. 50:8).

141. The throne was the highest position of power, and the one who sat on the throne wielded that authority. Judges, as here, would 'sit' to deliberate and render a verdict (*e.g.* Isa. 28:6; Ps. 9:4, 7-8 [9:5, 8-9]; 122:5; Exod. 18:3; Ruth 4:2ff; Matt. 25:31-46).

phrase **To judge** here goes beyond the concept of hearing the evidence and handing down a sentence; it includes the idea of punishment as well (cf. 1 Sam. 3:13). **All the surrounding nations** should not be restricted to those nations geographically adjacent to Israel. As the context clearly signifies, judgment is meted out to all nations, universally (3:2, 9, 12 [4:2, 9, 12]).

> *Put in the sickle, for the harvest is ripe.*
> *Come, Tread, for the wine press is full;*
> *The vats overflow, for their wickedness is great*
>   (3:13 [4:13]).

The command to commence the judgment, abruptly shouted out by the Judge, follows the sentencing immediately. Employing two metaphors taken from agriculture, the judgment scene is depicted and the execution vividly portrayed. The harvest depicts the cutting down of the armies while the wine-press picturesquely illustrates the accompanying bloodshed.[142]

The command to **put in the sickle** is directed to the 'mighty ones' of verse 11c.[143] As His 'reapers,' they are instructed to begin the harvest (cf. Matt. 13:39ff). The sickle was used to cut off the stalks of ripened grain, which were then transported to the threshing floor where the grain was separated from the stalks and chaff (cf. 2:24). Because **'sickle'** can possibly denote a vintager's knife, Wolff (80) and Bewer (136) are inclined to see only one metaphor in the verse, feeling that one figure is poetically more effective and thus preferable. The only other Old Testament use of Joel's word for sickle (Jer. 50:16) is non-committal. **Harvest** is also employed for the harvesting of both grain (Isa. 17:5)

---

142. Cf. Isa. 17:5-6; 63:3; Lam. 1:15; Rev. 14:14-20. The grain, wine and oil, used to denote literal crops in 1:10 and 2:24, are here employed figuratively.

143. In Isa. 63:1ff, it is Yahweh Himself who is treading the wine-press. In Micah 4:13, His people are doing the harvesting. In Zech. 14:5, the activity is attributed to His heavenly agents. While verse 13 does not specify, the involvement of the 'mighty ones' in verse 11c suggests that they are the ones who are given these responsibilities. However, His people may also assist, being empowered by Him (cf. Isa. 11:13-14; Zech. 12:8; 14:15).

and grapes (cf. Isa. 18:4, 5). **Ripe** can represent the ripening of grapes as well (cf. Gen. 40:10).

However, (a) because the figure of the sickle and grain harvesting is not an uncommon picture of divine judgment, (b) because both metaphors would connect nicely with the broader context of the prophecy (cf. 1:10; 2:24), and (c) given the fact that the available data does not allow closure, it seems best to let it stand here. Regardless of which avenue one takes on the issue, the picture is clear and the message pointed.

Moving from the grain harvest motif to that of the wine-press, the reapers are commanded to **come, tread, for the wine press is full**. The root of tread is debated, with most maintaining a connection with *radah* = 'to tread.' Others suggest an attachment with the verb 'to go down, descend' (*yarad*), noting that in order to tread grapes it was necessary to *go down* into the wine press.[144] Again, regardless of which translation is followed, the results are the same—the wine-press is full of grapes and in need of being pressed.

Not only is the wine-press full, but **the vats overflow**. Repeating the words of 2:24, where Joel describes the abundance of material blessings, the vast quantities of grapes lying in the vats waiting to be pressed depicts the innumerable numbers (cf. v. 14) that are to be judged. The weight of the enormous mass of grapes, piled high, initiated the flow of juice before they were pressed, **for their wickedness is great**. This final clause, introduced by the preposition **for**, amplifies and interprets the two metaphors. The ripe harvest and the full wine-press, expressed now in moral terms of great wickedness, symbolizes the overflowing evil of the nations assembled.

> *Multitudes, multitudes in the valley of decision!*
> *For the day of the LORD is near in the valley of decision*
>   (3:14 [4:14]).

The previous verse portrays the vast numbers of troops in figurative terms of grapes overflowing in the wine-press. Yahweh has summoned them there. Now, beholding the

---

144. Cf. Henderson, 121; S. R. Driver, 74. The former view is supported by the LXX, while the latter is followed by the Vulgate.

multitudes so obediently assembled, the prophet Joel bursts forth as the speaker. So amazed is he at the masses gathered together for judgment that he remarks repetitiously: **multitudes, multitudes!** The nouns, often rendered 'multitude' or 'crowd,' incorporate the idea of turbulence and unrest[145] and are predominantly employed in the Old Testament with reference to troops (cf. Ezek. 39:11, 15). The repetition as well as the plural forms express intensification and elevates the sense of awe at the innumerable hosts that were gathered.[146]

The multitudes were gathered **in the valley of decision**, so called because it is where Yahweh will finally execute His decision. Because the word **decision** is occasionally used with reference to a sharp threshing instrument (cf. Isa. 28:27; Amos 1:3), and because of the harvest motif in verse 13, some have translated it 'threshing board.'[147] However, the figurative element of the preceding verse is no longer present, causing most to abandon that rendering.[148] The term means 'to cut, sharpen, decide'[149] and, when referring to the rendering of a decision, depicts something which cannot be changed (cf. Isa. 10:22). The name defines the valley of Jehoshaphat further as a valley of that which is irrevocably determined (cf. Ezek. 39:17-29; Zech. 14:12-15; Rev. 19:17-21).

The last phrase **For the day of the LORD is near in the valley of decision** states the reason why the valley is full. The Day of Yahweh is present, it has arrived! Those summoned to it are present and thus its judgment can begin. The repetition of **the valley of decision**, as with the opening of the verse, serves to heighten the effect.

---

145. The same word is translated 'uproar' in Isa. 17:12a.

146 Hebrew characteristically repeats words to express intensification (cf. Exod. 8:14 [8:10]; Judg. 5:22; 2 Kings 3:16).

147. Cf. Von Orelli, 96; also Calvin.

148. S. R. Driver (75), responding to the 'threshing-board' translation, notes that 'there is nothing to suggest that sense here; nor does v. 13 (in which the figure of the wine-press *follows* that of the harvest) at all lead up to it.' Also cf. Laetsch, 134; Keil, 228.

149. BDB, 358.

> *The sun and moon grow dark,*
> *And the stars lose their brightness.*
> *And the LORD roars from Zion*
> *And utters His voice from Jerusalem,*
> *And the heavens and the earth tremble*
>   (3:15-16a [4:15-16a]).

That which was portrayed as a harbinger or prelude of the great and coming day of Yahweh in 2:10-11a is here depicted in its final reality. There the disruptions to the heavenly bodies, as a prelude to this day, were announced in connection with the massive locust invasion. Here, as promised, the final day of judgment upon the unrighteous and blessing of the righteous is accompanied by a display of cosmic upheaval,[150] demonstrating to the watching world the seriousness of the situation. The entire universe was experiencing convulsions on this day that belongs to Yahweh.

His presence in Zion and Jerusalem also causes the heavens and the earth to tremble (cf. Zech. 14:4; Isa. 29:6-8; Rev. 16:16-18). The nations, now gathered in the valley of decision, had roared in triumphal celebration against Yahweh and His anointed (Ps. 74:4; Isa. 5:25-30). Though sent by God to punish His people, they had exceeded their bounds, going beyond the orders of the Commander (cf. Zech. 1:15). In response, Yahweh now roars, thundering back in judgment (Jer. 25:30-33; also cf. Hosea 11:10-11).[151] The details of the day of Yahweh are not given; however, the awesome nature of this 'great and terrible day' is made explicit by the prophet's description of the cosmic events and Yahweh's roaring from Zion. The metaphor of a lion tearing its prey graphically portrays the terrible majesty with which He pours out His wrath on unrighteousness. One can only begin to imagine.

---

150. Cf. discussion in 2:10b, where the terminology is identical. In 2:30-31 [3:3-4], the verbs have been changed but many of the effects are similar.

151. Cf. further discussions on 2:10-11. Amos (1:2) almost certainly borrows from this passage, for 'in Joel it is the climax of a revelation; whereas Amos starts out with it, taking it, as it were, for his text' (Robinson, 38).

Blessing for the Righteous (3:16b-21 [4:16b-21])

> But the LORD is a refuge for His people
> And a stronghold to the sons of Israel
> Then you will know that I am the LORD your God,
> Dwelling in Zion My holy mountain.
> So Jerusalem will be holy,
> And strangers will pass through it no more
> (3:16b-17 [4:16b-17]).

For the nations, Yahweh's presence on Mt Zion, in conjunction with the cosmic display of power and the roaring of His voice from Jerusalem, generates fear and panic (cf. Rev. 6:12-17). The Judge of all the earth has taken up residence and is dispensing His righteous judgment upon the unrighteous. But for His own people, His presence and the sound of His voice provide assurances of protection. He is a **refuge** and **stronghold** for them. Found together in Isaiah 25:4, the words are here employed as synonyms. The temple in Jerusalem is a place of refuge, an asylum for Yahweh's people (cf. Isa. 14:32; Ps. 61:4),[152] resulting in manifold blessings (cf. Ps. 2:12; 17:7; 5:11 [5:12]; 31:19 [31:20]; Isa. 57:13). All who call on the name of the Lord truly will be delivered (2:32 [3:5]).

Both the judgment on the unrighteous and the protection of the righteous by Yahweh become visible proofs that **I am the LORD your God, dwelling in Zion**. Similar to the pouring out of material blessings (2:27), His retribution on the wicked and protection of the godly will also provide unmistakable attestation of His physical presence among them. As recipients of His punishment and judgment, the nations, as Israel had in the past (cf. Ezek. 6:7), would come to know whom Yahweh truly is (Ezek. 39: 6-7; 36:36ff).

Jerusalem will be holy, and strangers will pass through it no more becomes a reality (1) on the basis of Yahweh's actions, both toward the heathen in judgment (3:9-16a

---

152. The tradition of seizing the horns of the temple altar to secure protection from revenge (1 Kings 1:50) may have been foundational in this perspective. Also cf. Ps. 46:1 [46:2].

[4:9-16a]) and toward His people in protection (v. 16b), and (2) on the basis of His presence, dwelling in the midst of His people. The city has been set apart to Yahweh (cf. Isa. 52:1; Nahum 1:15 [2:1]; Zech. 14:21), providing a place where Israel can worship in truth and dwell in safety. Though the dwelling presence of Yahweh in Jerusalem will preclude any invasion by hostile nations, the emphasis emitted by the phrase **and strangers will pass through it no more** is on the eradication of moral and religious defilement. The contextual influence brought to bear by the preceding phrase that **Jerusalem will be holy** is significant and cannot be overlooked. Also, similar passages elsewhere connote the same idea (Isa. 52:1; Zech. 14:21; Nahum 1:15 [2:1]).

> *And it will come about in that day*
> *That the mountains will drip with sweet wine,*
> *And all the brooks of Judah will flow with water;*
> *And a spring will go out from the house of the LORD,*
> *To water the valley of Shittim* (3:18 [4:18]).

The temporal phrase **in that day**[153] introduces the final section of the prophecy, linking it with the preceding verses. The Day of Yahweh is not only a day of judgment on the unrighteous but is also a day of deliverance and blessing on the righteous. Both aspects of this theme are reiterated in these final verses. After the emphatic and universal judgment has been executed upon the heathen, the prophet summarizes the blessings which will flow from the throne of God and which will overflow the land of Israel (cf. Isa. 4:2). In comparison with Egypt and Edom (v. 19), each a long-time nemesis of Israel, the land of Palestine will enjoy abundant and fruitful harvests under the personal presence and rulership of Yahweh.

With poetical hyperbole, Joel's portrayal of the marvelous fertility of the land has an almost paradisiacal ring to it. **The mountains will drip sweet wine**[154] figuratively describes the exceptional fertility of the areas least known for their

---

153. Cf. 'in those days' (2:29) and 'at that time' (3:1).

154. Cf. 1:5 for a discussion of the nature of 'sweet wine;' also Amos 9:13.

productive soil. The sweet wine, at one time cut off due to the voracious appetite of the locusts (1:5), will once again be joyfully consumed by the repentant and restored people. So productive will be the vines that the flow of juice cannot await the treading of the wine-press.

With equal enthusiasm, the prophet sketches this millennial picture by recalling Yahweh's description of the land of Canaan. Looking back to their exodus from Egypt, when Canaan was depicted as 'a land flowing with milk and honey' (Exod. 3:8, 17; 13:5; Num. 13:27), Joel predicts that **the hills will flow with milk**. Possibly denoting a reversal of the fortunes lamented in 1:18, the hillside grazing lands will provide abundant nourishment for dairy cows and goats, dispensing a flow (figuratively) of uninterrupted milk.[155]

This profusion of blessing is made possible in part by abundant moisture (cf. 2:23), wherein **all the brooks of Judah will flow with water**. **Brooks** literally designates 'channels' or 'wadis' (cf. 1:20), for which Palestine is well known. In the semi-tropical climate of that region, the river beds (channels) generally flow with water only during the winter rainy season, and then only if there is ample rainfall. However, in the millennial age, all of them will be full of water,[156] being fed by **a spring** that **will go out from the house of the LORD**. As in the paradise of Eden, where a river streamed out to water the garden (Gen. 2:10), so there will be a river flowing out of Jerusalem and the Temple (cf. Zech. 14:8; Ezek. 47:1-12) **to water the valley of Shittim**.

Shittim, located to the north of the Dead Sea, was the final stopover for Israel prior to her march into the promised land (cf. Num. 25:1; Josh. 2:1; 3:1), camping there for several months. It is an area known for the shittim (or acacia) tree, a strong and durable hardwood tree that thrives in arid climates. Difficulties have prevented conclusive identification of the location of the valley associated with Shittim and

---

155. The text speaks figuratively of abundance and prosperity; yet it is not unusual for dairy cows whose udders are filled to capacity to involuntarily generate a flow of milk.

156. Cf. Isa. 30:25.

the significance for its mention here. Old Testament references to Shittim indicate that it was situated on the *plains* of
Moab (Num. 33:49); yet Joel speaks of it as lying in a *valley* or
gorge.[157] While the southern end of the Jordan River where
it enters the Dead Sea is spoken of as a plain, not a valley.[158]

This has led some to associate the valley of Shittim with the
Kidron valley. The Kidron valley, which runs along the east
side of the city of Jerusalem, is a gorge-like valley running
in a southeasterly direction toward the Dead Sea and thus
would fit the basic description.[159] Others lean toward a more
symbolic interpretation, highlighting the spiritual overtones
that accompany the historical events at Shittim. The shittim
tree, emblematic of arid, desert regions everywhere, figuratively speaks of the blessings of Yahweh that would go forth
into all the land.[160] As the place where Israel experienced
spiritual failure (Num. 25:1) and from which she began her
march of spiritual triumph into the promised land (Josh. 2:1;
3:1), and as the name of the wood from which the tabernacle
framing and furniture were constructed (Exod. 25-30), it
could serve as a symbol of renewed spiritual vitality. 'It thus
spoke of full redemption from past sin on the part of a people
who would claim God as their king (cf. Micah 6:1-5).'[161]

It seems best, however, to understand the text literally.
First, the other proper nouns in the immediate context denote
literal places. Second, the location of Shittim accords with
Ezekiel's mention that the river flowing out of the millennial
temple would flow in an easterly direction (Ezek. 47:1-12;

---

157. The designation is different than those translated 'valley' in 3:2, 12, 14
     [4:2, 12, 14].

158. It is possible that the topographical reconfiguration at the second advent
     of Christ (Zech. 14:4-5) could place Shittim in a newly-created valley.

159. Wolff, 83; Allen, 124.

160. Henderson (122-123) contends that 'consistency of interpretation requires
     us to understand this part of the verse figuratively of the most desert and
     arid spots, such as the acacia is fond of.'

161. Patterson, 265. So also Ahlstrom, 91-95. Wolff disagrees, claiming that
     'Joel, with his own meagre interest in the cultus, would hardly have
     thought of the fact that the acacia was important for the fashioning of
     cult objects' (84).

also cf. Zech. 14:8). Furthermore, Ezekiel notes that the river will 'heal' the waters of the Dead Sea (47:8ff), suggesting a location near the mouth of the Dead Sea. As a region which had decisively received the judgment of God (Gen. 19:24ff) and has over the centuries since vividly depicted His wrath upon sin, God will restore it to a place of beauty, fertility and life (cf. Ezek. 47:1-12). Any spiritual understanding should be seen as secondary.

> *Egypt will become a waste,*
> *And Edom will become a desolate wilderness,*
> *Because of the violence done to the sons of Judah,*
> *In whose land they have shed innocent blood* (3:19 [4:19]).

What was proclaimed earlier is here made explicit by the prophet—Yahweh will judge the nations. His presence will bring about material blessings and judgment on her enemies. There is little doubt that they are included in the group of nations gathered in the valley of Jehoshaphat (cf. 3:2, 11, 12 [4:2, 11, 12]). But here they are singled out as representatives of all of Israel's enemies, as perpetual antagonists of the nation of Israel, fighting for control of the 'land between.' Egypt was once a friend (cf. Gen. 46-47), but her animosity toward her neighbor to the north became a predominant feature of her history since the Exodus. As a result, Joel prophesies that she will become a desert (cf. Isa. 19:5ff; Ezek. 29:9; 32:15). Edom likewise will be turned into a desert (cf. Jer. 49:7-22). **Waste** and **desolate** are the same word in the Hebrew text. The additional description, **wilderness**, inserted with regard to Edom, provides a contrast to Egypt's Nile valley, long known for its fertility. Edom's mountainous terrain did not permit agriculture to flourish, limiting her primarily to sheep and cattle grazing.

Egypt and Edom are singled out **because of the violence done to the sons of Judah.**[162] The historical occasion referred to here is uncertain, although the subsequent reference to **innocent blood** may exclude killing done in battle. While

---

162. The Hebrew phraseology, which literally reads: 'the violence of the sons of Judah,' employs the genitive of object, meaning the violence done *to* them. Similar use of the genitive is found in Obad. 10 and Hab. 2:8, 17.

the term **violence** can signify wrongs of a physical or ethical nature, the reference to shedding innocent blood in the following phrase makes it obvious that the physical wrongdoing was definitely included. A few of the many suggestions include Pharaoh's order to kill the baby boys just prior to Israel's expulsion from Egypt (Exod. 1-2), Shishak's plundering of the temple during the reign of King Rehoboam (1 Kings 14:25-27), Pharaoh Neco's slaying of King Josiah on the plain of Megiddo in 609 BC (2 Kings 23; 2 Chron. 35), or the crimes inflicted during the wars between the Ptolemies and the Seleucids. One thing is certain; from the time of the Exodus onward, Egypt inflicted numerous wounds and casualties on Israel for which she is held accountable. Edom's violent role possibly includes her delight in Israel's overthrow by Babylon in 587 BC (Ps. 137:7; Ezek. 35:5; Amos 1:11; Obad. 10-14), even participating in the plundering of the city, slaughtering of her people, and occupying a portion of her land (the Negev) until the time of the Maccabees.[163]

In whose land probably refers to the land of Judah. While the expression **shed *innocent* blood** could signify the sudden and unprovoked attack on Jews who were residing in Egypt and Edom,[164] **Judah** is the closer antecedent and more accurate syntactically.[165] Furthermore, if these atrocities occurred in the land of Judah, with the perpetrators leaving their own lands to pursue His people, then the crime described is even more deserving of the retribution promised.

Was this prophecy fulfilled historically or is it yet future? The context suggests that this is an eschatological event. The obvious contrast with 3:18 [4:18] points to a judgment consisting of agricultural destitution and the absence of material prosperity. The productivity of the Nile River valley through the centuries does not support a historical event but rather implies a future time when even the perennially faithful

---

163. She was also guilty of refusing asylum to King Zedekiah and his men when fleeing Nebuchadnezzar in 587 BC (cf. 2 Kings 25:3ff).

164. So S. R. Driver, 78; Von Orelli, 97.

165. Wolff, 84.

Nile will no longer lend her strength. Fulfillment of this prophecy appears to be reserved for the time when Messiah returns to establish His millennial kingdom.[166]

> But Judah will be inhabited forever,
> And Jerusalem for all generations (3:20 [4:20]).

In contrast to Egypt and Edom, which will see her inhabitants lacking food to sustain the population, Israel can anticipate a future of prosperity and security. The verb **will be inhabited** is active, not passive as it is often translated. The land and the city is here personified; they will enjoy perpetual, flourishing occupation in the land, without fear of foreign invasion and forced exile (cf. Zech. 12:6). With Messiah dwelling in Zion (3:21 [4:21]), they will also dwell securely and prosperously (cf. Micah 5:4 [5:3]). This condition is promised to last **forever** and **for all generations**. Although the former term in English suggests time without end, in Hebrew it generally designates a long period of time, the length of which is predicated on the context in which it is found.[167]

> And I will avenge their blood which I have not avenged,
> For the LORD dwells in Zion (3:21 [4:21]).

Clearly emphasized throughout the chapter is the fact that the crimes carried out against Yahweh's people will not go unpunished (cf. vv. 2-8). The enemy will be punished in the same manner as it had punished Israel (cf. Deut. 30:7). Just retribution will descend on those to whom it is due; His people are guaranteed eventual vindication. There is an obvious connection with the close of verse 19, where innocent blood was shed, and therefore in need of righteous reprisal. The verbs **avenge/avenged** share the same root with **innocent** in 3:19 [4:19], making the translation difficult. A literal reading would be 'And I will hold

---

166. Henderson (123) suggests a figurative fulfillment, concluding that the political and military reduction of these two nations in the first millennium BC constitutes fulfillment.

167. *E.g.* Jer. 18:16 where it is used of the seventy-year Babylonian Captivity.

innocent [or cleanse] their blood which I have not held as
innocent [or cleansed].' S. R. Driver, following the literal
rendering, explains that so long 'as He permitted their
blood to remain unavenged, it might be supposed that
they had not been slain unjustly; but by the punishment of
the murderers (i.e. here, by the desolation of their country)
Jehovah declares (implicitly) what He had not declared
before, that their blood was innocent (*v.* 19*b*) and had been
unjustly shed.'[168] In this case, **their blood** would make reference to the innocent blood of the slain Israelites.

In another view, G. R. Driver maintains that the underlying sense of the verb is that of pouring out: 'The ACC.
niqu is used of pouring out water as well as blood and wine,
whether ordinarily or by way of libation, and then generally of offering sacrifices..., so that the text can be translated "and I will pour out their blood (which) I have not
poured out," i.e. I will destroy those whom I have hitherto
not destroyed.'[169] In this case, the antecedent of **their blood**
would be the blood of the Egyptians and the Edomites. The
LXX and Syriac translations render the verbs as 'avenge,'
while others have translated it 'Their bloodguilt, which
I have not pardoned, I will pardon,' thereby promising
that all of Judah's sins will be forgiven.[170] In each of the
first three, some concept of avenging the wrong is present,
a concept which its connection with 3:19 [4:19], together
with the larger context of 3:2-8 [4:2-8], seems to warrant.

The lament of the people (cf. 1:8, 13-14) as a result of
the locust plague and drought was heard—Yahweh has
promised material blessings (2:21-27). The penitence of their
hearts (2:12-17) was heard—Yahweh has promised spiritual blessings (2:28-32 [3:1-5]). The cry of injustice calling
for retribution was heard—Yahweh has promised vindication (3:1-21 [4:1-21]). It is guaranteed by the presence of

---

168. S. R. Driver, 78; also cf. Wolff, 84.

169. G. R. Driver, *JTS* 39:402; also cf. Kapelrud, 175.

170. So Patterson, 264. However, the direct verbal and clear contextual con-
      nections with verse 19 make this last possibility less likely. And, as noted
      by Allen, 'the book nowhere mentions Judah's bloodguilt' (126).

Yahweh who **dwells in Zion**. The verb **dwells** emphasizes His immanence or closeness with His people.[171] Yahweh has taken up residence in Zion, the place He has chosen for His name to dwell (Deut. 12:11; Ezek. 48:35).

---

171. Yahweh's presence is significantly described by the Hebrew verb *sakan* ['to dwell'], from which the noun *shekinah* ['shekinah glory'] is derived. Bursting with Old Testament meaning, this magnificent prophecy concludes by declaring that Yahweh's 'dwelling glory' will once again take up residence among His people. The synonym *yashab* ['to dwell'] is rarely used of God dwelling among His people, but is generally found with reference to His enthronement in the heavens.

Obadiah

OBADIAH: THE DAY OF THE LORD

THE JUDGMENT OF EDOM

THE JUDGMENT OF EDOM

The Judgment Enunciated (1-9)

Superscription (1a)

The Battle Summons (1b-c)

The Nation Subjugated (2-4)

The Treasures Stolen (5-7)

The Leadership Slain (8-9)

The Crimes Explained (10-14)

They Ignored Judah's Need (10-11)

They Rejoiced in Judah's Demise (12)

They Plundered Judah's Wealth (13)

They Prevented Judah's Escape (14)

The Judgment Expanded (15-21)

The Extent of the Judgment (15-16)

The Escapees of the Judgment (17)

The Execution of the Judgment (18)

The Effects of the Judgment (19-21)

HISTORICAL

ESCHATOLOGICAL

1.
Introduction to the Prophecy

The Man

There is little doubt that the book is named after the prophet who received the vision (1:1). Obadiah, meaning 'servant of the LORD,' is a compound form of *'ebed* (servant) and *Yah[weh]* (LORD). Though information about the author is scant and uncertain (even the customary identification of his father or the town from which he came is absent), the name itself speaks volumes about his faith and his faithfulness. His frequent mention of Jerusalem, Judah, and Zion suggests that he may have originated from or belonged to the southern kingdom (cf. verses 10-12, 17, 21).

References elsewhere to men of this name do not appear to be referring to this prophet. The name is relatively common in the Old Testament, occurring twenty times in the Old Testament and referring to as many as twelve other Old Testament individuals (1 Kings 18:1-16; 1 Chron. 3:21; 7:3; 8:38; 9:16, 44; 12:9; 27:19; 2 Chron. 17:7; 34:12; Ezra 8:9; Neh. 10:5; 12:25). Historically, the name is first mentioned as the great-grandson of Issachar (1 Chron. 7:3) and is last noted as the gatekeeper who is in charge of Nehemiah's storehouses (Neh. 12:25). Jewish tradition associates him with the steward in the royal court of Ahab, king of Israel (1 Kings 18:3-16), who acted with courage to save a hundred prophets.[1] Others have suggested that he was Jehoshaphat's official (2 Chron. 17:7), thereby placing the prophet in the reign of Jehoshaphat and Jehoram.[2] These traditions, however, seem to rest on nothing more than their shared names and their devotion to the LORD.[3]

The Date

Although the book contains some excellent historical references, the exact timeframe of these events is nevertheless difficult to assign. As a result, a wide spectrum of dates has been suggested, leading G. A. Smith to note that the prophet 'has been tossed out of one century into another by successive critics, till there exists in their estimates of its date a difference of nearly six hundred years.'[4] Some have posited a 9th century BC date,[5] while others have suggested an early 6th century BC (exilic) date.[6] Still others have pointed to a post-exilic time period (late 6th century BC to late 5th century BC).[7] Most would agree that the latest possible date would be late 5th century BC, since

1. Babylonian Talmud, San. 39b. Also see C. F. Keil, *Obadiah, Commentary on the Old Testament* (Grand Rapids: Eerdmans, reprint 1975), 1:337.

2. Jeffrey Niehaus, *The Minor Prophets: An Exegetical and Expository Commentary*, ed. by Thomas E. McComiskey (Grand Rapids: Baker, 1993), 502. Although this association supports Niehaus' date of authorship, he concedes that one 'cannot be sure of the identification of the author of this book' (503).

3. Given the inability to date the book with certainty, it seems best to leave the matter inconclusive.

4. G. A. Smith, *Book of the Twelve Prophets* (London: Hodder & Stoughton, 1928), 2:164.

5. E.g., Walter C. Kaiser, Jr., *Toward an Old Testament Theology* (Grand Rapids: Zondervan, 1978), 47; Niehaus, 496-502; Keil, 1:349; E. J. Young, *Introduction to the Old Testament* (Grand Rapids: Eerdmans, 1964), 260.

6. E.g., G. A. Smith, 2:172-173; Thomas J. Finley, *Joel, Amos, Obadiah; The Wycliffe Exegetical Commentary*, ed. by Kenneth Barker (Chicago: Moody, 1990), 342, 345; Douglas K. Stuart, *Hosea-Jonah, Word Biblical Commentary* (Waco, TX: WORD, 1987), 404.

7. E.g., Leslie C. Allen, *The Books of Joel, Obadiah, Jonah, and Micah; NICOT* (Grand Rapids: Eerdmans, 1976), 131; John Mauchline, *The Prophets of Israel: The Twelve* (London: Lutterworth, 1964), 35.

Malachi 1:2-5 speaks of Edom as having already fallen and lying in ruins.[8]

Efforts to determine the timing of Obadiah's words have generally followed three lines of evidence: the position of the prophecy in the canon, the historical allusions (primarily those in verses 10-14), and the literary similarities to the prophet Jeremiah. In each case, the evidence permits more than one possibility, making a dogmatic conclusion elusive.

Canonical Position

Situated among the first six Minor Prophets,[9] Obadiah's position in the Old Testament canon suggests an early date. While it is true that chronology does not appear to have been the controlling factor in determining the order of these prophets, neither can it be summarily dismissed as having no bearing. In fact, a general, overarching chronological pattern to their placement is obvious. Hosea, Amos, Jonah, and Micah are confidently assigned to the 9th and 8th centuries BC. Nahum, Habakkuk, and Zephaniah belong to the 7th century BC, while Haggai, Zechariah, and Malachi are undoubtedly post-exilic. The inclusion of Joel[10] and Obadiah within the earliest group does suggest that the framers of the canon viewed them as early. If Obadiah were post-exilic, one would certainly expect it to join the company of the other post-exilic prophets. As Leon Wood notes: 'This placement would be strange if Obadiah were written as late as the time of the exile.'[11]

Those adumbrating a later date have argued that the present canonical placement of Obadiah is due to a literary

---

8. Robert B. Chisholm (*Interpreting the Minor Prophets* [Grand Rapids: Zondervan, 1990], 110) remarks that 'Probably by the mid-fifth century B.C. Edom had experienced, at least to some degree, the divine judgment prophesied by Obadiah (cf. Mal. 1:3).' The Nabatean Arabs, after ravaging Edom for more than a century, eventually brought the Edomite capital of Petra under its control by 312 BC.

9. Obadiah stands fourth in the Masoretic Text and fifth in the LXX.

10. See discussion of Joel's date in the Introduction to Joel.

11. Leon J. Wood, *The Prophets of Israel* (Grand Rapids: Baker, 1979), 264.

relationship between Amos 9:12 and the theme of Obadiah.[12]
The Old Testament does, in fact, evidence such literary
binding elsewhere in the Old Testament canon. For example,
the closing verses of Chronicles 36 are repeated, in almost
verbatim fashion, in the opening verses of Ezra. However,
whereas the literary relationship between 2 Chronicles and
Ezra is virtually identical, such a relationship between Amos
and Obadiah is questionable. The phrase undergirding this
argument, 'That they may possess the remnant of Edom'
(Amos 9:12a), lacks the kind of evidence needed to compel
a definite literary connection with Obadiah.

Historical Allusions

A second line of evidence focuses on Edom's collaboration
with the enemy's invasion of Israel (vv. 10-14), for which
she receives a scathing denunciation by the prophet. Was
this something that had already happened, or was Obadiah
prophetically addressing a calamity still to come? Scripture
records at least five significant invasions of Jerusalem in
Old Testament history: (1) by Shishak, king of Egypt, ca.
925 BC during the reign of Rehoboam (1 Kings 14:25-26;
2 Chron. 12); (2) by the Philistines and Arabians between
848-841 BC during the reign of Jehoram[13] king of Judah
(2 Chron. 21:8-20); (3) by Jehoash, king of Israel, ca. 790
BC (2 Kings 14; 2 Chron. 25); (4) by Edom and Philistia in
the reign of Ahaz, who reigned in Judah from 735-715 BC
(2 Chron. 28:16-18); and (5) by Nebuchadnezzar, king of
Babylon, in the fall of Jerusalem in 586 BC.

Three of these invasions are doubtful. Shishak's invasion is
unlikely because Edom remained subject to Judah throughout the time period. Furthermore, the biblical record does not
indicate the kind of plunder and destruction mentioned by
Obadiah. The Edomite/Philistine alliance against Ahaz (ca.
735-715 BC) appears plausible at first glance. However, while

12. See discussion by A. K. Helmbold, 'Obadiah,' in *The Zondervan Pictorial Encyclopedia of the Bible*, ed. by Merrill C. Tenney (Grand Rapids: Zondervan, 1978), 4:480.

13. Also referred to as Joram (2 Kings 8:16-25).

captives were carried off during that incursion, no specific mention is made of the invasion of Jerusalem, which is specifically noted in Obadiah 11.[14] The attack by Jehoash, king of Israel, is unlikely as well. Obadiah 11 speaks of the invaders as 'strangers,' a name that is inappropriate for the northern ten tribes.

The debate is basically reduced to two possibilities— either the overrun of Jerusalem by the Philistine/Arabian coalition during the reign of Jehoram (852-841 BC) or the invasion and destruction of Jerusalem by Nebuchadnezzar (586 BC).[15] Before addressing these two options specifically, it should be noted first of all that the language of Obadiah 10-11 depicts the prophet's presence at the scene of the crime. Thus it is doubtful that the prophet is speaking prophetically in regard to the violence done by Edom against Judah. The brother of Jacob has acted wickedly and the prophet is demanding that it cease. 'As you have done, it will be done to you' (v. 15). Finley agrees, noting that this understanding is 'confirmed by verses 10-11, which clearly depict a past event in which Edom became guilty, and by the overall context of the book. Edom is soundly condemned for what she has done, not for something she will do in the future.'[16]

Proponents of an exilic time period enveloping Nebuchadnezzar's destruction of Judah's capital city point, first of all, to Obadiah's vivid description of the Edomite collaboration with the enemy invasion. The prophet repeatedly and graphically describes it as a day of 'violence,' 'misfortune,' 'destruction,' 'distress,' disaster,' and 'calamity' (vv. 10-14). Coupled with the 'day of Yahweh' (v. 15),[17] that future great day of judgment on the wicked so often associated with later prophets such as Zephaniah, it is easy to connect Obadiah's strong rebuke with the fall of

---

14. Cf. Wood, 263.

15. Evidence for a post-exilic date (late 6th century BC to late 5th century BC) is lacking. The commands of verses 12-14 are meaningless prohibitions during Israel's post-exilic existence since she no longer was fleeing an enemy attack nor did she possess wealth worth looting.

16. Finley, 340.

17. See the Day of Yahweh discussion in the Introduction to Joel.

Jerusalem in 586 BC.[18] Psalm 137:7, Lamentations 4:18-22,
Ezekiel 25:12-14 and Ezekiel 35, where the bitter hostilities so prevalent between Edom and Israel are enumerated,
are pointed out as well.[19] While the mention of Samaria
and Ephraim (v. 19) possibly 'suits a late date better than
an early date when Israel was in existence'[20] as a unified
nation, just the opposite may be the case. The mention of
the inhabitants of Esau and Philistia as still occupying their
own territories reflects an earlier, pre-exilic time period.
Similarly, it is better to see Samaria and Ephraim (i.e., the
northern tribes of Israel) as still occupying their territories
prior to their captivity.[21]

Those who espouse a ninth century BC date place it
during the reign of Jehoram (852-841 BC).[22] Seeking to throw
off the yoke of Judean control, the Edomites revolted against
Jehoram (2 Kings 8:20-21; 2 Chron. 21:8-9). Though able to
successfully defend himself, Jehoram continued to be militarily vulnerable. Shortly after the Edomite invasion was
repelled, a Philistine/Arabian alliance overran Jerusalem and
'carried away all the possessions found in the king's house
together with his sons and his wives' (2 Chron. 21:17).

First of all, it should be noted that the prophet's description makes no mention of the invading Chaldeans. Such
an omission is striking in light of the fact that every other
prophet who wrote of the fall of Jerusalem mentioned

---

18. Finley, 340-341. That the prophecy of Obadiah constituted God's answer to
    prayers of the godly exiles during the Babylonian captivity (so Willem A.
    VanGemeren, *Interpreting the Prophetic Word* [Grand Rapids: Zondervan,
    1990], 142 and C. Hassell Bullock, *Introduction to the Old Testament Prophetic
    Books* [Chicago: Moody, 1986], 254) may or may not be true. But it provides
    no verifiable support for an exilic date.

19. Homer Hailey (*A Commentary on the Minor Prophets* [Grand Rapids: Baker,
    1972], 28) adds that the 'we' of verse 1 includes other prophets from the
    time of the exile such as Jeremiah, Ezekiel, and the author of Psalm 137.

20. Helmbold, 4:481.

21. While the above argument is still valid, it should be noted that the context
    of verse 19 reflects an eschatological timeframe (see later discussion of
    text).

22. Jehoram co-reigned with his father Jehoshaphat until 848 BC.

the adversary by name. Nor is there any reference to the destruction of the city and especially the Solomonic Temple. In fact, as Archer notes, Obadiah's 'description hardly fits in with the complete and permanent destruction of the city such as was inflicted upon it by Nebuchadnezzar in 587-586.'[23]

Finally, the nations mentioned by the prophet are also noteworthy. Those identified are not exilic nemeses, but earlier foes (e.g., Philistia [v. 19], Phoenicia [v. 20]). Nor are there any Aramaic expressions or terms present in the book to point to a later timeframe. The absence of such bolsters the suggestion that the prophecy was penned in an earlier time period of Judah's history.

Literary Similarities

A third area of debate centers on the literary similarities between Jeremiah and Obadiah. Essentially, it is a question of who borrowed from whom. If Obadiah borrowed from Jeremiah,[24] then the prophecy against Edom must be dated during or after the exile. If Jeremiah borrowed from Obadiah, then Obadiah would of necessity be pre-exilic.[25]

There is no doubt that some similar material is found within the prophecies of Jeremiah and Obadiah. In fact, Jeremiah seems to utilize the material of previous writers

---

23. Gleason L. Archer, Jr., *A Survey of Old Testament Introduction* (Chicago: Moody, 1974), 300. Finley's observation that 'the prophet intends to focus on the guilt of Edom more than the event itself' (341), may be legitimate; however, such an explanation for the total absence of any mention of this most notable event is unconvincing.

24. Jeremiah's ministry is generally placed between 626 BC and the fall of Jerusalem in 586 BC. Shortly after the fall of Judah, Jeremiah was forcibly taken to Egypt (Jer. 43) where he most likely died.

25. Or, it could be that they both borrow from a third, unknown source, in which case their literary similarity would provide no chronological assistance whatsoever. Finley (344) observes: 'Given that many prophets ministered in Israel whose writings did not get recorded, it does not seem impossible that Obadiah and Jeremiah could have both relied on earlier traditional language, reshaping their own unique prophecies under the inspiration of the Spirit of God.' Though feasible, evidence to support this suggestion is lacking.

more than most. As Keil observes, Jeremiah often 'leans throughout upon the utterances of earlier prophets, and reproduces their thoughts, figures, and words.'[26] Certainly this does not preclude the possibility that Obadiah borrowed from Jeremiah. Many, if not most, of the writing prophets utilize to some extent the writings of their forebears. But Jeremiah does exhibit this characteristic with greater frequency than does Obadiah.

There are two major overlaps in wording between the two prophets Obadiah and Jeremiah. While both cases give evidence of notable linguistic similarities, significant differences abound as well. In the first instance (Obad. 5 and Jer. 49:9), a comparison indicates that Jeremiah not only presents an inverted version in comparison to Obadiah, but he also omits the more expansive version of Obadiah. In the case of the second (Obad. 1-4 and Jer. 49:14-16), the accounts differ in that Jeremiah announces the content of the envoy's message to the nations (49:14) while Obadiah records a response to the envoy's message (v. 1).

Furthermore, there is general concurrence that the shared material is a better fit contextually in Obadiah. 'It has been widely recognized that the material in Obadiah has more the appearance of an original than the fragments dispersed in Jeremiah, because the verses in Obadiah form a unified oracle with a sequence and an inner connection, while in Jeremiah they are scattered among other matters.'[27] Archer adds: 'By smoothing down the rugged places in Obadiah's style of expression, Jeremiah shows himself to have been the adapter rather than the original source....'[28]

---

26. Keil, 340. Jeremiah's frequent employment of phraseology from Deuteronomy is quite understandable in light of the newly found lawbook during King Josiah's temple reparations (2 Chron. 34).

27. Niehaus, 500. Commenting on Jeremiah 49, McKane adds: 'There is agreement that verses 14-16 have been appropriated from Obad. 1-4 (Duhm, Cornill, Peake, Volz, Rudolph, Weiser) and that they are better located at the beginning of an oracle as in the Obadiah passage' (William McKane, *A Critical and Exegetical Commentary on Jeremiah, ICC* [Edinburgh: T & T Clark, 1996], 1222).

28. Archer, 301.

Conclusion
When was the prophecy written? It is difficult to determine. The exilic date suffers from the fact that Israel wasn't around after 586 to be plundered. If that's the case, how could Obadiah's warning have any meaning? Embracing an early date has its problems as well. One difficulty is the fact that the Chronicler makes no mention of a role by Edom in the attack on Jerusalem during the reign of Jehoram. In fact, the writer of 2 Kings doesn't even record it. Nor is there any indication that Jerusalem suffered to the degree described by Obadiah. As Finley observes: 'It hardly seems like the kind of national catastrophe depicted by Obadiah.'[29]

However, the canonical position given to the prophecy coupled with the apparent use of Obadiah by Jeremiah suggest an earlier date, possibly during the reign of Jehoram.[30] In addition, the historical allusions within the book itself do carry enough strength to adequately explain an invasion during the days of Jehoram, but they seem too insufficient to account for the atrocities that accompanied the Babylonian destruction of Jerusalem. Without any mention of the destruction of the temple or the royal palace, it is unlikely that Obadiah is making reference to the Babylonian invasion. Furthermore, it would make no sense to warn Edom about entering Jerusalem's gates or having her possessions plundered after the Chaldean forces had reduced the city to rubble.[31] Instead of picturing the mass exodus of exiles to Babylon or refugees to Egypt, the language reflects a continuation of Jerusalem residents living in the city during the prophet's time.

The Historical Setting
The Edomites trace their origin to Esau, the firstborn twin son of Isaac and Rebekah (Gen. 25:24-26) who struggled with Jacob even while in the womb (Gen. 25:22). Esau's name means 'hairy,' because 'he was like a hairy garment

---

29. Finley, 342.
30. Even Finley, who suggests an exilic date, admits that 'The relationship between Jeremiah and Obadiah is the major positive argument in favor of an early date for the latter prophet…' (345).
31. Niehaus, 502.

all over' (Gen. 25:25). He is also called Edom, meaning 'red,' owing to the sale of his birthright in exchange for some 'red stew' (Gen. 25:30). He showed disregard for the covenant promises by marrying two Canaanite women (Gen. 26:34) and later the daughter of Ishmael (Gen. 28:9).[32] He loved the out-of-doors and, after having his father's blessing stolen from him by Jacob, was destined to remain a man of the open spaces (Gen. 25:27; 27:38-40).

Esau settled in a region of mostly rugged mountains south of the Dead Sea (Gen. 33:16; 36:8-9; Deut. 2:4-5) called Edom (Greek, 'Idumaea'), an area approximately 40 miles wide and 100 miles long and stretching from the Brook Zered south to the Gulf of Aqabah. It was also known as the land of Seir,[33] an ancestor of the Horites (Gen. 36:20-21; Deut. 2:12), whom the Edomites had dispossessed.

Edom occupied a land dominated by vast wilderness, narrow valleys and rugged mountains. Her cities, perched among these natural fortresses, were endowed with an impenetrable defense (cf. Jer. 49:16). Great wealth was bestowed on her as well. An extensive copper mining and smelting industry in the region of Punon also provided considerable wealth. The fabled King's Highway, beginning in Ezion-geber (Elat) at the northern tip of the Red Sea and running along the eastern plateau to Damascus and points north, provided an essential caravan route linking North Africa with Europe and Asia (cf. Num. 20:17). The Edomites controlled about seventy miles of this lucrative route, exacting tolls from the passing caravans. In addition to her material wealth, Edom was also known for her wisdom. Eliphaz, Job's friend, came from Teman, a city in southern Edom (Job 15:1, 18; Obad. 7-8).[34]

---

32. The language of Genesis 28:8-9 is unclear as to whether Esau's marriage to the daughter of Ishmael represented a deepening of the rift between him and his parents or if it demonstrated an attempt on his part to heal the breach.

33. Meaning 'hairy,' the name represents a further connection with Esau.

34. Her geographical location on the King's Highway allowed the wisdom of many different cultures to be deposited within her borders. Bullock (255) adds that 'Job also likely hailed from some place like Edom, for Lamentations 4:21 puts Edom and Uz in parallel lines, suggesting that Uz was located within the bounds of Edom'.

The struggle and birth of Jacob and Esau (Gen. 25) form the ultimate background to the prophecy (Gen. 25:23, 'two nations are in your womb'). Although the need to subdue a mutual enemy occasionally required a joint effort (cf. 1 Kings 3:9), the descendants of Esau seemed to hold the descendants of Jacob in perpetual contempt. When Israel came out of Egypt, Edom denied her brother Jacob passage through her land (Num. 20:14-21), requiring Israel to travel vast distances around her (cf. Num. 33:41-44), a situation that undoubtedly contributed to the fiery serpent incident (Num. 21:4-7). In spite of this violation of fraternal relations, Israel was instructed by God to be kind to Edom (Deut. 23:7-8). Yet Edom harbored a perpetual hatred toward Israel throughout her history (Amos 1:11; Ezek. 35:5, 11-12).[35]

In confirmation of Isaac's prophecy (Gen. 27:40 'And by your sword you shall live'), the Edomites were frequently at odds with Israel and her neighbors. They opposed Saul (ca. 1043-1011 BC; 1 Sam. 14:47), but were later subdued under David (ca. 1011-971 BC; 2 Sam. 8:13-14). They were also subjugated by Solomon (ca. 971-931 BC; 1 Kings 11:14-25), allowing him to build a fleet of ships at Ezion-geber 'in the land of Edom' (1 Kings 9:26). They fought against Jehoshaphat (ca. 873-848 BC; 1 Kings 22:47; 2 Chron. 20) and successfully rebelled against Jehoram (ca. 852-841 BC; 2 Kings 8:20-22; 2 Chron. 21:8-10). They were again conquered by Judah under Amaziah (ca. 796-767 BC; 2 Kings 14:7), but they regained their freedom during the reign of Ahaz (ca. 735-715 BC). Edom was later controlled by Assyria and Babylon. In the fourth century BC the Edomites were forced by the Nabateans to leave their territory. They moved to the area of southern Palestine and became known as Idumeans. Judas Maccabeus gained victory over them in 164 BC, and when his nephew, John

---

35. While 'No Ammonite or Moabite shall enter the assembly of the Lord; none of their descendants, even to the tenth generation, shall ever enter the assembly of the Lord' (Deut. 23:3), the third generation of Edomites was granted permission to enter (23:7-8).

Hyrcanus, came into power in 120 BC, he compelled the Idumeans to adopt Judaism.[36]

Herod the Great, an Idumean, became king of Judea under Rome in 37 BC. In a sense, the enmity between Esau and Jacob was continued in Herod's attempt to murder Jesus. The Idumeans participated in the rebellion of Jerusalem against Rome and were defeated along with the Jews by Titus in AD 70. After that time they were never heard of again. As Obadiah predicted, they would be 'cut off forever' (v. 10), 'and no survivor shall remain of the house of Esau' (v. 18).

The Theme

While the recipients of this national oracle are undoubtedly the Edomites,[37] the promise of Yahweh's retribution on them provided comfort and hope for the beleaguered nation of Israel. Specifically, the book is a case study of Genesis 12:1-3. Edom's vaunted spirit of pride and her uninhibited hatred of her twin made her the object of God's wrath. She had failed to comprehend the intensity of God's love for Israel—that 'he who touches you touches the apple of His eye' (Zech. 2:8). The book also vividly illustrates the sowing/reaping principle of Galatians 6:7. 'The principle operative in Obadiah's announcement of the Day of the Lord for Edom was that of retributive justice: 'As you have done, it will be done to you. Your dealings will return on your own head' (v. 15).'[38]

In keeping with the dual aspects of the Day of Yahweh (v. 15), the focus of Obadiah's words constitutes both judgment and blessing. The judgment on Edom, and on all nations that share her hostility toward the Lord (vv. 15a, 16), would eventuate in blessing and prosperity for the remnant of Israel. 'The message of judgment on Judah's enemies was

---

36. Flavius Josephus, *The Works of Josephus: The Antiquities of the Jews*, tr. by William Whiston (Peabody, MA: Hendrickson, 1987), 13:9:1.

37. Other subsequent prophecies against Edom include Isa. 34:5-15, Jer. 49:7-22, Ezek 25:12-14, and Amos 1:11-12.

38. Bullock, 262.

a message of comfort and encouragement for the...Jews. The prophetic word assured them that Yahweh would save his people and that he would avenge their enemies.'[39]

Like Joel's prophecy, Obadiah's Day of Yahweh encompasses both a historical aspect and an eschatological aspect. The historical aspect, describing the historical demise of the Edomites at the hands of other nations in verses 1b-9, is followed by a description of her cruelty toward Israel in verses 10-14. The eschatological aspect of the Day of Yahweh is highlighted in verses 15-21. Ironically, just as Edom's hostile action was joyfully directed against her ally and very own brother Israel, so too Edom herself will suffer desolation without compassion from an ally-led attack (v. 7) in the course of history, and again eschatologically at the hands of her own brother Jacob (v. 18).

> The first prophecy concerns judgment by Edom's allies, the second is about judgment by Israel herself. Yet in both sections the personal participation of the Lord is also prominent. That the Lord will use the nations as instruments of wrath against Edom is clear from the message He has sent out among the nations (v. 1b).... The second prophecy is of the Lord's own day of vengeance against the nations. Then he will summon not the other nations but Israel as His tool to destroy Edom.[40]

Finally, the prophecy looks beyond the nation of Edom and the charges that led to her indictment. Because Edom is no different than any nation that engages in actions contrary to God's purposes, the prophet serves notice that all nations will receive the same sentence of judgment (v. 15). The Lord will ultimately rule over all the nations (v. 21c).

The Composition

Unity

Under the influence of the Documentary Hypothesis, higher criticism has in recent centuries attacked the unity

---

39. VanGemeren, 144. Bullock agrees: 'No words of comfort or hope appear, at least not for Edom. Yet the effect of the oracle for Judah is greatly comforting, both directly and indirectly' (257).

40. Finley, 350.

of the prophecy. It is contended that the historical portion
(vv. 1-14, 15b) comes from the hand of a different writer than
does the eschatological portion (vv. 15a, 16-21). Some advocate
an even more radical dissection of the oracle of Obadiah.
Bewer, for example, suggests at least three different authors,
divided between verses 1-14, 15-18, and 19-21: 'With v. 15a we
enter upon a different range of thought. The writer does not
describe a present calamity but hopes for the punishment of
Edom on the day when Yahweh will judge all nations. These
verses have therefore grown out of a different situation.... It
is not likely that Obadiah was the writer of these verses.'[41] He
divides verses 15-21 still further, adding that 'we must probably
conclude that verses 19-21 are by a different author....'[42]

In the face of this growing perspective, Keil[43] maintained
the unity of the prophecy. Later, Young added his endorse-
ment of the book's unity: 'But in opposition to the above
views we would assert that it is best to regard the entire
prophecy as having been written by Obadiah and that he
lived before Jeremiah.'[44] More recently, Allen[45] and Finley
have argued convincingly for its unity as well. 'Even though
the second half focuses on the Lord's judgment of the nations
in addition to His judgment of Edom, this new theme has
its motivation in the first half of the book.... Moreover, the
second half underlines the theme of just retribution and
extends its scope to include all the countries that have participated in the scattering of Israel and Judah.'[46]

---

41. J. A. Bewer, *A Critical and Exegetical Commentary on Obadiah and Joel. ICC*
(Edinburgh: T & T Clark, 1974), 3-4. Owing to the belief that the current
Old Testament text was constructed at the hands of a multiplicity of editors
and redactors, there is little agreement among higher critics as to which
divisions or arrangements are correct (see Allen, 133-135 and Hans Walter
Wolff, *Obadiah and Jonah*, translated by Margaret Kohl [Minneapolis:
Augsburg, 1986] 18-19).

42. Bewer, 4.

43. Keil, 337-338.

44. E. J. Young, *Introduction to the Old Testament* (Grand Rapids: Eerdmans,
1975), 260.

45. Allen, 133-135.

46. Finley, 349.

Style

Obadiah displays a flair for the dramatic. His oracle against Edom and ultimately against the nations is filled with descriptive imagery, rhetorical questions and irony. The prophet describes Edom's proud and invincible perch among the cliffs of Petra as an eagle's nest nestled among the stars (v. 4). He addresses her overindulgent aggression against Judah with the rhetorical questions, 'If thieves came to you, if robbers by night…, would they not steal only until they had enough? If grape gatherers came to you, would they not leave some gleanings?' (v. 5). The prophet's notable use of irony to announce Edom's judgment is vividly set forth in verses 7, 15, and 16, while the repeated warnings 'Do not …' (vv. 10-14) herald an inescapable admonition. As Niehaus notes: 'Whoever Obadiah was, he possessed literary skills appropriate to his calling. He had a repertoire of poetic devices that earn him an honorable place among the writing prophets.'[47]

Arrangement

The oracle basically falls into three sections, with the first (vv. 1-9) and third (vv. 15-21) portions revolving around the second (vv. 10-14). In the first major section, Yahweh pronounces His judgment upon Edom, describing the dramatic and far-reaching effects of the sentence. The second major section announces the core of the indictment, revealing the nature of the evidence and substantiating the severity of the sentencing. Edom's proud and haughty spirit (vv. 3-4), coupled with an insatiable appetite (v. 5), fueled unrestrained violence against her brother. The third section broadens the Day of Yahweh concept, already revealed earlier (v. 8: 'in that day'), to include with Edom all nations who attack God's chosen people.

---

47. Niehaus, 503-505.

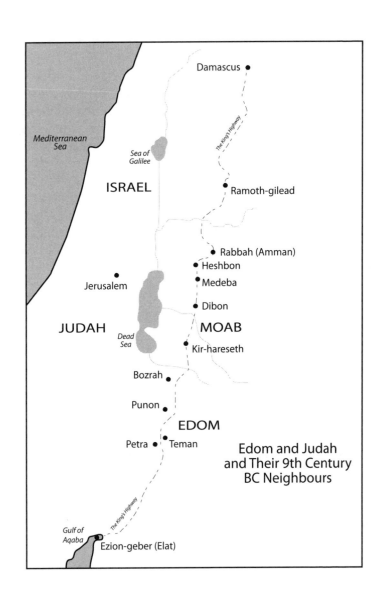

Edom and Judah
and Their 9th Century
BC Neighbours

2.

The Judgment of Edom
Enunciated (1-9)

The Superscription (1a)

The vision of Obadiah (1a)

The prophecy opens with a relatively simple yet dignified introduction. Serving as both the book's heading and title, it is the shortest of the prophetic writers. While divine revelation was given through various means (Num 12:6-8; Heb. 1:1), this message came by means of a vision.[1] The nomenclature chosen by Obadiah on this particular occasion leaves little doubt as to the origin of the message, since the term usually serves to designate divine revelation. 'Literally meaning 'see,' it is a technical term of prophecy which developed to refer not only to visions but to the wider perception of divine revelation.'[2]

---

1. The only other prophecies to be called a vision are Isaiah (1:1) and Nahum (1:1), though Micah (1:1) does use the verb form of 'vision' to depict his reception of the divine message.

2. Allen, 265. Although the Hebrew term can be used to denote natural eyesight (e.g., Job 15:17; Ps. 58:8[9]; Isa. 33:20) or seeing God (Exod. 24:11; Ps. 17:15; 63:2[3]), it is used predominantly to designate the content of the prophetic revelation (Bewer, 19).

The Battle Summons (1b-c)

Thus says the Lord GOD concerning Edom—
We have heard a report from the LORD,
And an envoy has been sent among the nations saying,
'Arise and let us go against her for battle.'

Lest there be any lingering doubt as to the origin, the prophet continues with a common phrase for announcing divine oracles, **Thus says the Lord GOD**.[3] The message of Obadiah was not generated from a heart of unholy vengeance but came supernaturally from the Lord God Himself by means of a revelatory vision. The combination of **Lord GOD**, though not uncommon, is found predominantly in the latter prophets. Literally rendered 'Adonai Yahweh,' the former name means 'master, owner' and in this context announces God's sovereign ownership of the world and history. He is the Overlord of the nations. The latter name, which speaks of eternal existence and eternal presence,[4] embraces a definite covenant perspective in which the covenant relationship with Israel is reiterated.[5]

The oracle concerns **Edom**,[6] Israel's relative, neighbor and intermittent enemy. The Edomites are addressed directly; however, the immediate recipients of the message are the inhabitants of Judah.[7] As ones who had recently

---

3. Cf. Isa. 7:7; Jer. 7:20; Ezek. 2:4. Since the phrase does not immediately introduce the direct speech of the Lord, it is best to view it as a preface to the entire prophecy, with the oracle itself beginning with the next phrase. 'In all likelihood the introductory formula in this line forms a subtitle to Obadiah's brief work, which is really an extended ode or oracle dealing with the downfall of Edom' (Niehaus, 513; also see Allen, 145).

4. See comments on Joel 1:1.

5. The inclusion of the name of Yahweh in such pronouncements conveyed significant meaning to the people of Israel, especially during difficult times, reminding them of His unfailing love and commitment. It is noteworthy that this combination first occurs in Genesis 15:2, in a context that foretells of Israel's sojourn in Egypt (Gen. 15:18; Exod. 3:13-18). Nor is its connection with 'I am,' the verb form of the name Yahweh, lost in Jesus' day (John 8:24, 58-59; 18:4-8).

6. See Introduction.

7. Similarly, Nahum delivered within his own country an oracle against a foreign power. In contrast, Jonah was called to deliver the Lord's message against a foreign power in person (Jonah 1:2).

experienced the ransacking of their city, the looting of their wealth, and the slaying of their fugitives, the words serve as an encouragement and promise of hope. 'This small book is both a warning to nations and individuals who do not serve the Lord and as a lesson for those who follow Him.'[8]

We have heard a report. In the prophet's use of the plural **we**, he is most likely identifying himself with his people. In doing so, Obadiah may have been underscoring the importance of the message for his own people. 'Strictly the message came to the prophet, but it reached him as representative of his people and was not for his ears alone.'[9] The term **report** does not mandate a particular meaning; its essence is derived only from the context. Though used in Scripture to designate many different things, such as rumors or false reports, the context of verse 1 as well as the entire book leaves little doubt as to the meaning here. It is a divine message given to Obadiah through the means of a vision. And, for the third time, the prophet reiterates the source of the vision—it is **from the LORD.**

The vision sees that **an envoy has been sent among the nations.** The **envoy**, or messenger, may refer to a human messenger, as in Proverbs 13:17; Isaiah 18:2; 57:9. However, here the envoy's identity is most likely angelic, as in Jeremiah 49:14. Though on occasion the prophets personally confronted the dignitaries of foreign nations (cf. Jer. 27:1-3), it is doubtful that a personal emissary was sent to rally the nations against Edom. Israel's suffering at the hands of Edom and others at this time in her history would render such efforts doubtful.

Although Obadiah utilizes the prophetic perfect (**has been sent**) to describe the envoy's mission, the context of the prophecy indicates that Edom's ruination is still future.[10] By employing a past tense verb to describe an event yet future, a sense of certainty is given to the coming demise of Edom. The demise will come from **among the nations**, apparently

---

8. Finley, 354.

9. Allen, 145. Contending that the phrase should be understood as parallel to the following phrase, 'an envoy has been sent,' Henderson (188) suggests that the plural is intended as an editorial 'we' and thus should be rendered in a passive sense (e.g., 'a report has been heard').

10. Cf. verses 7-9 where the verbs are clearly futuristic.

referring to a coalition of neighboring states whom the Lord will arouse against them.[11]

Arise and let us go against her[12] **for battle** is the succinct message so urgently proclaimed by the messenger. The summons begins with the imperative **arise,** and is immediately followed by the cohortative of the same verb, **let us arise.** The redundancy depicts the urgency of the moment and begs for an immediate response. The term **arise** frequently denotes an initial call to military action[13] and reflects an element of stealth and the expectation of victory.[14] It is not necessary to conclude that the plural **us** 'reflects the presence of Yahweh's envoy, who identifies Yahweh with the armies he is calling up.'[15] It is even more doubtful that the prophet expects Israel to participate in this military action, since her recent desolation would make her military participation difficult, if not impossible.[16] The plural may simply identify the envoy with the nations that he summons.[17] The expectation of certain victory invites the messenger to include himself with the hostile nations.

The Nation Subjugated (2-4)

> *Behold, I will make you small among the nations;*
> *You are greatly despised.* (2)

Although the prophet is delivering the message to his own people, the oracle is directed against Edom in the first person

---

11. Cf. Ps. 76:10[11]; Isa. 44:28; 45:1; Jer. 43:10. The summons is not unlike Joel 3:7-10 or Zechariah 14:2, where the nations' armies are stirred to action, responding to God's sovereign will.

12. Though one might expect a masculine pronoun, the feminine is used because the prophet views Edom as a country, which is normally referred to as feminine, both in OT times as well as today.

13. E.g., Deut. 2:24; Josh. 8:1; Judg. 4:14; 5:12; 18:9; 1 Sam. 23:4; Isa. 21:5; Jer. 6:4; Micah 4:13.

14. Finley, 356. He adds that such confidence 'contrasts starkly with the picture of Edom's ensuing sense of security' (356).

15. Niehaus, 514.

16. Finley, 356. The participation of the house of Jacob and Joseph in the demise of Edom noted in verse 18 appears to be eschatological and thus would not have reference to Edom's historical downfall spoken of here.

17. Henderson, 189.

from the Lord Himself. He begins with **Behold**, arresting with urgency and immediacy the attention of the hearers/ readers. When used, it often unveils some surprise or the unexpected, marking the importance of the statement that is to follow. The phrase, **I will make you small**, is literally 'I have made you small.' Most interpret the verb as a prophetic perfect, describing the desolation of Edom, though still future to Obadiah, as already accomplished. Her punishment is so certain and her judgment is so sure that it is spoken of as done.[18]

As a result of her judgment, Edom will be **small**. The term can connote periods of time, size, or status. Although Edom was comparatively small in geographical size, that is not the sense here. The subsequent phrase, **You are greatly despised**, clarifies the authorial intent, indicating that she will be reduced to insignificance, both numerically and politically. The attitude of the nations toward Edom will not stop at a neutral indifference and insignificance; rather, their disdain and contempt for her will encompass an active and open hostility.[19]

> *The arrogance of your heart has deceived you,*
> *You who live in the clefts of the rock,*
> *In the loftiness of your dwelling place,*
> *Who say in your heart, 'Who will*
> *bring me down to earth?'* (3)

Edom's strategic location, nestled comfortably in the rugged mountains between the deep Arabah that extends in a southerly direction from the Dead Sea and the Arabian desert, gave her a feeling of military impregnability and invincibility. Deep, terrifying gorges emanating from peaks

---

18. See Niehaus, 516; Stuart, 417; Allen, 147. Finley, however, suggests that 'it is possible to see the verse as referring to the nation's present condition. Then a better contrast results with the secure pride that Edom feels... Moreover, the Lord later promises to reduce the nation to nothing (vv. 9, 18). The force of these threats seems greater than the threat alleged to be present in verse 2' (357).

19. Paul R. Raabe, *Obadiah*, in *The Anchor Bible* (NY: Doubleday, 1996), 122. See verses 5-7.

reaching 5,700 feet surrounded her like a fortress, generating a proud, false security.

> The gigantic cliffs and steep gorges of Edom, even from the more gentle slopes of Punon's pass, represented an inaccessible objective that at Edomite whim would continue to exist in splendid isolation. Situated adjacent to the western Edomite mountains about 21 air miles south of Punon is a cavity-like canyon containing the impressive remains of Petra.... The site of Petra was approached through a one-mile corridor flanked on either side by high perpendicular cliffs that almost touch at a few points. The basin that actually housed Petra was itself surrounded by cliffs of colorful sandstone into which have been carved the structures and tombs of what in antiquity was a city laden with wealth.[20]

While other nations were more vulnerable, both economically and militarily, Edom's setting generated a heart of self-assured pride. Using a term that describes water that boils under heat or pressure, the prophet depicts figuratively her **arrogance** as inflated self-exaltation, suggesting an exaggerated, unwarranted presumption.[21] Her excessive arrogance had **deceived** her. Her superiority was based on presumption, not on fact. Similar to Eve in the Garden of Eden (Gen. 3:13), she had believed a lie.

The source of Edom's self-deception is noted by their dwelling place **in the clefts of the rock**. Though the writer is almost certainly referencing the rocky canyon walls surrounding the Edomite kingdom, the term **rock** (*sela'*) may also include an intentional reference to Sela, the well-protected capital city of Edom located on the high plateau of Umm el-Biyara.[22] If so, the prophet seems to be pointing his finger directly at the capital city itself and noting that

---

20. Barry J. Beitzel, *The Moody Atlas of Bible Lands* (Chicago: Moody, 1985), 24-25.

21. Jeremiah 49:16 implies that 'the fear Edom created among the nations led the nation to even greater presumption against God' (Niehaus, 516).

22. Allen, 147. Finley (358) notes that while the ancient Sela had been identified with the modern Petra (which also means 'rock' in Greek), archaeologists now place it farther north at the modern city of Sela.

even her phenomenal natural defenses would be incapable of providing adequate protection. **In the loftiness of your dwelling place** reiterates her inaccessibility. Ancient cities were built on the tops of hills for increased security and fortification. Few cities, if any, could match the imposing fortifications and protections Edom enjoyed.

An exaggerated arrogance, fueled by a presumption of invincibility and a heart of deception, propels Edom to defiantly flaunt a challenge to any who will listen, **Who will bring me down to earth?** The rhetorical question loudly shouts the defiant answer that no one can! Edom's taunt is reminiscent of Goliath's mockery of the God of Israel (1 Sam. 17:36, 45) and Nebuchadnezzar's proud boast on his palace roof-top (Dan. 4:28-31).[23] Without God, she failed to realize that 'Pride goes before destruction, and a haughty spirit before stumbling' (Prov. 16:18).

> *Though you build high like the eagle*
> *Though you set your nest among the stars,*
> *From there I will bring you down, declares the LORD.* (4)

The arrogant challenge of verse 3 is answered in verse 4. The imagery is clearly that of birds nesting in the remote, inaccessible cracks and crevices of the sheer mountain walls surrounding Edom like a walled compound. A popular motif in ancient Near East, the **eagle**[24] in the Old Testament illustrates strength (Exod. 19:4), swiftness (2 Sam. 1:23; Jer. 4:13; Lam. 4:19), loftiness (Prov. 23:5) and tireless flight (Isa. 40:31). Nesting **among the stars** heightens the metaphor, reminding the inhabitants of Edom, who already dwell on the heights, that even if they were able to dwell among the stars they would be unable to elude their sentence of judgment (cf. Amos 9:2-4; Ps. 139:8).

---

23. Similar taunts are given in Isa. 14:13-14; 37:22-29; Ezek. 27:4-9; 28; 29:3; 32:2 (also cf. Matt. 11:23; 23:12).

24. The word can designate either an 'eagle' or a 'vulture.' Occurring twenty-six times in the Old Testament, it is usually translated 'eagle,' though it is rendered 'vulture' when the eating of carrion or baldness is involved (Milton Fisher, *Theological Wordbook of the Old Testament* [Chicago: Moody, 1980], II:606).

In bold contrast to Edom's boast, 'Who will bring me down to earth?' (v. 3), Yahweh replies, **'From there I will bring you down.'** Even when making their abode in the highest and most inaccessible place, they would be accessible to the hand of the Sovereign of the universe; He would bring them down. Lest the certainty of the Judge's sentence is doubted, the prophet punctuates the matter with an emphatic, **'declares the LORD.'** The root is employed exclusively of divine speaking and frequently introduces or concludes a prophetic oracle. It draws special attention to the origin and authority of what has been said. It will definitely come to pass!

The Treasures Stolen (5-7)

> *If thieves came to you,*
> *If robbers by night —*
> *O how you will be ruined! —*
> *Would they not steal only until they had enough?*
> *If grape gatherers came to you,*
> *Would they not leave some gleanings?* (5)

Obadiah launches a series of rhetorical questions, illustrating the unrelenting extent of Edom's punishment. While verses 2-4 establish that the punishment is inevitable, verses 5-7 stress its thoroughness. They are 'rhetorical questions designed to focus attention on the completeness of Edom's coming loss by contrasting to it theoretical instances of partial loss.'[25] The first interrogative illustration highlights the normal practice of thieves. Thieves would seize only that for which they came or what they could hurriedly gather and carry away. Because of the rugged mountains and narrow access through the gorges, robbery usually came only **by night**. The terrain encompassing the cities of Edom was strongly

---

25. Stuart, 417. The questions introduced by the particle 'if' are followed by perfect verbs. Best taken as prophetic perfects, they indicate that the condition, though yet future, was realized in the writer's mind (Niehaus, 520). 'With solemn effect the prophet finally turns from direct address of Edom to a mournful soliloquy, as if Edom is already dead and gone, unable to hear this pronouncement of its doom' (Allen, 149).

fortified by nature, and its elevation afforded a view of the surrounding regions. Stealth under the cover of darkness was a mandatory ingredient for making a successful theft. The word **thieves** can designate individuals accused of various kinds of thievery, but it always speaks of something done in secret. On the other hand, **robbers** is a much stronger term, referring to those guilty of plundering destructively. 'It basically denotes acts of physical violence done to property and persons, taking the desired items and destroying all the rest.'[26]

The second rhetorical question is also taken from customs familiar to the inhabitants of Edom. The lower slopes provided excellent locations for productive vineyards (cf. Num. 20:17). **Grape-gathers**, unable to do a perfect job of harvesting, will inevitably leave some fruit still hanging on the vine.[27] At the close of both illustrations, the prophet completes the rhetorical query, **Would they not? Would they not?** thereby driving home the point of the metaphor. Robbers would pilfer only that for which they came, leaving the rest. The grape harvesters would inevitably leave some grapes in the field. The contrast is vividly clear. Contrary to the normal practice of thieves and grape gatherers, the aroused nations would strip Edom utterly bare! Her well-stocked cities, laden with goods purchased from the merchants traveling the King's Highway, will be completely ravaged.

In the midst of the two illustrations, the prophet interrupts the contextual flow and blurts out with intense emotion the exclamatory declaration, **O how you will be ruined!** The reality and extent of her devastation is overwhelming, provoking the writer's astonishment! The Hebrew verb **ruined,** rendered as a prophetic perfect, connotes an even stronger sense of 'to be silenced, to cease to exist.'[28] Its certainty and

---

26. Raabe, 140.

27. Israelite harvesters were to leave gleanings for the poor and needy (Lev. 19:9-10; Deut. 24:19-21; Ruth 2). Occasionally gleanings would be left for other reasons, such as if they were not yet ripe or too small.

28. The silence, in most instances total, is usually produced by violent destruction (cf. Isa. 15:1; Jer. 47:5; Zeph. 1:11).

its thoroughness combine to add to its impact. 'The prophet
breaks out into a shocked exclamation which had its prov-
enance in a funeral lament and similar expressions of grief,
and was then applied satirically to add weight to prophetic
denunciations.'[29]

> O how Esau will be ransacked,
> And his hidden treasures searched out! (6)

Obadiah continues to contrast the devastation of Edom with
the normal custom of robbers and grape gatherers. Whereas
thieves take only the best and whereas grape harvesters
generally leave some grapes on the vine, Edom's destruction will be thorough and complete. As before, the prophetic
perfect verbs describe the certainty of her desolation. With
poetic parallelism, Obadiah announces that Edom will be
ransacked and **searched out**. The former verb speaks of
mining or digging out, conveying the idea of a thorough
search and seizure—nothing will be left.[30] The latter verb,
a synonym, depicts searching out something that is hidden
or covered (cf. Isa. 21:12). The **hidden treasures,** for which
these invasion forces will deliberately search, is a word used
only here in the Old Testament. It may speak of hiding places
where individuals would hide in order to elude capture or
where treasures are hidden for safe keeping, or it may refer
to the treasures themselves. The context seems to imply
each of these concepts. 'Neither the descendants of Esau nor
their riches will go undetected by the enemies in spite of
their hiding places. Ordinary thieves and plunderers might
not have the necessary time to discover such secret places,
but Edom's enemies will painstakingly and extensively seek
after them and find them.'[31]

---

29. Allen, 149. While the phrase does interrupt the flow of the text by its
insertion between the protasis and the apodosis, Allen's suggestion that
it should therefore be moved to the end of the verse (148-149) is unnecessary. Its present location adds to the shock value and impact on the hearer
(Niehaus, 520).

30. Amos 9:3 uses the word to depict Yahweh hunting down Israel, whether
she is hiding on Mt. Carmel or concealing herself on the floor of the sea
(cf. Zeph. 1:12).

31. Raabe, 146; cf. Henderson, 191.

All the men allied with you
Will send you forth to the border,
And the men at peace with you
Will deceive you and overpower you.
They who eat your bread
Will set an ambush for you.
(There is no understanding in him). (7)

After a summons is sent to the nations to gather for battle (v. 1) and Yahweh announces Edom's inevitable downfall (vv. 2-4), the prophet begins to describe the extent of her desolation (vv. 5-6). But the question of how this can be accomplished remains. How can a nation so richly endowed and so naturally fortified on all sides be success-fully invaded and overrun? Verse 7 reveals the strategy, identifying three specific groups who will conspire against them and invade this impregnable fortress and accomplish the devastation.

The first group is designated as **men allied with you**. The phrase, literally rendered 'all the men of your covenant,' appears only here in the Old Testament.[32] In Old Testament times, covenants were held essentially as sacred trusts; to break a covenant constituted a very serious breach, often punishable by retribution or death (cf. Ps. 55:20[21]; Jer. 34:18-20; Amos 1:9).[33] These are nations with whom Edom had entered into a covenant or treaty.[34] Her relatively small population could not provide for a large army and fortunately the fortifications of her natural boundaries pre-cluded the need for one. Thus, when undertaking military

---

32. A similar phrase, 'the woman of your covenant,' is used in Malachi 2:14 to refer to one's wife.

33. 'To cut a covenant' is the most common OT covenant phraseology, refer-ring to the animal sacrifice that often accompanied the ratification ritual. For other covenant terminology, see Irvin A. Busenitz, 'Introduction to the Biblical Covenants; the Noahic Covenant and the Priestly Covenant,' *The Master's Seminary Journal* (Fall 1999)10:2:174-180.

34. Because many details of Edomite history are lacking, identifying the his-torical setting or the allies cannot be done with certainty. It is most likely a reference to their displacement during the fourth century BC by the Nabateans (see Introduction).

forays, she had to rely on her allies for assistance. Instead of rushing to their assistance, the allies will renege on their commitment and instead **send you forth to the border.** The intensive verb **send** implies a compelled expulsion, a description of 'transportation into a state of captivity.'[35]

A second group, **the men at peace with you,** describes Edom's neighboring states. They were the ones with whom she enjoyed a common relationship of trust and friendship (cf. Ps. 41:9[10]; Jer. 20:10; 38:22). But instead of furthering her prosperity and security, **they will deceive you and overpower you.** Not only will the Edomite inhabitants be **deceived,** they will be overpowered—through the treachery of friends! Deception eventually leads Edom's friends to **overpower** her through calculated hostility. 'Thus Edom's self-deception [v. 3] is now accompanied by deception from allies, belying its vaunted claim to independence.'[36]

They who eat your bread signifies a third group who share in the bounty of the Edomite prosperity. In the cultural setting of the Ancient Near-East, eating together signaled a bond of friendship.[37] The mention of eating bread within the context of a covenant reference may have reference to food shared by parties to a covenant (cf. Josh. 9:12-15).[38] On the other hand, it may designate some of the poorer tribal groups inhabiting Edom's outlying areas, denoting those to whom some of her bounty would inevitably extend.[39] But the prophet explains that even these will abuse the bond of loyalty expected by Edom's hospitality;[40] instead **they will**

---

35. Henderson, 191. Allen (151) presents an alternative, suggesting that it 'could refer to a courteous farewell to be given to Edomite envoys, sent home again with their appeal for help against their foes refused.' If true, as Niehaus (521) contends, it would not necessarily denote hostile military action.

36. Armerding, 345.

37. E.g., Gen. 18:1-8; 24:33, 54; Deut. 2:4[5]; Judg. 19:21; 1 Kings 2:7; Ps. 41:9[10].

38. See Niehaus, 522; cf. Gen. 26:28-31; 31:44-54; Exod. 24:3-11; Josh. 9:14-15; 2 Sam. 3:12-21.

39. Henderson, 191.

40. Ps. 41:9[10] notes the shocked disbelief when a friendship is so violated.

set an ambush for you. The meaning of the term **ambush** is unclear, though the thought of treachery is definitely present. 'It should probably be derived from the root *mzr*, 'to weave' or 'twist,' attested in post-biblical Hebrew. Then it would be possible to adopt the meaning of 'trap' or 'net' given in the ancient versions.'[41] The Edomites had no place to look for assistance. Her allies, her friends, and even her very dependents would actively seek their ruination.

The verse closes with a parenthetical thought: **There is no understanding in him.** The phrase does not imply that Edom will have no understanding *of* it. Rather, she will have no understanding [literally] *in* it, making the **ambush** the antecedent. They will fall into the ambush/trap without anticipation, taken by her enemies by complete surprise![42]

The Leadership Slain (8-9)

The Lord, through the vision given to Obadiah, declares in verses 2-4 that Edom will be brought to justice. In verses 5-7, He vividly describes the extent of their desolation, first by a series of rhetorical questions (v. 5) and then by declarative pronouncement. Now that same theme is revisited. Here the statement of judgment against the descendants of Esau, as in verses 2-4, is combined with description of the extent, as in verses 5-7.

> *Will I not on that day, declares the* LORD,
> *Destroy wise men from Edom*
> *And understanding from the mountain of Esau?* (8)

The prophet, relaying the words of Yahweh, opens with the question, **'Will I not...?'** There is little doubt that an affirmative answer is expected from this rhetorical question. After all, Yahweh's omnipotence over Edom is made clear in verses 2-4. No fortification or hiding place is secure enough

---

41. Finley, 361. Niehaus (522) suggests the meaning of 'wound' as it is elsewhere (Jer. 30:13; Hosea 5:13); but it is difficult to see how a wound could be placed 'for' (literally 'under') the Edomites.

42. Cf. Deut. 32:28 where an almost identical phrase depicts the nation of Israel similarly.

to thwart the hand of Yahweh. If Yahweh is able to facilitate a physical ruination that is so complete and thorough, will He not also have the power to confound her wisdom and understanding? The answer is a resounding 'yes!'

The seer continues, specifying the timeframe—**on that day.** The reference is obviously to the day of judgment just described in verses 6-7. But the designation is often employed by the prophets to denote the Day of Yahweh at the end of the age as well.[43] Edom's initial judgment (vv. 2-9) will have a Day of Yahweh essence about it, while awaiting a more distant eschatological fulfillment (v. 15).[44] The question is interrupted by the phrase, **declares the LORD.** The terse phrase picks up the language and theme of verses 2-4, emphatically declaring that the covenant-keeping Yahweh will bring His promises to pass![45]

Obadiah's record of the vision integrates a theme from the previous verse as well. The absence of understanding (v. 7) results from the fact that Yahweh will **destroy the wise men from Edom and understanding from the mountain of Esau** (v. 8). Edom was well known for her wise men and sages (Job 4:1; Jer. 49:7). Her location on the King's Highway afforded her immense opportunity to engage in intellectual intercourse with the numerous merchant caravans who not only peddled their wares but also their wisdom from the distant lands of India, Europe and North Africa. But her wealth of traditional wisdom will forsake her,[46] for Yahweh will eliminate her wise

---

43. Cf. Joel, Introduction. The Day of Yahweh passages often incorporate both an historical (near) fulfillment and an eschatological fulfillment. The historical fulfillment appears to be in view here, with the eschatological fulfillment taken up in vv. 15-21.

44. Cf. Finley, 362; Armerding, 346.

45. Cf. discussion in verse 4.

46. Job 12:20, 24 describe Yahweh's power in this realm. Allen (151) observes that 'the emphasis upon deception [v. 7] appears to be a taunting allusion to the famed wisdom of the Edomites, to which verse 8 explicitly refers. The ironic truth is that those who know so much are to come to their downfall by their lack of knowledge.'

men from the land.[47] The verb **destroy** is written in the causative stem, thereby indicating the ultimate source. Though the devastation would come at the hands of the nations (v. 1), it is aided by Yahweh's strong arm. **The mountain of Esau**, while making an allusion back to her lofty dwelling place (v. 3), is undoubtedly a reference to Edom and the mountainous setting that so defines her physical terrain (cf. Gen. 36:8).

> *Then your mighty men will be dismayed, O Teman,*
> *In order that everyone may be cut off from*
> *   the mountain of Esau by slaughter.* (9)

Because wisdom and understanding are absent, Edom's **mighty men will be dismayed.** The warriors, deprived of the leadership and counsel of their commanders, will not know what course of military action to follow. They will be **dismayed**, denoting a demoralized state that results in frustration (Job 32:13) and terror (Job 7:14). The **mighty men,** known for their physique and military abilities, will be rendered unable to resist the onslaught of the enemy forces or protect the inhabitants. **Teman**, named after a grandson of Esau (Gen. 36:9-11) and the home of Job's friend Eliphaz (Job 2:11; 4:1), was one of the major cities of Edom, along with Bozrah and Sela. Some think the city was situated historically in the northern part of the country;[48] others suggest that it designates a region with a more southerly location.[49] Its usage here, however, designates the nation as a whole.

The purpose for the withdrawal of Edom's wisdom and understanding is **in order that everyone may be cut off**

---

47. The Hebrew term 'destroy' can refer to both death and removal (cf. Lev. 23:30; Jer. 49:38; Ezek. 25:7). However, the focus here is not specifically on the death of the Edomite wise men themselves, though that may occur (cf. v. 9), but on the elimination of the wisdom and understanding for which they were famed and on which their populace depended.

48. Allen, 347.

49. Finley, 362. The southern region suggestion may have its origin in the fact that the name itself means 'south' as a direction.

from the mountain of Esau by slaughter.[50] Yahweh will
cause the mighty men to be ineffective so that the people are
rendered defenseless and the full extent of His judgment will
be brought down on them. When compared to the thieves
and grape harvesters (v. 5), who inevitably leave something behind, Edom will experience a massive dispposses-
sion. It should be noted that **everyone**, in Hebrew thought,
often reflects a majority rather than *every* human being.[51]
Apparently, a remnant of Edomites will be left to enter the
millennial kingdom (Amos 9:12), possibly from the offspring
of those exiles who were sent forth to the border (v. 7).[52]

---

50. Henderson, following the LXX, connects 'by slaughter' with 'because of
violence' (v. 10). Suggesting that both nouns form an objective genitive
relationship with 'your brother,' he believes it should be rendered: 'the
slaughter of and the violence done to your brother' (193). Keil, however,
contends that such textual manipulation is 'opposed not only by the
authority of the Masoretic punctuation, but still more decisively by the
fact, that the stronger and more special word [slaughter] cannot precede
the weaker and more general one [violence]' (359-360; also cf. Bewer,
26, 41).

51. Finley (362-363) correctly observes that 'in Hebrew thought to speak of
'all' or 'every' often means a majority or a very large number. For example,
David struck down 'every male in Edom' (1 Kings 11:15), yet the nation
of Edom continued.'

52. Joel 3:19 [4:19] also speaks of a remnant of Edomites who are judged in
the eschatological Day of Yahweh (also cf. Isa. 11:14; Dan. 11:41; Obad.
15-21).

3.
The Crimes of Edom
Explained
(10-14)

In the opening portion of the prophecy, the author vividly sets forth the certainty and extent of Edom's judgment. Though the natural fortifications of her mountainous location were impressive, they would not provide the needed protection from her divinely empowered enemies. Her vast storehouse of riches, accumulated from the incessant flow of merchant caravans through her land, would be inadequate to purchase the loyalty of her allies. Her famed wisdom and military strength would be insufficient to protect her inhabitants. Edom would be overrun. Her nation would be devastated, her people ravished, and her land denuded—well beyond normal limits. Now the prophet turns to enumerate and explain the charges leveled against her, providing the evidence that underlies the judicial sentences of verses 2-9 and verses 15-21. Verse 10 is transitional, setting the stage for the more specific charges of verses 11-14.[1]

---

1. Allen, 154.

They Ignored Judah's Need (10-11)

> *Because of the violence to your brother Jacob,*
> *You will be covered with shame,*
> *And you will be cut off forever.* (10)

The first indictment begins with the general statement, **Because of violence to your brother Jacob.** The reality of Galatians 6:7 is made powerfully clear: 'Do not be deceived, God is not mocked; for whatever a man sows, this he will also reap.' The Old Testament law of retaliation [*lex talionis*] (Exod. 21:24-25; Deut. 19:21) is also elevated to the fore (and reiterated again in verse 15). The promise to Abraham that 'I will bless those who bless you, and the one who curses you I will curse' (Gen. 12:3) is put on vivid display.

The gravity of Edom's offenses is magnified by the fact that they were committed against **your brother Jacob.** In fact, her behavior was in direct violation to the divine stipulations regarding family relationships: 'You shall not detest an Edomite, for he is your brother' (Deut. 23:7). By referring to Israel as **Jacob**, the prophet intentionally draws the reader's attention back to the birth of the twins and the origin of their struggles. As the subsequent verses demonstrate, Edom had a long history of treating Israel with disdain and hatred. There was turmoil between them while still in the womb (Gen. 25:22), followed by Jacob's deception and theft of Esau's blessing (Gen. 27:1-29, 40-41). When Israel came out of Egypt, Edom's animosity toward Israel emerged once more. She denied Israel permission to travel through her territory (Exod. 15:15; Num 20:14-21; Judg. 11:17), in spite of Israel's generous offer to not take any food or water while traveling on the King's Highway (Num 21:17).

Although the prophet introduces the charges here only generally, addressing the crimes specifically in the subsequent verses, the strength of the term **violence** should not be underestimated. It is almost always used for violence resulting from sinful actions, and is often used for describing extreme wickedness, such as murder (Gen. 49:5-6), rape (Jer. 13:22), and the wicked behavior that caused the flood

(Gen. 6:11, 13).[2] In other words, the charges are not insignificant. Allen notes: 'Whatever the rights and wrongs of this habitual hostility, the prophet can see no sufficient warrant for this unforgettable instance of Edom's treatment of a brother nation already overwhelmed by crisis. Kinship creates obligation, which cannot be neglected by impunity.'[3] Consequently, Edom **will be covered with shame.** A proud nation that enjoyed immense abundance—security, wealth, wisdom, power—would become the laughing-stock of the nations. Not only would she experience the loss of honor and prestige, but **you will be cut off forever.** As a result of her crimes, Edom will no longer exist as a nation. The exact timeframe of this occurrence is difficult to determine. Was this sentence of judgment fulfilled by the end of the first century AD, when the Romans overran Israel and Idumea? Or do the words of the prophet understand a more distant fulfillment? The Hebrew term **forever** ['olam] often connotes the idea of eternity. However, it is not always so restricted, but may specify a long period of time, the exact length of which is determined by the context.[4] The occasional statements regarding Edom in eschatological contexts (cf. Isa. 11:14; Dan. 11:41; Joel 3:19 [4:19]; Amos 9:12) suggest that the author has the more distant future in view here.[5]

> *On the day that you stood aloof,*
> *On the day that strangers carried off his wealth,*
> *And foreigners entered his gate*
> *And cast lots for Jerusalem—*
> *You too were as one of them.* (11)

Having charged the descendants of Esau with the general crime of violence toward their ancestral twin brother Jacob (v. 10), the prophet now gets up close and personal, unveiling

---

2. R. Laird Harris, *TWOT* (Chicago: Moody, 1980) I:297. Allen's (155) reference to this violence as 'a basic disregard for human rights' probably understates the term's full impact.

3. Allen, 154-155.

4. Anthony Tomasino, *NIDOTTE* (Grand Rapids: Zondervan, 1997), III:346.

5. See discussion on verse 9 above.

and amplifying the specific charges of the indictment against
them. He begins by repeating the phrase, **On the day, On
the day**. It is a repetitive theme trumpeted throughout the
immediate context, repeated ten times within the confines
of these four verses. It is an obvious reference to Judah's suffering when **strangers** and **foreigners** [6] invaded the city of
Jerusalem.[7] Rather than identify these intruders, the prophet
instead chooses to refer to them as anonymous infiltrators,
thereby accentuating the true nature of Edom's absence of
brotherly kindness and duty. Even when Israel was suffering at the hands of complete strangers, she wouldn't even
come to her aid—her very own brother!

Though Edom did not actually participate in the crimes,
You too were as one of them indicates that Edom was not
without guilt. They were fully cognizant of their brotherly
duty and responsibility, but they had chosen to 'pass by on
the other side' (Luke 10:31-32). Out of a spirit of arrogance,
they were guilty of the sin of omission (cf. James 4:16-17).
The Hebrew text records the clause without a verb (literally,
'Also you as one of them'), making it void of any specific
time designation. Raabe observes: 'This temporal neutrality
allows the clause both to refer to Edom's past actions (v. 10)
and to lead into the following prohibitions (vv. 12-14), as if
to say "you were like one of them and you still are".' [8]

The first indictment is that Edom **stood aloof**. Rather than
maintaining a truly neutral position of observation, as the terms
initially suggest, the context (vv. 12-14) indicates that Edom
stood aloof in a hostile sense (cf. 2 Sam. 18:13; Dan. 10:13).
Obadiah describes what happened on that terrible day. Edom
stood aside, waiting like vultures to enrich themselves after
the enemy had **carried off his wealth**. While the Hebrew term
wealth connotes a rather wide range of meanings, it usually
speaks of 'wealth' (Job 31:25; 19:29), 'might, strength' (Ps. 33:17;
1 Chron. 26:7, 9), or an 'army' (2 Kings 25:5). Its usage in verse 13

---

6. While the term occasionally denotes a person outside one's family circle
   (Ps. 69:8[9]), it usually refers to another ethnic group of the people of
   another country (Deut. 17:15; 29:22; 2 Sam. 15:19; 1 Kings 8:41) (Raabe, 174).

7. See Introduction for a discussion of the timeframe of this invasion.

8. Raabe, 176.

refers to wealth and goods; here, however, the prophet may
have military strength in view, as is suggested by a possible
progression of thought. Before an invader may enter the city
and cast lots for it, it must first subdue its defenders.[9]

The foreigners **entered his gate and cast lots for Jerusalem**. The **gate** is a reference to the capital city of Judah,
as the subsequent phrase reveals. Once the enemy had
subdued the enemy, they **cast lots** for it, depicting the
division of spoils among themselves.[10]

They Rejoiced in Judah's Demise (12)

> *Do not gloat over your brother's day,*
> *The day of his misfortune.*
> *And do not rejoice over the sons of Judah*
> *In the day of their destruction;*
> *Yes, do not boast*
> *In the day of their distress.*

The initial indictment (v. 11) charges Edom with standing
aloof, disregarding her brother's desperate need of assistance. Now the accusation is explained with greater speci-
ficity. As the charge that they too were as one of them (v. 11)
hints, they rejoiced at the downfall of Judah. The eight rhetorical prohibitions each begin with the Hebrew negative *'al*
('not'), expressing 'not a general prohibition but a specific,
individual-circumstance prohibition.'[11] The prophet thrusts

---

9. Finley (366) correctly warns, however, that this argument 'cannot carry too
   much weight since the events are not necessarily arranged chronologically.'

10. E.g., Joel 3:3 [4:3]; Nahum 3:10. Zech. 14:1 refers to a similar division of
    booty, although the mention of casting lots is absent.

11. Stuart, 419. Raabe (177) observes: 'To express a past subjunctive—'you
    should not have'—Hebrew uses *lmh* + perfect, 'Why did you gloat?'
    but the construction used in vv. 12-14, a'al + second person jussive, is
    the standard way to make a vetitive or negative command, as Hebrew
    does not negate the imperative form. Therefore it should be translated
    'Do not do so-and-so.' The construction expresses the will and desire that
    the addressee not engage in the activity, often with the sense of urgency.
    By definition vetitives concern present or future time. One does not say
    'Do not gloat yesterday.' They can be rendered 'Do not begin an action'
    (e.g., Gen. 22:12; 37:22) or 'Stop doing an action' (e.g., Amos 5:5; Pss 35:19;
    75:5-6 [4-5]). The context dictates.'

himself (figuratively) into the midst of the Edomites, passionately admonishing them (apparently to no avail), **Do not gloat
over your brother's day**.[12] Though omitted in many translations, a conjunction stands at the head of the verse. It seems
best to translate it as an adversative, setting up a contrast with
the preceding verse. 'You have witnessed, to your delight,
the downfall of Judah, but do not gloat,' because (note the
'for' or 'because' [*ki*] at the beginning of verse 15) your day of
judgment is coming!' Literally written, 'Do not look at/upon,'
the context requires the phrase to be translated with the idea
of staring with scorn and triumph (cf. Judg. 16:7; Ps. 54:7 [9];
Micah 7:10). By referring to Judah as **your brother**, the writer
adds weight to his pointed protest, exhorting them to refrain
from gloating.

The prophet continues to reprimand them, **do not rejoice
over**[13] and **do not boast**. The former phrase warns Edom
not to celebrate with malicious joy at the downfall of the
sons of Judah.[14] The latter prohibition is more descriptive.
It is literally rendered, 'do not make large your mouth' and
is thought to depict an enlarged mouth so as to multiply
words (cf. Ezek. 35:13). The context suggests that these multi-
plied words were full of arrogance and pride (cf. v. 3).

The **brother's day** is identified by the three subsequent
descriptions **The day of his misfortune, the day of their
destruction,** and **the day of their distress.** The term **misfortune** is found only elsewhere in Job 31:3 where it stands
as a synonym for 'disaster' (also used in verse 13a).[15]
Destruction is derived from a rather strong word, generally meaning 'to die/be destroyed.' Wolff suggests that

---

12. Edom was not the only nation who relished the thought of Israel's demise
    (cf. Ezra 4; Neh. 4:1-8).
13. Though usually with the sense of 'rejoice over,' in Job 21:12 it connotes
    'rejoice at' (Niehaus, 531).
14. Raabe (179) notes that similar phraseology generally depicts a malicious
    delight over another's misfortune (Isa. 14:8; Ps. 30:1 [2]; 35:19, 24) and was
    condemned (Prov. 17:5; 24:17).
15. Job's form of the word is slightly varied. Its etymology signifies something
    foreign or strange, thus possibly depicting a foreign or abnormal hap-
    pening, such as misfortune.

the meaning of 'being dispersed' is an occasionally valid rendering as well (cf. Ps. 119:176).[16] The third description, **distress**, connotes a variety of meanings, such as pain in childbirth (Jer. 4:31; 49:24), anguish (Gen. 42:21; Ps. 25:17), and Jacob's trouble (Jer. 30:7) in the eschatological Day of Yahweh. Derived from a root meaning 'to be hard pressed,' it here expresses the distress brought upon the nation of Israel by an enemy invasion.

They Plundered Judah's Wealth (13)

> *Do not enter the gate of My people*
> *In the day of their disaster.*
> *Yes, you, do not gloat over their calamity*
> *In the day of their disaster.*
> *And do not loot their wealth*
> *In the day of their disaster.*

The sequence of parallel thoughts continues to reverberate through the indictment of Edom. With each stanza, the prophet's repetitive warnings increase in intensity. The series of prohibitions are followed by the recurring phrase, **in the day of their disaster.**[17] The noun **disaster** is parallel to 'misfortune' (Job 31:3; cf. v. 12), 'doom' (Deut. 32:35), 'wrath' (Job 21:30), and 'punishment' (Jer. 46:21). Raabe argues that it is to be associated with a root meaning 'to be bent,' thus implying calamity or distress—something under which one might bend (cf. Ezek. 35:5).[18]

The three prohibitions represent an escalation in Edom's role. In the previous verses, she spied on the military action from afar, maliciously gloating over her brother's calamity. In the following verse, her involvement is a secondary one

---

16. Wolff, 54.

17. The second and third lines are literally 'his disaster.'

18. Raabe, 182. Finley rightly adds that the changes in the LXX translation, 'his trouble…his distress…his destruction' lacks textual warrant. 'Apparently the translator of LXX, like the modern versions, smoothed out the pronominal references. Also, different terms were chosen to give more variety than the Hebrew. MT is preferred because of the impact of repetition on the passage and the wordplay on Edom' (369).

in which she maintains her distance. However, the present
verse reveals a more active role—entering the city and
looting the wealth. Finley observes, 'The verse is framed
by two scenes of the Edomites standing outside the city.
The effect is to focus on the disaster within the city itself.'[19]
Do not enter the gate depicts Edom taking advantage of
Jerusalem's ruined state. The Edomites, realizing that the
enemy had left the city vulnerable and defenseless, now see
their chance to enrich themselves handsomely.

Having entered the city, they begin gorging themselves on the enemies' leftovers, all the while continuing to
gloat[20] **over their calamity**. The combination of **calamity**
and **disaster** in this middle prohibition makes a two-fold
reference to Judah's misfortune, highlighting the depths of
her distress. Because of the **calamity**,[21] Edom was given to
rejoicing over her good fortune and Israel's misfortune. The
purpose for entering was to **loot their wealth**. The phrase
harkens back to the prophet's earlier accusation in verse 11,
'You too were as one of them.' Though they did not participate with the desolation of Judah, they plundered her just
like the enemy. She has gone from being a passive (though
malicious) observer to an active participant. Instead of
assisting her twin brother, she engages in plundering the
helpless, all the while continuing to gloat.

Finally, the reference to **My people** should not be overlooked. Though the text has left little doubt as to Yahweh's
love and zeal for His chosen people, it is the first time that
the text reveals it so blatantly. Edom has failed to account
for the fact that is not just dealing with the sons of Jacob,
but with the God of Abraham, Isaac and Jacob. The phrase
not only depicts ownership but also speaks of an enduring
relationship between Yahweh and His covenant people (cf.
Hosea 1:10; 2:23; 1 Sam. 12:22).

---

19. Finley, 368.

20. See discussion in verse 12.

21. The noun in a general sense speaks of evil. Here it denotes the broader
idea of trouble and misfortune. The Hebrew term also forms a wordplay
with Edom, 'which the listener would not miss and from which he would
rightly glean a suggestion of ill omen' (Allen, 158).

They Prevented Judah's Escape (14)

And do not stand at the fork of the road
To cut down their fugitives;
And do not imprison their survivors
In the day of their distress.

The prophet sets forth two final prohibitions. In doing so, he makes two additional accusations against Edom, revealing the grim details of Edom's increasing involvement in Judah's downfall. He passionately pleads for Edom to **not stand at the fork of the road to cut down their fugitives**. The precise meaning of the term **fork** is difficult to determine. The etymology of this rare word suggests some kind of splitting or dividing, such as a 'breach' in a city wall, a 'narrow pass' in the mountains, or a 'fork in the road.'[22] These were common avenues of escape during times of foreign invasion (cf. 2 Kings 25:4; Jer. 39:4). Apparently, the inhabitants of Edom would station themselves at strategic locations, whether at a breached wall, a mountain pass or a fork in the road, **to cut down their fugitives**. The language reflects the earlier statement of judgment against Edom—she will be cut off (vv. 9, 10) in a manner corresponding to her treatment of her brother. The verb **to cut down** may mean 'to kill,'[23] in which case Obadiah would be accusing Edom of seeking to eradicate the inhabitants of Judah. In light of the following prohibition, however, it seems best to understand the verb to mean 'to intercept.'[24]

The prophet concludes with the final admonition, **And do not imprison their survivors**. The verb **imprison** is used at times to speak of 'isolating' or 'closing off' an impure person from contact with others (e.g., Lev. 13:4, 5, 11, 21; 14:38, 46). Here, however, the causative stem of the verb

---

22. BDB, 830.
23. Cf. Keil, 365; Wolff, 55-56.
24. Cf. Allen, 159; Niehaus, 532. Raabe (185) remarks: 'Although one assumes murder for some contexts with the verb, the verb *per se* does not denote this. A reference to murder here would render the next bicolon anticlimactic, since it speaks of Edom handing captives over to others.' Finley (369) suggests that the Edomites 'slaughtered some of the refugees but captured others....'

means 'to deliver up,' a meaning that is reflected in its use in most other passages outside the levitical prescriptions.[25] Edom stood aloof, watching the enemy ravish the nation of Israel. She plundered the leftovers of the people after the invasion forces had departed. By guarding the escape routes, she betrayed, intercepted, and handed over to the enemy those who were fleeing the travesties of war.

---

25. Cf. Deut. 32:30; Josh. 20:5; 1 Sam. 23:11; Ps. 31:8 [9]; Amos 1:6; 6:8).

4.
The Judgment of Edom Expanded (15-21)

The Extent of the Judgment (15-16)

*For the day of the L*ORD *draws near on all the nations.*
As you have done, it will be done to you.
Your dealings will return on your own head. (15)

With the opening of this final section, the prophet once again turns his attention toward Yahweh's judgment. Earlier, in verses 2-9, the sentence of judgment upon Edom was explicitly set forth in all its fullness. This proud and arrogant nation would be brought down with certainty. The treasures of her overflowing storehouses would be thoroughly emptied and her strong, wise leadership would be cut off. Following this explicit statement of eventuality is Yahweh's stinging indictment of Edom (vv. 10-14), declaring His justification for the severity of the sentence.

In comparison with Yahweh's previous declaration of judgment, a broader perspective is now heralded. Judgment is no longer focused solely on the inhabitants of

Edom. Rather, it is said to encompass **all the nations**. God's
judgment of Edom in history (vv. 2-9) is a preview of His
future judgment on all nations who refuse to bow to His sovereignty.[1] Edom has exemplified the character of all nations
who fail to acknowledge their Creator and Sovereign. Thus
the sentence expands beyond Edom to include all nations.

Obadiah introduces the urgency of the state of affairs with the
phrase **For the day of the LORD draws near**. Literally rendered,
'For **near** is the day of the Lord,' the expression emphasizes
the imminence of the day.[2] The drama is further heightened
by the fact that it is **the day of the LORD**.[3] While the reference
to **that day** in verse 8 contains a Day of Yahweh essence, the
full zeal of Yahweh's definitive intervention into the affairs of
human history eschatologically is depicted here. Allen observes
that the prophet here 'shows how his special message fits into
the eschatological pattern of God's final triumph. The conquest
of Edom already predicted is now presented as a signal inau-
gurating that traditional widespread demonstration of divine
justice and grace which is associated with the Day of Yahweh.'[4]

Obadiah opens both verse 15 and verse 16 with the same
Hebrew conjunction. Translated **For** or **Because**, they not only
introduce the reason for the preceding prohibitions but also
depict the relationship of the punishment to the crime. **As you
have done, it will be done to you**. The penalty corresponds
precisely to the nature of the infractions. Edom's judgment is
perfectly just.[5] The law of retaliation,[6] demanding an exact

---

1. Finley (370) notes that Edom will first suffer at the hands of other nations
   (cf. v. 1) but later at the hands of the Lord and at the hands of His people.
   'It is this later judgment that is in focus in verses 15-21.'

2. A number of other prophetic writers speak of the Day of Yahweh similarly
   (Isa. 13:6; Ezek. 30:3; Joel 1:15; 2:1; 3:14 [4:14]; Zeph. 1:7, 14). Not to be overlooked are the ten references to 'day' in verses 11-14. Edom had her day
   against Yahweh's chosen people; now Yahweh will have His day!

3. Cf. Joel Introduction for a full discussion on the Day of Yahweh.

4. Allen, 160. Finley (370) adds: 'It is His 'day' when He brings the era of the
   control of the world by the nations to an end. He pours out His wrath,
   rescues and restores His people, and finally establishes His kingdom on
   earth.'

5. The prophet Joel speaks of a similar punishment in 3:6-8 [4:6-8]. The New
   Testament reiterates the standard in Matt. 7:1-2 and Rom. 2:1-11

6. See discussion on verse 10.

correspondence between crime and punishment, is reiterated by the last phrase, **Your dealings will return on your own head.** The term **dealings** often denotes recompense, whether good or bad.[7] In the case of Edom, God will recompense her in a manner similar to her reprehensible actions toward her brother.

> *Because just as you drank on My holy mountain,*
> *All the nations will drink continually.*
> *They will drink and swallow,*
> *And become as if they had never existed.* (16)

The prophet continues the theme of recompense. He begins by referring to the time when **you drank on My holy mountain.** Commentators have had difficulty identifying the people who **drank on My holy mountain.** Henderson argues that, because the pronoun **you** is singular in verse 15 but plural in verse 16, the reference can no longer be to Edom. Instead, Judah must be the one drinking on God's holy mountain. In other words, Obadiah is assuring the Jews that, though the sufferings to which they had been subjected were great, still greater punishment would be inflicted upon the hostile nations.[8] Armerding agrees, adding that 'The second person plural pronoun in verse 16 is without precise parallel in the prophecy; and it is therefore quite appropriate for this isolated address to Judah...' [9] In this view, the comparative clause set up by **just as** is not correlating the crime with the punishment but the experience of the two different groups—the people of Judah and the people of Edom.[10]

Others argue that the subject of verse 16a refers to Edom. Edom's drunken celebration of Judah's demise is compared with the turn of events in which they, together with all the

---

7. Ps. 103:2 and 2 Chron. 32:25 use the term to speak of the Lord's 'benefits.' Also cf. Judg. 9:16; Joel 3:4, 7 [4:4, 7].

8. Henderson, 195.

9. Armerding, 353.

10. Raabe, 203.

nations, would be made to drink of Yahweh's wrath. In this case, the comparative clause introduced by **just as** is correlating the crime and the punishment, not the experience of two different groups. Since gloating, rejoicing, and boasting accompanied Edom's bold march into the gates of Jerusalem, drunken revelry may have attended her arrogant behavior as well. Furthermore, it is claimed that the change from singular to plural need not depict a change in antecedent. Fluctuations between singular and plural are particularly common when a nation is in view. Finley's contention that 'it is very difficult to accept linguistically that Judah is suddenly introduced with only a pronoun'[11] is not without merit. As in the previous verse, this understanding views the judgment as both retributive and distributive—'as Edom has drunk on the Lord's mountain, so the other enemies of his people will drink.'[12]

The difficulty with this view, however, is that it attributes a different meaning of the drinking to the first line than it does to the drinking of the second and third lines. Drinking the cup of God's wrath is not an uncommon metaphor in the Old Testament for divine judgment. Yet if one sees Edom as the referent in the first line, one must view the drinking not as the cup of God's wrath but the cup of revelry. Notwithstanding its abruptness, it seems better to understand the first line as a reference to Judah.[13] This allows one to keep the drinking metaphor in all three lines parallel; in each instance it describes the cup of wrath. Consequently, the comparison is between the people of Judah and Jerusalem, who were made to drink the cup of divine judgment, and all the nations, who too will have to drink of His wrath. Judah drank temporarily, but Edom and the nations will drink continually.

---

11. Finley, 371-372. He adds: 'The ancient versions continue to make Edom the center of attention' (372; also cf. 'their distress' and 'his distress' in v. 13).

12. Niehaus, 536. If not literally, Edom surely had reveled figuratively in the defeat of Jerusalem.

13. Raabe (203-204) admits that one would expect a vocative to signal a change of addressee. However, he notes that a vocative is not absolutely necessary, pointing to Nahum 1:2 as evidence.

My holy mountain undoubtedly refers to Mount Zion on which Israel's capital city, Jerusalem, was built. The reference to Mount Zion in the next verse confirms this identification.[14] The city and temple were holy, not because of any inherent virtue but because that is where Yahweh had chosen to establish His place of worship. Edom had violated it by entering her gates, looting her wealth, and gloating over her demise. Judah had drunk of God's judgment; now Edom together with all the nations will be made to **drink continually** of divine retribution.[15] The psalmist poignantly describes how God the Judge causes the wicked of the earth to 'drain and drink down its dregs' (Ps. 75:8 [9]).[16] The nations will be caused to continually imbibe, to drink and **swallow**. This rare verb conveys the idea of gulping down the wrath of God's vengeance, perhaps with the sense of having to drink without stopping. Zechariah, speaking also of Yahweh's activity on His day, describes how Yahweh will 'make Jerusalem a cup that causes reeling to all the peoples…' (12:2).

They will drink until they **become as if they had never existed**. This motif, literally rendered, they will 'be as though they had not been,' frequently occurs in the prophetic oracles against the nations.[17] The prophet declares that they will cease to exist as nations, having been driven to insignificance and inconsequence.[18] Though the phrase speaks with rather bold finality, other Old Testament texts indicate that a believing remnant of the nations,[19] including Edom, will survive. The prophet Jeremiah states that Edom's orphans and widows will be given Yahweh's protection (49:11). But as a nation she will exist no longer; her territory will be possessed and judged by Israel (v. 21).[20] Furthermore, because

---

14. See Ps. 2:6; Isa. 11:9; Joel 2:1.

15. Cf. Jer. 25:15-29; 49:12; Lam. 4:21; Isa. 51:17-23; Hab. 2:15-16.

16. Also cf. Isa. 51:39, 57.

17. Cf. Isa. 29:7-8; 41:11-12; Zeph. 1:3, 18.

18. Raabe, 205.

19. E.g., Isa. 2:2-4; Amos 9:12; Micah 4:1-3; Zech. 14:16-19.

20. Jeremiah adds that the cities of Edom will become an object of horror, a reproach, a curse, and perpetual ruins, causing those who pass by it to be horrified and to hiss at all its wounds (49:13, 17-18).

the context is one of enmity between the nations and God's chosen people, the phrase may indicate that the nations will become as if they had never existed in their relationship to Israel. Under Messiah's millennial rule, national enmity toward Israel will cease to exist. The nations 'will be under one King and no longer a threat to Israel's existence. Therefore, the nations as we presently know them will exist no more once the Millennium begins. In any case, Obadiah dwells only on the destruction of the old order as far as the nations are concerned.'[21]

The Escapees of the Judgment (17)

> *But on Mount Zion there will those who escape,*
> *And it will be holy.*
> *And the house of Jacob will possess their possessions.*

A reversal of Judah's plight, so dramatically depicted in the indictment on Edom (vv. 10-14), will come about when Messiah intercedes on her behalf.[22] The Day of Yahweh will bring judgment on Edom and the nations, but will usher in a period of unprecedented blessing and prosperity for Israel.[23] In comparison to the nations (v. 16), there will be **those who escape** on Mount Zion. The noun **escape** is employed frequently to describe God's preservation and purification of a remnant in Israel (Ezra 9:8-13; Isa. 4:2; 10:20; 37:31-32; Jer. 50:28; 51:50; Ezek. 6:8-9; 7:16; 14:22; 24:26-27). Joel describes this elect remnant as those who call on the name of Yahweh (Joel 2:28 [3:5]).[24] Formerly, Edom endeavored to cut down and imprison those who attempted to escape (v. 14). Now there is a complete reversal. Yahweh will provide protection and a means of escape for His elect remnant (Isa. 31:5; Amos 9:8; Zech. 12:8).

---

21. Finley, 372.
22. Cf. the prayer of Asaph in Ps. 74:2.
23. See extensive discussion in Introduction to Joel.
24. Cf. Isa. 4:2-3; 37:31-32.

It is doubtful that the return from the Babylonian captivity is in view.[25] The context indicates that their occupation will be extensive, with boundaries reaching well beyond those enjoyed by the returning Babylonian exiles. Rather, the context points to the millennial rule of Messiah, who will reside in their midst and provide a safe haven for them (Prov. 18:10). His presence will make Mount Zion **holy**.[26] Everything will be set apart solely for the manifestation of His glory, even the cooking pots, and the bells on the horses will be inscribed with 'Holy to the Lord' (Zech. 14:20-21).

The prophet continues his focus on the restoration of Judah, designating her as **the house of Jacob**. As the following verse confirms, the reference includes the northern and southern tribes. However, by employing this nomenclature, he accentuates her relationship with Edom. Edom had looted her brother's wealth; now Jacob would **possess their possessions**. Whether one follows the variant reading, 'possessing their possessors,'[27] or whether one advocates the reading handed down by the Masoretes, the sense of the passage remains evident—Israel will possess the inheritance promised to her (Exod. 6:8; Ps. 136:21-22; Ezek. 11:15; 33:24).[28]

The Execution of the Judgment (18)

> *Then the house of Jacob will be a fire*
> *And the house of Joseph a flame;*
> *But the house of Esau will be as stubble.*
> *And they will set them on fire and consume them,*
> *So that there will be no survivor of the house of Esau,*
> *For the LORD has spoken.*

Obadiah once again takes up the theme of annihilation announced earlier. In verses 9 and 10, he utilizes a military

---

25. Henderson (196) suggests that the escapees are those Jews restored from the Babylonian captivity (so also Wolff, 64)

26. Cf. Ps. 48:1-2 [2-3].

27. So Allen (163), who contends that 'it provides a better link with the reference to the nations in the previous stanza and to Edom in the next.' Jeremiah 49:2 suggests a similar understanding, as well as the LXX, Syriac Peshitta, Vulgate and the Targums.

28. For a fuller discussion, see Finley, 378-379.

motif, declaring that the inhabitants of Edom would be **cut off**. In verse 16, he describes how they will **drink continually** until it will be **as if they never existed**. Here the **fire/flame** metaphor is employed to depict the divine destruction of Edom.[29] Yahweh had enlisted the aid of the nations to bring judgment on Edom (vv. 1, 7); now those who escape (v. 17) will be divinely empowered to dispose of the house of Edom (v. 18) and the surrounding nations (vv. 19-20). They become His instruments of judgment, acting at the behest of the Sovereign of the Universe.[30] The metaphor continues by likening Esau to **stubble**, a highly flammable substance that illustrates the swiftness and completeness of the judgment.[31] Just as Edom had attempted to cut down Judah's fugitives and **survivors** (v. 14), so now the devouring flames of Jacob and Joseph will not leave any **survivors**. All will be consumed.

The **house of Jacob** not only provides a strong connection to the preceding verse; it also forms a bold contrast to the **house of Esau**. As before, the prophet again highlights this ancestral relationship, reminding the descendants of the familial bond between the fathers of their two nations (cf. vv. 6, 8, 9, 10, 12, 17). The nature of their criminal actions and the severity of their punishment must be seen against the backdrop of the fact that they were blood brothers. The **house of Joseph** is apparently mentioned so as to include the northern ten tribes, a designation so used repeatedly by the Old Testament prophets elsewhere.[32] Even though the northern tribes had been removed from the land by the Assyrians (722 BC), they too will be returned to the land. Together once again, the twelve tribes of Israel will collectively subdue the house of Esau. And, lest there be any lingering doubts, the prophet provides a dramatic punctuation to the prediction of

---

29. Cf. Deut. 32:22; Isa. 29:5-6; Matt. 3:12; Luke 3:17.

30. Cf. Isa. 11:14; Zech. 12:5-8; Mal. 4:3 [3:21].

31. Frequently throughout Scripture, fire, flame and stubble become vivid pictures of divine visitations of judgment on the wicked (e.g., Exod. 15:7; Isa. 10:17; Joel 2:5; Nahum 1:6; Zech. 12:6; Mal. 4:1 [3:19]).

32. Isa. 11:12-14; Hosea 1:11; Ps. 77:15 [16]; Zech. 10:6.

judgment: **For the LORD has spoken.**[33] The phrase reiterates the certainty of Yahweh's oracle. It will occur!

Generally speaking, there are three perspectives regarding the fulfillment of this judgment. Some believe that the prediction finds its fulfillment in the sixth century BC conquest by the Babylonians, first by Nebuchadnezzar (ca. 606-562 BC) and later by Nabonidus (ca. 556-539 BC), one of his successors.[34] Others understand the passage to have been fulfilled in the second century BC. The Edomites, eventually driven out of their homeland by the Nabateans in the fourth century BC, settled in the regions of the Negev and southern Judah. In the second century BC, this remnant of Edomites, known as Idumeans, were subdued by the Maccabeans and Hasmoneans, who compelled them to be circumcised and observe Jewish law.[35]

There are a number of factors, however, that render these possibilities doubtful. First, the Day of Yahweh context suggests a time period when all nations are judged (vv. 15, 16). Furthermore, Edom's subjugation comes at the hands of both the house of Jacob and the house of Joseph (v. 18); Israel had no involvement in Edom's demise in the sixth century BC, and the northern tribes were not involved in her second century BC conquest. Finally, the extension of Israel's borders that is concomitant with her desolation (vv. 20-21) has not been realized since the days of David and Solomon. Consequently, given these factors, it seems preferable to understand that, while a partial fulfillment may be seen historically, a complete realization is yet future.

---

33. Stuart (420) correctly argues that the interjection of this phrase cannot be judged a statement of closure as if verse 19 began a new section, since its placement internally in oracles is routine (e.g., Isa. 1:2; Jer. 13:15).

34. Kenneth G. Hoglund, 'Edomites,' *Peoples of the Old Testament World*, edited by Alfred J. Hoerth, Gerald L. Mattingly, and Edwin M. Yamauchi (Grand Rapids: Baker, 1994), 342-343. Malachi (1:3) speaks of Edom's desolation as past, though he also intimates an ongoing existence (1:4).

35. Henderson, 196; Josephus, *Antiquities*, 13:9:1. But Armerding (355) notes, 'They continued to haunt the Jews, however, for the family of Herod the Great was of Idumaean descent....' Also, see Introduction comments.

The Effect of the Judgment (19-21)

Then those of the Negev will possess the mountain of Esau,
And those of the Shephelah the Philistine plain;
Also, they will possess the territory of Ephraim and the
    territory of Samaria,
And Benjamin will possess Gilead. (19)

As a result of the divine judgment, Yahweh will empower his remnant to repossess the former territories once held by David and Solomon.[36] Expansion will be effected in all directions, fulfilling the promises made to Jacob in his ladder dream at Bethel (Gen. 28:14). The list begins and ends (v. 20) with the mention of the **Negev**, the dry, mountainous area in southern Judah. The double reference to the **Negev** seems to be an intentional effort to accentuate the conquest of Edom. Though not the original territory of Edom, it was the area in which she had most recently settled. The prophecy makes it clear that the land occupied by the descendants of Edom will be regained (Amos 9:12). Because of their relative nearness to the **mountain of Esau**, the settlements of the Negev will extend into the territory of ancient Edom.

To the west, the inhabitants of the **Shephelah** will reclaim the lands of the **Philistines**. The Shephelah is a region of fertile valleys and low-lying hills on the west. The coastal plain, extending along the shores of the Mediterranean Sea down to the Brook of Egypt (Josh. 15:4, 47),[37] was predominantly occupied by the Philistines. Originally, however, it had been given to the children of Israel; now it would once again belong to them.[38]

---

36. Verses 19-20 contain grammatical challenges, leading some to propose that 'the text has been amplified by means of explanatory notes…' (Allen, 170; also cf. Stuart, 420-421). Caution should prevail, however, since manuscript evidence to support such speculation is lacking. Furthermore, the text as we now have it seems adequate to provide the general sense (cf. Finley, 375-376; Niehaus, 355).

37. It formed the southwest boundary of the territory of Judah and is probably to be identified with the Wadi el-Arish.

38. Gen. 15:18; Num 34:5; Josh. 13:2-3.

To the north, they would possess **the territory**[39] **of Ephraim** and **the territory of Samaria. Ephraim**, by the fact that it encompassed the largest segment of the ten northern tribes, represents the entirety of the northern tribes. **Samaria** was the capital of the northern tribes. The two are occasionally mentioned together (Isa. 7:9; 9:8 [9]; Jer. 31:5-6; Hosea 7:1), much like Judah and Jerusalem. And Benjamin will possess **Gilead**. The name **Gilead,** frequently depicting all of the TransJordan (Josh. 22:9-32; 2 Kings 10:33), refers to the lush highland region east of the Jordan River. Though the tribe of Benjamin never occupied the TransJordanian area,[40] Finley suggests that her expansion into that territory may have historical roots. Saul, from the tribe of Benjamin himself, won Jabesh-gilead for Israel (1 Sam. 11), while later his son Ish-bosheth was briefly made king over Gilead (2 Sam. 2).[41] It may also be that since most foreign invaders crossed over the Jordan River and infiltrated the Benjamite territory first, she would be given opportunity to secure her borders.

And the exiles of this host of the sons of Israel,
Who are among the Canaanites as far as Zarephath,
And the exiles of Jerusalem who are in Sepharad
Will possess the cities of the Negev. (20)

The judgment on Edom permits **the exiles of this host** to return to the Promised Land and to settle in regions beyond those described in the previous verse. The textual difficulties of the previous verse continue here. Is the reference to the exiles living in Canaan who will occupy the territories of Zarephath and the Negev?[42] Or is the prophet making reference to the Jewish slaves who, having been sold into Phoenician slavery, will now return from there? (Joel 3:4-7

---

39. Though literally rendered 'field,' it designates the whole of Ephraim (cf. Niehaus, 539). In Gen. 32:3, the country of Edom is referred to as the 'field of Edom.'

40. It was settled by the tribes of Gad, Reuben and Manasseh (Josh. 13:15-33).

41. Finley, 375.

42. So Finley, 376.

[4:4-7]).[43] Since expansion is the focal point of this section, it seems best to translate it: 'And the exiles of this host belonging to the sons of Israel [will possess][44] what [is] the Canaanites' as far as Zarephath.'[45] This perspective does not restrict the origin of the returning exiles; it merely indicates that upon their return they will possess the land previously occupied by the Canaanites well into the land of Phoenicia. The prophet's choice of the term **host**, frequently translated 'army,' here presents the more general idea of 'company' or 'band.'[46] **Zarephath**, located along the Phoenician coast between Tyre and Sidon (1 Kings 17:9; Luke 4:26), was a part of the original settlement plan under Joshua (Josh. 19:28). However, only during the reign of David was it under Israel's control.

The location of **Sepharad** is uncertain. Some of the more common suggestions include Spain,[47] Hesperides in North Africa,[48] Sardis in ancient Lydia (modern day Turkey),[49] and Saparda (also spelled Sparda), a colony in ancient Media.[50] Sardis remains the best possibility, though it too lacks sufficient evidence. Regardless, the essence of the prophecy is unmistakable — the distant exiles of the houses of Jacob and Joseph will enjoy the fruits of Yahweh's day of judgment against Edom and the nations. They will **possess the cities of the Negev**. The prophet now ends where he began in verse 19. The Negev territory previously occupied by the descendants of Edom will once again be possessed by Yahweh's chosen

---

43. So Henderson, 197; cf. Ezek. 27:13.

44. Because the text supplies no verb, the same verb is borrowed from the parallel statement in the last half of the verse.

45. Cf. Allen, 170-171; Wolff, 61.

46. Raabe, 264. Similar uses include 1 Kings 10:2; Ezek. 37:10.

47. The Syriac Peshitta and the Targums so designate, and thus the term 'Sephardic' came to be applied to Jewish people from Spain in the Middle Ages.

48. J. D. W. Watts, *Obadiah: A Critical Exegetical Commentary* (Grand Rapids: Eerdmans, 1969), 64.

49. Armerding, 356; Allen, 170.

50. Niehaus, 540. Assyrian inscriptions record that Sargon II transplanted prisoners from the northern tribes of Israel there (cf. 2 Kings 17:23).

people. The references to possessing the land and dwelling in cities that they had not built recall the days of the conquest and settlement of the land under Joshua (e.g., Lev. 20:24; Num 33:53; Deut. 1: 8, 21; 6:10-11; Josh. 24:13).

> The deliverers will ascend Mount Zion
> To judge the mountain of Esau,
> And the kingdom will be the LORD's. (21)

In a summary fashion the prophet continues his description of the effects of the judgment on Edom and the nations. Not only will Yahweh empower the descendants of the houses of Jacob and Joseph to assist in bringing about the judgment. Not only will He make it possible for the exiles to return[51] and to possess the land promised to their forefathers.[52] He will also provide divinely empowered **deliverers**.[53] Rendered in the causative stem, the term depicts those whom God causes to bring about the deliverance.[54] Just as Yahweh raised up judges to deliver His people during the time between the conquest and the monarchy, so He will appoint similar leaders to help rule in the millennial kingdom.

Their responsibility is to **judge the mountain of Esau.** Although the verb can speak of rendering judicial decisions, the broader sense of governance seems evident here. Given the fact that the context expands the judgment on Edom to include all the nations (v. 15), it can be assumed that the scope of governance extends beyond Edom to embrace all the nations.[55] **Mount Zion** is the administrative center of Messiah's rule in the Millennium (Isa. 2:1-4).

---

51. Isa. 11:15-16.

52. Gen. 12:7; 13:15, 17; 17:8; Deut. 34:4; Ps. 105:9-11.

53. The passive [hophal] translation given the term by the LXX and the Syriac Peshitta, 'those who have been delivered,' lacks support since the hophal form occurs nowhere in the OT.

54. The term is occasionally used to refer to those who were raised up in the time of the Judges (e.g., Judg. 3:9, 15; Neh. 9:27; also cf. 2 Kings 13:5).

55. Stuart (421) observes: 'Edom, indeed, becomes in the OT a kind of metonymy for "hostile nations".'

From the location of their escape, Yahweh will empower His people to rule—to participate in the rulership of His earthly kingdom.[56] Obadiah envisions the restoration of Israel to her divinely appointed role of leadership among the nations.[57]

The prophet concludes with the remark, **And the kingdom will be the LORD's**.[58] Throughout her history, Israel frequently slipped away from her monotheistic moorings. Whether it was while wandering in the wilderness for forty years[59] or when Solomon built altars for his idolatrous foreign wives,[60] Israel was repeatedly seduced into worshipping other gods. Obadiah anticipates the time when the kingdom will belong exclusively to the Lord.[61] Three centuries later, the prophet Zechariah states that when He returns to set up His millennial kingdom, 'The Lord will be king over all the earth; in that day the Lord will be the only one, and His name the only one' (14:9). Indeed, the entire prophecy of Obadiah speaks of Yahweh's great love for His covenant people and His omnipotent intervention into the affairs of human history on behalf of His people so that He might reign over the nations. The closing phrase reflects the eventuality of Revelation 11:15: 'The kingdom of the world has become the kingdom of our Lord, and of His Christ; and He will reign forever and ever.'

---

56. Cp. Gen. 2:26, 28 with Rev. 5:9-10; 20:4; also cf. Dan. 7:27; 1 Cor. 6:2.

57. Cf. Exo. 19:6a.

58. Note the same terminology in Ps. 22:28 [29]

59. Cf. Amos 5:25-26.

60. Cf. 1 Kings 11:1-8.

61. It is doubtful 'That Obadiah is thinking in terms of the survivors of the earlier conflict rather than of some distant event in the future...' (Allen, 164). The passage depicts a united people, northern and southern together, subjugating, possessing, and extending the borders to the extremities of the land—a reality that has not occurred since the Davidic monarchy. Furthermore, the Day of Yahweh context anticipates an eschatological timeframe that exceeds any historical fulfillment.

Bibliography

Abba, R. 'The Divine Name Yahweh.' *Journal of Biblical Literature* 80 (1961): 323.

Ahlstrom, Gosta Werner. *Joel and the Temple Cult of Jerusalem.* Supplements to *Vetus Testamentum*, Vol. 21. Leiden: Brill, 1971.

Albright, William F. 'Book Review of *Introduction to the Old Testament*, by Robert H. Pfeiffer.' *Journal of Biblical Literature* 61 (1942): 111-126.

Allen, Leslie C. *The Books of Joel, Obadiah, Jonah, and Micah.* New International Commentary on the Old Testament. Grand Rapids: Eerdmans, 1976.

Allen, Ronald B. ' 'arapel.' *Theological Wordbook of the Old Testament*, Vol. 2, edited by R. Laird Harris, Gleason L. Archer Jr. and Bruce K. Waltke. Chicago: Moody, 1980.

Anderson, B. W. 'God, Names of.' *Interpreter's Dictionary of the Bible*, Vol. 2, edited by George A. Buttrick. New York: Abingdon Press, 1962.

Archer, Gleason L., Jr. *A Survey of Old Testament Introduction.* Chicago: Moody, 1974.

Armerding, Carl E. 'Obadiah.' *Expositor's Bible Commentary*, Vol. 7, edited by Frank Gaebelein. Grand Rapids: Zondervan, 1985.

Barabas, S. 'Day.' *The Zondervan Pictorial Encyclopedia of the Bible*, Volume 2, edited by Merrill C. Tenney. Grand Rapids: Zondervan, 1975.

Barker, Kenneth L. 'Zechariah.' *Expositor's Bible Commentary*, Vol. 7, edited by Frank Gaebelein. Grand Rapids: Zondervan, 1985).

Beitzel, Barry J. *The Moody Atlas of Bible Lands.* Chicago: Moody, 1985.

Bewer, Julius A. *A Critical and Exegetical Commentary on Obadiah and Joel.* International Critical Commentary. Edinburgh: T. & T. Clark, 1974.

Bic, Milos. *Das Buch Joel.* Berlin: Evangelische Verlagsanstalt, 1960.

Bornkamm, Gunther. 'presbus, ktl.' *Theological Dictionary of the New Testament*, Vol. 6, edited by Gerhard Friedrich; translated by G. W. Bromiley. Grand Rapids: Eerdmans, 1968.

Bratt, J. H. 'Sackcloth.' *The Zondervan Pictorial Encyclopedia of the Bible*, Volume 5, edited by Merrill C. Tenney. Grand Rapids: Zondervan, 1975.

Brown, Colin. 'Day of the Lord (Yahweh).' *The Zondervan Pictorial Encyclopedia of the Bible*, Volume 2, edited by Merrill C. Tenney. Grand Rapids: Zondervan, 1975.

Brown, Francis, S. R. Driver, and Charles A. Briggs. *A Hebrew and Chaldean Lexicon of the Old Testament*. Oxford: Clarendon, 1968.

Bullock, C. Hassell. *An Introduction to the Old Testament Prophetic Books*. Chicago: Moody, 1986.

Busenitz, Irvin A. 'Introduction to the Biblical Covenants: The Noahic and the Priestly Covenant.' *The Master's Seminary Journal* 10 (1999): 174-180.

Calkins, Raymond. *The Modern Message of the Minor Prophets*. New York: Harper, 1947.

Calvin, John. *Commentaries on the Twelve Minor Prophets*, translated by John Owen. Grand Rapids: Baker, reprint 1979.

Cannon, W. W. 'The Day of the Lord in Joel.' *The Church Quarterly Review* 103 (1927): 32-63.

Cansdale, G. S. 'Locust.' *The Zondervan Pictorial Encyclopedia of the Bible*, Volume 3, edited by Merrill C. Tenney. Grand Rapids: Zondervan, 1975.

Cerny, L. *The Day of Yahweh and Some Related Problems*. Prague: Nakladem Filosoficke Fakulty University Karlovy, 1948.

Chisholm, Robert B., Jr. *Interpreting the Minor Prophets*. Grand Rapids: Zondervan, 1990.

Chisholm, Robert B., Jr. 'The Polemic Against Baalism in Israel's Early History and Literature.' *Bibliotheca Sacra* 150 (1994): 280-282.

Cohen, Gary G. 'sqq.' *Theological Wordbook of the Old Testament*, Vol. 2, edited, R. Laird Harris, Gleason L. Archer Jr. and Bruce K. Waltke. Chicago: Moody, 1980.

Coker, W. B. 'Solemn Assembly.' *The Zondervan Pictorial Encyclopedia of the Bible*, Volume 5, edited by Merrill C. Tenney. Grand Rapids: Zondervan, 1975.

Conzelmann, Hans. 'skotos, ktl.' *Theological Dictionary of the New Testament*, Vol. 7, edited by Gerhard Friedrich; translated by G. W. Bromiley. Grand Rapids: Eerdmans, 1968.

Cornhill, Carl H. *The Prophets of Israel: Popular Sketches from Old Testament History*. Norwood, PA: Norwood Editions, reprint 1977.

DaCruz, Daniel. 'Plague Across the Land.' *Aramco World* (Nov-Dec 1967): 21.

Dahood, Mitchell. *Psalms II – 51-100*. The Anchor Bible. Garden City, NY: Doubleday, 1974.

Davidson, A. B. *The Theology of the Old Testament*. New York: Scribner's, 1907.

Deane, W. J. *The Book of Joel*. TPC. Grand Rapids: Eerdmans, reprint1975.

Driver, G. R. 'Notes and Studies, Joel.' *Journal of Theological Studies* 39 (1938): 400-402.

Driver, G. R. 'Notes and Studies: Studies in the Vocabulary of the Old Testament VI.' *Journal of Theological Studies* 34 (1933): 375-385.

Driver, S. R. *The Books of Joel and Amos.* Cambridge: Cambridge University Press, 1907.

Eissfeldt, Otto. *The Old Testament, An Introduction*, translated by Peter R. Ackroyd. New York: Harper and Row, 1965.

Everson, A. Joseph. 'The Days of Yahweh.' *Journal of Biblical Literature*93 (1974): 329337.

Feinberg, Charles L. *The Minor Prophets.* Chicago: Moody, 1977.

Feinberg, Charles L. ed. *Prophecy and the Seventies.* Chicago: Moody, 1971.

Finley, Thomas J. *Joel, Amos, Obadiah.* Wycliffe Exegetical Commentary. Chicago: Moody, 1990.

Fowler, Henry T. 'The Chronological Position of Joel among the Prophets.' *Journal of Biblical Literature*16 (1897): 146-154.

Frankfort, Therese. '*Le ki de Joel I 12.*' *Vetus Testamentum* 10 (1960): 445-448.

Freeman, Hobart E. *An Introduction to the Old Testament.* Chicago: Moody, 1968.

Friedrich, Gerhard. '*salpigx.*' *Theological Dictionary of the New Testament*, Vol. 7, edited by Gerhard Friedrich; translated by G. W. Bromiley. Grand Rapids: Eerdmans, 1968.

Gaebelein, A. C. *The Prophet Joel.* New York: Our Hope Publications, 1909.

Garrett, Duane. 'The Structure of Joel.' *Journal of the Evangelical Theological Society* 28 (1985): 289-297.

Gianotti. C. 'The Meaning of the Divine Name YHWH.' *Bibliotheca Sacra* 142 (1985): 45-48.

Gilchrist, Paul R. '*yalal.*' *Theological Wordbook of the Old Testament*, Vol. 1, edited by R. Laird Harris, Gleason L. Archer Jr. and Bruce K. Waltke. Chicago: Moody, 1980.

Gill, John. *Gill's Commentary.* Grand Rapids: Baker, reprint 1980.

Gray, G. B. *Critical Introduction to the Old Testament.* New York: Scribner & Sons, 1913.

Gray, G. B. 'The Parallel Passages in "Joel" and Their Bearing on the Question of Date.' *Expositor* 8 (1893): 208-225.

Hailey, Homer. *A Commentary on the Minor Prophets.* Grand Rapids: Baker, 1972.

Hamilton, Victor P. '*Shaddad.*' *Theological Wordbook of the Old Testament*, Vol. 2, edited by R. Laird Harris, Gleason L. Archer Jr. and Bruce K. Waltke. Chicago: Moody, 1980.

Harris, R. L. '*'asis.*' *Theological Wordbook of the Old Testament*, Vol. 2, edited by R. Laird Harris, Gleason L. Archer Jr. and Bruce K. Waltke. Chicago: Moody, 1980.

Harrison, R. K. *Introduction to the Old Testament.* Grand Rapids: Eerdmans, 1969.

Hartley, John E. *Leviticus.* Word Biblical Commentary, Vol. 4. Dallas: Word, 1992.

Helmbold, A. K. 'Obadiah.' *The Zondervan Pictorial Encyclopedia of the Bible*, Volume 4, edited by Merrill C. Tenney. Grand Rapids: Zondervan, 1975.

Henderson, Ebenezer. *The Twelve Minor Prophets*. Grand Rapids: Baker, reprint 1980.

Hengstenberg, E. W. *Christology of the Old Testament*. Grand Rapids: Kregel, reprint 1973.

Henry, Carl F. H. *God, Revelation, and Authority*. Waco, TX: Word, 1976.

Hoglund, Kenneth G. 'Edomites.' *Peoples of the Old Testament World*, edited by Alfred J Hoerth, Gerald L. Mattingly and Edwin M. Yamauchi. Grand Rapids: Baker, 1994.

Holzinger, Heinrich. 'Sprachcharakter and Abfassungszeit des Buches Joel.' *Zeitschrift für die Alttestamentliche Wissenschaft*. Giessen: J. Rickersche Buchhandlung, 1889: 89-136.

Horst, J. 'ous.' *Theological Dictionary of the New Testament*, Vol. 5, edited by G. Friedrich; translated by G. W. Bromiley. Grand Rapids: Eerdmans, 1968.

Israel, Richard D. 'Joel 2:28-32 (3:1-5 MT): Prism for Pentecost.' *Charismatic Experiences in History*, edited by Cecil M. Robeck, Jr. Peabody, MA: Hendrickson, 1985.

Kaiser, Walter C. *The Messiah in the Old Testament*. Grand Rapids: Zondervan, 1995.

Kaiser, Walter C. 'The Promise of God and the Outpouring of the Holy Spirit: Joel 2:28-32 and Acts 2:16-21.' *Living and Active Word of God: Studies in Honor of Samuel Schultz*, ed. by M. Inch and R. Youngblood. Winona Lake, IN: Eisenbrauns, 1983.

Kaiser, Walter C. *Toward an Old Testament Theology*. Grand Rapids: Zondervan, 1978.

Kapelrud, A. S. *Joel Studies*. Uppsala: Almquist and Wiksells, 1948.

Keil, C. F. *Amos*. Commentary on the Old Testament. Grand Rapids: Eerdmans, reprint 1975.

Keil, C. F. *Joel*. Commentary on the Old Testament. Grand Rapids: Eerdmans, reprint 1975.

Keil, C. F. *Obadiah*. Commentary on the Old Testament. Grand Rapids: Eerdmans, reprint 1975.

Keil, C.F. and Franz Delitzsch. *Exodus*. Grand Rapids, Eerdmans, reprint 1975.

Kennedy, J. Hardee. 'Joel.' *Hosea to Malachi*, Broadman Bible Commentary, Volume 7, edited by Clifton J. Allen. Nashville: Broadman Press, 1972.

Kirkpatrick, A. F. *The Doctrine of the Prophets*. New York: Macmillan, 1897.

Kittel, Gerhard. 'akouo.' *Theological Dictionary of the New Testament*, Vol. 1, edited by G. Friedrich; translated by G. W. Bromiley. Grand Rapids: Eerdmans, 1968.

Klein, Ralph W. 'The Day of the Lord.' *Concordia Theological Monthly* 39 (1968): 517-525.

Koehler, L. *Lexicon in Veteris Testamenti*. Leiden: Brill, 1953.

Ladd, George Eldon. *The Presence of the Future*. Grand Rapids: Eerdmans, 1974.

Laetsch, Theodore. *The Minor Prophets*. St. Louis: Concordia, 1970.

Laney, J. C. 'The Role of the Prophets in God's Case Against Israel.' *Bibliotheca Sacra* 138 (1981): 318-323.

Lange, John Peter. *Joel*. Commentary on the Holy Scriptures. Grand Rapids: Zondervan, n.d.

Lightner, Robert P. *The God of the Bible*. Grand Rapids: Baker, 1978.

Longenecker, Richard N. 'The Acts of the Apostles.' *Expositor's Bible Commentary*, Vol. 9, edited by Frank Gaebelein. Grand Rapids: Zondervan, 1985.

MacRae, A. A. 'Prophets and Prophecy.' *The Zondervan Pictorial Encyclopedia of the Bible*, Volume 4, edited by Merrill C. Tenney. Grand Rapids: Zondervan, 1975.

Mauchline, John. *The Prophets of Israel: The Twelve*. London: Lutterworth, 1964.

McKane, William. *A Critical and Exegetical Commentary on Jeremiah*. International Critical Commentary. Edinburgh: T & T Clark, 1996.

Milman, Henry H. *History of the Jews*. 3 vols. London: J. Murray, 1883.

Motyer, J. A. 'Old Testament History.' *Expositor's Bible Commentary*, Vol. 1, 253-281, edited by Frank Gaebelein. Grand Rapids, Zondervan, 1985.

Motyer, J. A. *The Revelation of the Divine Name*. Leicester: Theological Students Fellowship, 1959.

Mowinckel, Sigmund. 'The Name of the God of Moses.' *Hebrew Union College Annual* 32 (1961): 126-127.

Mowinckel, Sigmund. *Psalmenstudien*. 2 vols. Amsterdam: P. Schippers, 1961.

Murtonen, A. *The Appearance of the Name YHWH Outside Israel*. Studia Orientalia. Helsinki: Suomalaisen Kirjallisuuden Seuran Kirjapainon Oy, 1951.

Myers, Jacob M. 'Some Considerations Bearing on the Date of Joel.' *Zeitschrift für die Alttestamentliche Wissenschaft* 74 (1962): 177-195.

Niehaus, Jeffrey. *The Minor Prophets: An Exegetical and Expository Commentary*, edited by Thomas E. McComiskey. Grand Rapids: Baker, 1993.

Oswalt, John N. 'bosh.' *Theological Wordbook of the Old Testament*, Vol. 1, edited by R. Laird Harris, Gleason L. Archer Jr. and Bruce K. Waltke. Chicago: Moody, 1980.

Patterson, Richard D. 'Joel.' *Expositor's Bible Commentary*, Vol. 7, edited by Frank Gaebelein. Grand Rapids: Zondervan, 1985.

Pentecost, J. D. *Things to Come*. Grand Rapids: Zondervan, 1958.

Pfeiffer, Robert H. *Introduction to the Old Testament*. New York: Harper, 1941.

Price, Walter K. *The Prophet Joel and the Day of the Lord*. Chicago: Moody, 1976.

Pritchard, James B., ed. *Ancient Near Eastern Texts relating to the Old Testament*. Princeton: University Press, 1955.

Pusey, E. B. *The Minor Prophets*. 2 vols. Grand Rapids: Baker, 1973.

Raabe, Paul R. *Obadiah*. The Anchor Bible. Garden City, NY: Doubleday, 1996.

Reed, Oscar F. *The Book of Joel*. BBC. Kansas City: Beacon Hill, 1966.

Robinson, George L. *The Twelve Minor Prophets*. Grand Rapids: Baker, 1979.

Ryrie, Charles. 'The Significance of Pentecost.' *Bibliotheca Sacra* 112 (1955): 334.

Sellers, Ovid R. 'Stages of Locust in Joel.' *American Jornal of Semitic Literature* 52 (1935/36): 82-84.

Smith, G. A. *The Book of the Twelve Prophets*. 2 vols. London: Hodder & Stoughton, 1898-99.

Soggin, F. Alberto. *Introduction to the Old Testament*. Philadelphia: Westminster, 1976.

Stählin, Gustav. '*threneo; threnos*. B. *threnos* in Near Eastern Culture.' *Theological Dictionary of the New Testament*, Vol. 3, edited by G. Friedrich; translated by G. W. Bromiley. Grand Rapids: Eerdmans, 1975.

Stigers, H. G. '*dor*.' *Theological Wordbook of the Old Testament*, Vol. 1, edited by R. Laird Harris, Gleason L. Archer Jr. and Bruce K. Waltke. Chicago: Moody, 1980.

Stuart, Douglas. *Hosea—Jonah*. Word Biblical Commentary, Vol. 31. Waco, TX: Word, 1987.

Tasker, R. V. G. *The Biblical Doctrine of the Wrath of God*. London: Tyndale, 1951.

Thompson, J. A. 'Joel's Locusts in the Light of Near Eastern Parallels.' *Journal of Near Eastern Studies* 14 (1955): 52-55.

Tomasino, Anthony. '*'olam*.' *New International Dictionary of Old Testament Theology and Exegesis*, Vol. 3, edited by William A. VanGemeren. Grand Rapids: Zondervan, 1997.

Treves, Marco. 'The Date of Joel.' *Vetus Testamentum* 7 (1957): 149-156.

VanGemeren, Willem A. *Interpreting the Prophetic Word*. Grand Rapids: Zondervan, 1990.

von Orelli, C. *The Twelve Minor Prophets*, translated by J. S. Banks. Minneapolis: Klock & Klock, reprint 1977.

von Rad, Gerhard. '*'emera*. A. "Day" in the Old Testament.' *Theological Dictionary of the New Testament*, Vol. 2, edited by Gerhard Kittel; translated by Geoffrey W. Bromiley. Grand Rapids: Eerdmans, 1968.

von Rad, Gerhard. 'Origin of the Concept of the Day of Yahweh.' *Journal of Semitic Studies* 4 (1959): 97-108.

Vos, Gerhardus. *Biblical Theology*. Grand Rapids: Eerdmans, 1948.

Wade, G. W. *Micah, Obadiah, Joel and Jonah*. London: Methuen, 1925.

Waltke, Bruce K. '*btl*.' *Theological Wordbook of the Old Testament*, Vol. 1, edited, R. Laird Harris, Gleason L. Archer Jr. and Bruce K. Waltke. Chicago: Moody, 1980.

Watts, John D. W. *The Books of Joel, Obadiah, Jonah, Nahum, Habakkuk and Zephaniah*. Cambridge Bible Commentary. Cambridge: Cambridge University Press, 1975.

Watts, John D. W. *Obadiah: A Critical Exegetical Commentary*. Grand Rapids: Eerdmans, 1969.

Wenham. Gordon. '*Betulah* "A Girl of Marriageable Age."' *Vetus Testamentum* 22 (1972): 326-348.

Wolff, Hans Walter. *Joel and Amos*, translated by W. Janzen, S. D. McBride Jr. and C. A. Muenchow. Philadelphia: Fortress, 1977.

_____. *Obadiah and Jonah*, translated by Margaret Kohl. Minneapolis: Augsburg, 1986.

Wood, Leon J. *The Prophets of Israel*. Grand Rapids: Baker, 1979.

_____. '*za'aq*.' *Theological Wordbook of the Old Testament*, Vol. 1, edited by R. Laird Harris, Gleason L. Archer Jr. and Bruce K. Waltke. Chicago: Moody, 1980.

Young, E. J. *Introduction to the Old Testament*. Grand Rapids: Eerdmans, 1977.

Scripture Index

Subject Index

Y

Z

Other
Mentor
Commentaries

Galatians

A MENTOR COMMENTARY

David McWilliams

Galatians

A MENTOR COMMENTARY

David McWilliams

While Dr. McWilliams' exposition of Galatians keeps in mind the various mischaracterizations of Paul's epistle that have become dominant, his purpose is not primarily polemical. The author sees Paul's paramount concern to be acceptance with God through the work of Christ. McWilliams affirms: "everywhere in every way Paul's concern is with the gospel; he is concerned with the personal salvation of sinners." Written principally, though not exclusively as an aid to preachers, Galatians is an exposition that is scholarly yet readable, combining the rare qualities of depth and brevity. Galatians is sent out to the reading public with the prayer that it might be used of God to extend the gospel of Jesus Christ and the truth of justifying righteousness through the proclamation of free grace to sinners who need the message of salvation through Christ alone!

"Timely, lucid, and reliable, this is an excellent commentary for preachers, Bible study leaders and others. David McWilliams admirably succeeds in his aim for brevitas and claritas, the two qualities in commentators that Calvin most commended. He distils a great deal of scholarship into uncluttered and readable prose. Paul's message in Galatians has rarely been so urgently needed as today, when justification only by faith is under attack from many sides. McWilliams explains it with judicious care."

Robert Letham,
SENIOR TUTOR, SYSTEMATIC & HISTORICIAL THEOLOGY,
WALES EVANGELICAL SCHOOL OF THEOLOGY, BRIDGEND, WALES

David McWilliams has been the senior pastor at Covenant Presbyerian Church, Lakeland, Florida for 20 years. He has a passion for Christ-centred preaching and wished to apply the theology of the life of the church.

ISBN 978-1-84550-452-6

Lamentations

A MENTOR COMMENTARY

John L. Mackay

Lamentations

A MENTOR COMMENTARY

John L Mackay

The five chapters of Lamentations may be easily overlooked. Not only is it brief, but it is also sadnwiched between the two giants of Old testament prophecy, Jeremiah and Ezekiel. Lamentations also deals with realities which we rather wish were not discussed - consequently the book is little studied. However, although there much here to challenge faith, there is much that builds it up. Lamentations was not written in the first instance to serve as warning to others, or to even keep alive the present memory of past suffering, it is the present that dominates the thought of the book.

And in that present are overiding thoughts - 'has God left us?'; 'Have we blown our chance as God's covenant people?' 'Is there a way forward towards the restoration?'

A popular view today is that Lamentations is a deary book with nothing to say to today's society. The reality is that it could not be more relevant, more authentic.

Mentor combines a high view of Scripture with access to the latest academic theological research. This unique combinations allows the reader to see what recent scholarly research has discovered without losing sight of scripture.

John L. Mackay is internationally known as an Old Testament scholar and is also in demand for church retreats where his skill in the practical exposition and application of doctrine are well respected. He is professor of Old Testament in the Free Church College.

ISBN 978-1-84550-363-5

Leviticus

Robert I. Vasholz

Leviticus

A MENTOR COMMENTARY

Robert I. Vasholz

"Vasholz's commentary on Leviticus provides another helpful resource for students of the Scriptures. His work on this often-neglected biblical book will take its place next to a comparatively small group of commentaries that combine an evangelical focus, a high view of Scripture, careful attention to the text, and an avoidance of overemphasis on symbolism and typology. Throughout the volume, he interacts with other commentaries on Leviticus as well as various monographs, writes clearly in an expositional fashion, and provides helpful explanations of a book whose meaning and importance eludes many of its readers."

Michael A Grisanti,
PROFESSOR OF OLD TESTAMENT,
THE MASTER'S SEMINARY, SUN VALLEY, CALIFORNIA

""Dr Vasholz claims that Leviticus, far from being a book to avoid or skip over, is of basic importance to the Bible and to our understanding of what it teaches. His commentary proves the claim to the hilt. It is a high treat to enter into huge scholarship wedded to patient, detailed explanation and exposition of the sacred text. Here is Leviticus brought out of obscurity into the light, off the sidelines into the mainstream. The patience of his scholarship calls for patience in our reading, and rewards it."

Alec Motyer,
WELL KNOWN BIBLE EXPOSITOR AND COMMENTARY WRITER

Robert I. Vasholz is Professor Emeritus of Old Testament at Covenant Theological Seminary in St Louis, Missouri. Though Dr. Valshoz retired in 2007, he continues to serve God's people through his teaching, preaching and publishing projects.

ISBN 978-1-84550-044-3

Christian Focus Publications
publishes books for all ages

Our mission statement –

STAYING FAITHFUL

In dependence upon God we seek to impact the world through literature faithful to His infallible Word, the Bible. Our aim is to ensure that the Lord Jesus Christ is presented as the only hope to obtain forgiveness of sin, live a useful life and look forward to heaven with Him.

REACHING OUT

Christ's last command requires us to reach out to our world with His gospel. We seek to help fulfil that by publishing books that point people towards Jesus and help them develop a Christ-like maturity. We aim to equip all levels of readers for life, work, ministry and mission.

Books in our adult range are published in three imprints.

Christian Focus contains popular works including biographies, commentaries, basic doctrine and Christian living. Our children's books are also published in this imprint.

Mentor focuses on books written at a level suitable for Bible College and seminary students, pastors, and other serious readers. The imprint includes commentaries, doctrinal studies, examination of current issues and church history.

Christian Heritage contains classic writings from the past.

Christian Focus Publications, Ltd
Geanies House, Fearn,
Ross-shire, IV20 1TW, Scotland, United Kingdom
info@christianfocus.com

Our titles are available from quality bookstores and
www.christianfocus.com